JOURNEY
TO
SELF

Discovering Paths Beyond My Dreams

Barry D. Hampshire

Andrew Benzie Books
Martinez, California

Published by Andrew Benzie Books
www.andrewbenziebooks.com

Salutes/Salaams
I have been unable to contact a number of individuals mentioned in the
story and have, therefore, renamed them in the following account. I suspect a
few of these people have already died—I'm saddened I couldn't share this book
with them. I offer my condolences to their families and may this book be a
tribute to their adventurous spirits.

Printed in the United States of America
First Edition: September 2019

10 9 8 7 6 5 4 3 2 1

Hampshire, Barry
Journey to Self: Discovering Paths Beyond My Dreams

ISBN: 978-1-950562-02-2

Cover and book design by Andrew Benzie
www.andrewbenziebooks.com

I dedicate this memoir to those who suffer, no matter if it be caused by ill health, social injustice, or financial inequalities. I also dedicate this account to all the people who have chosen to spend their careers or volunteer some of their time to work with these people in their time of suffering. And lastly, I dedicate this book to the adventurers who explore the world and who, in doing so, are willing to discover themselves.

CONTENTS

Map of England to Greece (1977) 1

Map of Turkey to Saudi Arabia (1977) 2

Map of Saudi Arabia (1977) 3

Foreword 5

Chapter 1: A Different Paradigm 7

Chapter 2: Camp Life 15

Chapter 3: Preparations 27

Chapter 4: Unto Europe 35

Chapter 5: Old Familiar Places 47

Chapter 6: New Territory 61

Chapter 7: West Meets East 85

Chapter 8: Ancient Worlds 101

Chapter 9: Getting Hotter 121

Chapter 10: Being Tourists for a While 133

Chapter 11: Home-Style Cooking 149

Chapter 12: Indiana Jones—You and Me, Both 167

Chapter 13: A Couple of Minor Incidents 181

Chapter 14: The Home Stretch 195

Chapter 15: Post Journey 207

Chapter 16: Al Hofuf 211

Chapter 17: Diving in the Red Sea 219

Chapter 18: Uplifting Winds 233

Chapter 19: Spelunking in the Desert 243

Chapter 20: What Next? 253

Chapter 21: The Empty Quarter 255

Chapter 22: Life Thereafter 277

Epilogue—Part I 283

Epilogue—Part II 289

Appendix 295

Acknowledgements 297

About the Author 299

MAP OF
ENGLAND TO GREECE
(1977)

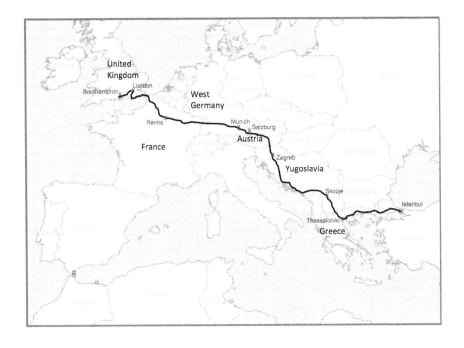

MAP OF
TURKEY TO SAUDI ARABIA
(1977)

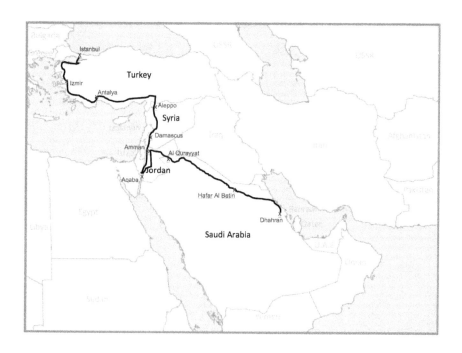

MAP OF
SAUDI ARABIA
(1977)

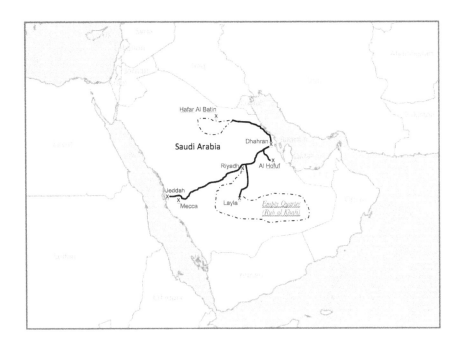

FOREWORD

This is the travel story of a stubborn, determined young man with a taste for adventure, who 40 years ago drove an American car from London to Dhahran. His journey took him through Europe and into Syria, much of which has now been devastated by conflict.

Often in the face of adversity, encountering crooked officials and bureaucracy, Barry and his friends pressed on.

On reaching his destination his love for exploring led him into the deserts of Arabia, 'spelunking' down a massive sink hole and other deeper caverns, discovering archaeological sites, and contending with the hazards of driving in such a scorched, remote region.

This self-confessed rebel eventually discovered the importance of faith and compassion, thereafter devoting his life to the service of those who suffer. Perhaps the emptiness of deserts has this effect; as a great spiritual leader found 2,000 years ago.

Colonel John Blashford-Snell
President, the Scientific Exploration Society

CHAPTER 1
A DIFFERENT PARADIGM

الله ه شاء ان   الله ه شاء ان   الله ه شاء ان   الله ه شاء ان   الله ه شاء ان   الله ه شاء ان

"Why did you buy this great big American car?" Mother demanded to know as she sat erect, dressed in a fawn-colored tweed skirt, stockings, and light cardigan. She looked intently into my eyes as if reading my mind. "Why didn't you buy a nice English car here? You plan to drive that monster all the way back to Saudi Arabia? Couldn't you have bought one there? It's 1977. They sell cars there, don't they?" Her volley of questions battered me as we sat drinking tea.

I fidgeted. I thought. I folded my arms across my chest. "I need it for getting around camp. Maybe you've forgotten the size of our camp in Saudi; it's about the size of a small English town. And the average temperature is over 100 degrees for much of the time. Most vehicles in camp are American, they're bigger than what we drive here."

When she realized my brief answer hadn't explained my decision to drive back, her brow furrowed and her eyes narrowed. Her stare held me while she fired another salvo. "What will happen if you need help while you drive all the way from England back to Saudi Arabia?"

I had no answer, proving her constant criticism. She felt I never thought thoroughly about situations. My hands glistened with sweat and twitched. "Oh, many friends have driven back, and they say getting help isn't any big deal."

Mother's exasperation boiled over. "Barry, you're so infuriating. I just want to know what you're planning to do. I don't understand this trip. It sounds dangerous and not a good idea."

Words failed to form, I sat in silence, unable to reply. In that moment, I realized nothing in her experience allowed her to connect with my plans to drive across Europe and the Middle East. I wished I could give her some reassurances, but outcomes of adventures were never foreseeable. I had already bought the Blazer and arranged to take two friends with me on the trip. When I purchased the vehicle, I informed my mother of my plans in a letter. However, I realized in later conversations she had dismissed the letter as just another crazy idea of mine. At the time of my mother's barrage of questions, my Chevy Blazer sat at the curb outside her house; my intentions were concrete and real. In Mother's eyes, the prospect of driving all the way to Saudi Arabia looked frightening but, for me, it looked like an exciting adventure—full of unknowns.

Her shoulders slumped forward, I felt relieved to see the tension in her arms ease as she placed her cup on her lap, and her stare softened as it drifted down towards the floor. I sat waiting and drank another mouthful of tea; she had no more questions. She shook her head in disbelief and took another sip of her tea—I wondered if it was a sign of her resignation that I would do what I intended. I let out a long breath to assuage a sense of guilt because I'd just lied to her.

The truth is only a few of my friends have ever made the journey. They've told me finding help with mechanical repairs, money problems and paperwork issues would be a headache for most of the trip.

I couldn't admit these details to my mother and minimized them for myself. I found comfort in an internal state of denial where I could hide from my concerns and fears. If she knew how vague my plans were, she would have picked holes in them causing herself to be more worried which would have heightened my own level of angst. I felt the need to protect both of us and thought it best to shut down.

Her worried thoughts stayed with me over the next few weeks. Being a rather arrogant 28-year-old British guy didn't help my unpleasant sense of being cornered by my more sensible and much wiser mother. I grew up in London in the post-World War II 1950s, and life had its challenges and its blessings. Through it, I developed a false sense of self-resiliency, whereas my mother who had survived the war and witnessed much hardship had a better sense of what I needed to be considering. However, her war-time experiences had left her with a need to control situations. My proposed trip was far beyond her control which my rebellious side purposefully sought. On the few occasions I did listen to her, she talked about my safety, the security of the Blazer, potential health problems, communicating with people who didn't speak English, and my ability to contact British embassies. I believed her concerns were well founded, but my immature stubbornness prevented my listening to her words or engaging in a meaningful dialogue.

I was aware driving across the Middle East in 1977 presented a few challenges despite the region enjoying a reasonably peaceful period. The main potential problem was Lebanon, which verged on becoming a powder keg, so I plotted a course around it. Back then, terrorism was rare so I had no reason to alter my plans due to such worries. Possible Bader-Meinhoff terrorists in Germany caused me more concern than what I thought I might encounter in Syria.

Considering our current environment, it may sound naïve but people had a greater trust in others and didn't automatically suspect the worst of them. Many of my interactions with people during the journey could never happen today. Did I behave foolishly? No, I don't believe that was true; we lived in a different world back then. At times, bad people perpetrated terrible deeds. However, their actions didn't have a hold over everyone else or force the rest of the world to live in fear.

Also being 28, I thought myself to be invincible and prepared for life. It is interesting to contrast my late twenties to modern day people of a similar age. When I looked around me, I understood my immediate surroundings, but to understand much of what was beyond my everyday experience was another matter. I had to listen to others who, hopefully, had some real experiences or to read the limited book selection that I found at a library. Nowadays, the internet brings the world to everyone, but it only gives us a glimpse of what is out there, no real experience. It is like if I watched a waiter walk by me carrying an incredible entrée with its aromas dancing in my nostrils, and I then said that I knew the greatest cuisine in the world. I would be totally incorrect. I may have witnessed it, but I had no real experience of it and no emotional connection to it. To me, the internet and social media provides some people with an essential means of connection, but for the vast majority of people, they provide a distraction from engaging with authentic life. The unknown sounds much more inviting to me than a superficial glimpse of what others consider to be incredible or interesting. Yes, some of these on-line videos and articles are wonderful, but I would encourage viewers of these items to hold them as the just an aperitif that invites us to engage with the entrée at a personal level, experience the unknown, move to living life with depth—not just skimming along the surface. So, in hindsight, I'm glad I grew up in the era before computers and people drowning in too much information, most of which is actually unnecessary. My sense of being invincible or prepared may have been immature and invalid, but it allowed my eyes to be open to what was around me and not be fogged by a misconceived notion that I knew what I was doing.

Sensing my mother's exasperation with my unwillingness to discuss my plans about the journey in detail, I assumed she worried about me for the next few weeks while I made preparations and then drove into the unknown. Having seen her through various stressful times while I grew up, I had no doubt she spent tormented nights imagining terrible scenarios, while I inched my path across the map all the way to Saudi Arabia. I would drive with two friends from London to Dhahran in the eastern province of Saudi Arabia, about 5,500 miles, over a two-week period. To drive over 350 miles each day for 15 days through foreign lands was not a simple undertaking, nor for the faint of heart. Today, this route would be impossible to navigate due to war, terrorism, genocide, and refugee migrations; but, my journey took place over 40 years ago when the Middle East looked relatively quiet.

I worked for the Arabian American Oil Company—Aramco—in the eastern province of Saudi Arabia. I had moved there the previous year, intending to work in the desert for one year. I thought I could earn enough money for a down-payment on a small three-bedroom house in England. When I first arrived in Saudi Arabia—I thought I would stay for just twelve months.

I found life in the Aramco camp to be engaging, challenging, and to my liking. The camp accommodated the several thousand ex-pats employed by the oil company. I was delighted to find the camp had facilities such as a theater, a supermarket, a library, a swimming pool, tennis courts, squash/racquetball courts, and a golf course to keep us entertained. Ex-pats also enjoyed a private swimming beach and a boating facility 15 miles south of camp. When I decided to stay longer than the one year and considered the heat, I determined a vehicle was a necessity to take advantage of all that camp offered.

After I checked several car dealers near to camp, I was disheartened to realize I didn't trust the salesmen enough to buy a pint of oil from them, let alone a car. I considered flying to Kuwait to buy a British 4-wheel drive, which I soon heard had a reputation for unreliability. After I considered several other options, I decided to follow what several friends had done. I bought an American 4-wheel drive from a New York car dealer who shipped it to England. From there, I would drive it to Saudi Arabia.

My mother was most concerned about my planned drive while my step-father Fred never expressed an opinion about it. Having seen how they had settled into their newly-married routine, I suspected he felt the full angst of my mother's feelings on the matter when she thought I couldn't hear her.

Mother's three-bedroom house looked similar to others in the northern suburbs of London. The 'burbs comprised a huge swath of housing around central London; I found them monotonous. Variations included the color of the external paint or the layout of the front garden, however I viewed the sameness and repetition as uninspired, verging on being depressing. The thought of becoming another face lost in that sea of humanity, tending to my front yard or painting the house sent my spirit on a search for a different paradigm and a life I could love. My mother's vision of a secure future for me was to tie myself down with a mortgage for a house in the 'burbs. I wonder how my life would have turned out if I had followed her path. But instead, I moved to Saudi Arabia and, a year later, I drove my Blazer there. How would those decisions affect the rest of my days?

For the three years before I moved to Saudi Arabia, I worked in central London with a long daily commute. I loved everything about the job. Our team of mathematicians, engineers, and computer programmers enhanced a computer system, which analyzed the designs of supertankers and offshore oil structures to ensure their sea-worthiness. Being a member of a multiple academic discipline team challenged and satisfied me in ways that I never found in later career paths. I was happy in my work; however, I had a hankering deep inside which left me unsatisfied. I sought opportunities that would challenge me in different ways.

During one morning commute, I read a newspaper article about the first ever successful Darien Gap expedition. A 100-mile band of impenetrable jungle in Central America, known as the Darien Gap, had been successfully crossed by a British expedition with two Range Rovers. The Scientific Exploration Society—SES—had arranged the expedition and the British Army had backed it. SES had been founded by Colonel John Blashford-Snell OBE DSc(Hon) FRSGS. Reading about this expedition caught my imagination and when I saw a contact address at the end of the article, I had found the opportunity to challenge myself.

In reply to my inquiry, I received information about the society and an application for membership. I was intrigued to learn that SES had arranged a number of expeditions, primarily humanitarian endeavors such as creating access to remote areas where clinics, hospitals, or schools needed supplies. I sensed my heart rate increase when I read they had also organized the first complete 4,000-mile navigation of the Blue Nile, from its source in the Ethiopian mountains to the Mediterranean Sea. I felt intimidated and unnerved by the application form; SES sought highly specialized and qualified people like doctors, engineers, journalists, bankers, and other professionals, as well as ex-military commanders. Despite feeling unqualified, I submitted my application. If I didn't try, I would never know. Surprisingly, they accepted me and invited me to their offices to help with administrative duties. The prospect to join an expedition wasn't implicit in the opportunity, but I was humbled to be invited to be a member of such a group.

After work, one evening, I navigated to an address, close to Downing Street. I was ushered into the lobby of a grand Georgian house with highly polished wood paneling and marble flooring. It, along with its neighboring houses, had become government offices. After a few minutes, a member of the SES staff came to collect me. We crossed the lobby to a waiting elevator which, to my astonishment, descended three floors below street level. He headed into a warren of poorly-lit underground passageways which extended out in multiple directions. As I kept pace with my guide, I occasionally had to duck my head to avoid steaming pipes and gantries that hung from the ceiling.

We entered an office lit by a few desk lamps allowing me to see the cramped quarters which overflowed with books, papers, and equipment. The staff member introduced me to the two men who sat at a desk in the middle of the office. I sensed being in a hallowed place where only great men walked, when one of them turned out to be Colonel John Blashford-Snell himself. I shook his outstretched hand, my own hand became limp and sweaty in his vice grip, and I struggled to form a comprehendible phrase of greeting. Even in the semi-darkness, his manner spoke of his undeniable sense of authority, zeal, decisiveness, leadership, and tradition. A feeling of self-doubt gripped my shoulders and neck, and my feet shuffled uncomfortably.

Having finished his conversation, the Colonel turned to me. "Right. Mr. Hampshire, I want you to tackle a task we've talked about for a while. The society needs a tie." From my reading of the society's information and a quick survey of the office, the society resembled the military as closely as possible, but without being so. Hence in my mind, the need for a uniform or even a tie felt consistent with who they were.

I sensed I could handle this task and my shoulders relaxed. I asked for a little clarification. "You want me to buy ties for the members of the society?"

He turned back to me almost knocking over a pile of papers. "Oh, no, no. I want you to design a motif for the tie, select the colors, and arrange to have one hundred manufactured."

I frowned. "But I don't know any manufacturers."

He stopped me. "No problem. I'm sure we've got several tie companies on file. You can talk to them to get the best price."

"Okay. That should be fun." This was probably the only time the word 'fun' had ever been mentioned in those august, historic offices.

I designed the tie and negotiated the manufacture of one hundred. Over the following months, I performed other administrative tasks, during which I talked with several members about expeditions. My appetite for adventurous travel was whetted by these conversations, and they convinced me I lacked the necessary experience, talents, or qualifications to join an SES expedition.

Mixed thoughts of adventurous travel and my lack of experience stayed in my mind while I worked in London. In many ways, those thoughts persuaded me I should go to work in Saudi Arabia. But, ultimately, they contributed to my decision to drive a Blazer back to Saudi Arabia which allowed me to undertake my own self-directed mini-expedition. Did I have the necessary qualities to achieve this endeavor?

CHAPTER 2
CAMP LIFE

الله ه ش اء إن   الله ه ش اء إن   الله ه ش اء إن   الله ه ش اء إن   الله ه ش اء إن   الله ه ش اء إن

My plans to stay working for Aramco for a longer term caused my mother much consternation. She still held to my original idea to work in the desert for just one year.

During one conversation, she observed, "I thought I knew my son who left home last year."

I tried to anticipate her thought. "But you're puzzled as to who's returned in his place, for a vacation?"

She recognized I was trying to make light of her comment. "Well, yes. However, I'm not sure I feel comfortable with how you've changed under the influence of those people in Saudi Arabia. I know it's 1977 and you're 28 years old, but you make such major decisions without thought about possible consequences."

I had to admit I'd changed. In camp, I'd discovered a different person from the version of me who grew up in England. My eyes had been opened to the world, people, and their cultures. The restrictive vision of my potential life in England, with a house and mortgage, had dissolved. I may have lived in the confined cocoon of the Aramco camp which emulated American life but, among the camp residents, I had found people who exhibited a more-worldly engagement that intrigued and seduced me. Having been raised in England in the 1950s, my schooling had portrayed England as a world leader that still hung onto the final vestiges of its empire. Even with this skewed background, I had been inculcated with an interest in the world, other ethnicities, and people. Once I physically moved beyond the borders of England, I recognized a desire to experience the world and to engage with different cultures coursed through my veins. I knew to buy a house in England couldn't be my future.

Looking back at my upbringing now, I'm dismayed when I think of our annual school photographs, in which about 360 boys stood in lines, all dressed in the same uniform, with no allowance for individualism. Conformity ruled. To buy a house with a mortgage represented conforming to what my mother wanted for me, and I rejected that expectation totally. I accepted she wanted me to have a safe and secure future, but her version felt too restrictive to me.

School hadn't been a pleasant experience for me. I learned to read, but I didn't enjoy it. I disliked reading so much that I wouldn't do any reading assignments I needed for class. As a result, I was an extremely poor student which was frustrating to both my mother and myself as I was intelligent. Mathematics was my saving grace; it came quite naturally to me and I loved it. I knew I had the capability to be successful and needed to find a way to maximize my potential. I saw working in Saudi Arabia as a possible path to fulfill that objective. Obviously, I had to prove myself qualified to be offered the job with Aramco. Thankfully, I was asked to write a piece of computer code at my interview in London. Apparently, my coding impressed my future boss, Keith, sufficiently that he overlooked my lack of good scholastic grades.

In Saudi Arabia, I lived in the main Aramco camp in Dhahran, close to the city of Al Khobar in the eastern province. Al Khobar had originally been built on the shores of the Persian Gulf where trading caravans met with dhows, small sail driven craft used to transport cargo or passengers, that sailed to ports along the edge of the gulf. Dhahran comprised our camp, the University of Petroleum and Minerals, the International Airport, and the original two oil wells which had started the Saudi Arabian oil boom back in the 1930s. Our camp covered between fifteen and twenty square miles. Within its boundary lay housing and facilities for thousands of ex-pats, multiple office blocks, as well as industrial work yards. The camp housing had been expanded multiple times over the years so that one section of housing always looked modern and new. The camp even boasted having a 27-hole golf course, which didn't have greens of green grass, they had greens made of fine sand, mixed with light grade oil. These greens required perpetual attention; a single worker was assigned to each green, he dragged the green with a weighted piece of carpet after each group played through, ensuring the green's surface was always perfectly even. These workers stayed at their posts for 12 hours every day, no matter the weather, even during sandstorms.

The camp's size plus the heat made an automobile essential. This thought hit me hard one day when I misjudged the time to leave for a game of squash. I rushed out of my efficiency, a single occupancy studio apartment, for the squash courts with only five minutes before the start of the game. I decided to run; not a smart move as the courts were about a mile away and the temperature was over 100 degrees. After fifty yards, I slowed to a jog, and after only a hundred yards, I had been reduced to a puddle of exhausted sweat. I literally lay in the gutter on the side of the road. I immediately decided three things: I needed to purchase a vehicle, I needed to be fitter, and I would walk to the game and be late. I lost the game too. Life could be so harsh.

Several friends in Saudi Arabia talked about their decisions to drive their vehicles back from England rather than buying from one of the local car dealers. A good friend, Hughie, gave me the name, address, and fax number for a Chevrolet dealer in New York. In those days, the Internet and email didn't exist. Communications complicated my negotiations for a car; they were slow, unreliable, and frustrating. To send questions to the dealer, and hopefully, receive answers by standard mail took about two weeks. Despite its being slow, postal mail was seen as the most reliable form of communication. On the other hand, facsimile transmissions were slightly uncertain, but they could be much faster than postal mail. I used both, and over a number of weeks I negotiated the purchase of a Chevrolet Blazer that the New York dealer would ship to England. I had reservations about the one vehicle they had in stock that met most of my specifications. Its black bodywork didn't align with my ideals when it came to the best color for a blistering hot climate. However, by then, the date for my return to England loomed closer, and I needed to have the vehicle shipped ahead of my vacation.

Finally, I faxed my bank in England to have them transfer money to the New York dealer. It took more than a little courage to send that fax. In doing so, I committed myself to spend almost all of my savings from my first year in the desert on a vehicle which I would have to drive from England to Saudi Arabia. I could see no way to recoup this outlay if my plans didn't work out. Looking back now, I'm sure many of my mother's friends must have considered me to be insane after she told them about my plans and her concerns. But being 28 years old, I arrogantly thought myself infallible and never allowed myself the time to consider the reality of the drive. The stress of driving through eleven countries, about which I knew little, was a detail I didn't spend much thought on. Interacting with people whom I didn't know I could trust was a concern that never crossed my mind. I had a dream with a few not insignificant concerns. Deep down, I knew my mother's doubts and concerns had validity, but I chose to ignore them, minimize them. I kept my tunnel-vision on my goal to drive to Saudi Arabia, and I saw no reason to back away from giving my dream a shot.

While I negotiated the car deal, I talked with several friends who had made the drive back, and they all offered pieces of advice. Keeping a wad of US currency handy to bribe officials was the most common suggestion. That didn't feel comfortable with my British sense of correctness. Thankfully, I did take their advice and later purchased U.S. currency when I returned to London.

In my first year at the Aramco camp, I had quickly realized a vibrant social life existed, especially among the bachelors, based on a substantial supply of alcohol. This may come as a surprise because Saudi Arabia considered itself a "dry" country as Muslims were not supposed to drink alcohol. However, a simple economic expediency necessitated this incongruity. The Saudi's required ex-pats to run the oil industry and as they needed to keep ex-pats happy in the scorching desert, they bowed to the most obvious Western vice— alcohol. Thus, any ex-pat employee who lived on one of their main camps, could request a hand-made 10-gallon stainless steel still, provided they made assurances the resulting liquor stayed within the camp. To produce good quality alcohol took time and patience. As a result, many people—primarily bachelors—supplemented their income by producing and then selling liquor to other camp residents. I decided to be a purchaser rather than a producer. As a result of this lucrative sideline for producers and a large group of thirsty consumers, pure alcohol flowed freely and copiously through certain sections of the camp.

Sadly, the cheap supply of pure alcohol became problematic as I later heard the World Health Organization published an annual report that ranked communities by the number of alcoholics per thousand capita. Apparently, our camp made the top ten in the world while I lived there. As to the truth of that reporting, I'm not sure how the data was collected. But, I sensed the report might have been close to the truth. Camp residents nicknamed a gallon of the spirit, "*Sid*," which was short for Siddiqi, Arabic for the English phrase, "my friend."

One might wonder how we functioned, as heavy drinking normally resulted in hangovers. If we cut pure alcohol, 182 proof, with water, down to drinkable strength, 110 proof, and drank it with ice and soda, then we certainly became inebriated. Surprisingly, in the morning, we felt fine with no hangovers—a little tired, which could quickly be cured with coffee. So imbibing became a nightly occurrence.

One evening, while still back in Saudi Arabia, I attended a small party where I bumped into my manager's secretary, a young English woman called Penny. I enjoyed her company as we shared a curiosity about people and cultures. We chatted for a while, during which I mentioned I had been toying with the idea of driving a vehicle back from England at the end of my first annual vacation.

"Would you mind if I came on the trip with you?" she hesitantly asked. I hadn't expected such a question as I had thought of her as a little timid and not too adventurous. Her question sent my mind reeling. *Did she understand what the journey could entail? This wouldn't be moving from hotel to hotel.* On the other hand, the thought of a companion for the trip felt good.

"Are you sure you understand this could be rough at times? I imagine we'll sleep out under the stars quite often. Have you listened to Hughie and Trevor talk about their trips?" I threw these thoughts her way so that she could feel comfortable if she wanted to withdraw her request.

"Yes. I've heard a few stories and I'm fine with a little adventure," she replied, and suddenly I had a traveling companion. From being around her in the office and while out socializing, I knew she could be quiet and withdrawn, as at times I could be too. During one exchange with her, I discovered she hadn't completed her undergraduate degree, but had switched to a secretarial college, where she had excelled. That qualification was sufficient to apply successfully for the job with Aramco.

I asked. "I'm intrigued. Why would you want to join me on an insane adventure like this?"

She looked me in the eyes. "Barry, I trust you and we're good friends, so I felt comfortable asking you. I hadn't travelled much before I came to Arabia and want to see some of the world. Not many people drive back to Arabia and so this sounds like a perfect opportunity."

"Great. It's good to know you have an adventurous spirit. We may need it somewhere along the way. I'll keep you posted with details, as things get resolved. I'm really pleased you want to come."

I was relieved as I had worried about the prospect of making the journey back to Dhahran alone. I enjoyed being on my own, but I would have found 15 days on the road extremely hard. I'd imagined a male buddy would possibly join me, as significantly more men than women lived in the Aramco camp. Instead, I had a determined woman who hopefully would contain any ill-considered notions that I may have.

I now wonder if anything else could have been going on for us at that time. I can't answer for Penny, but for me, I liked her as a friend. She was a bright and intelligent young woman with a tall, slender frame, which she carried with poise and a little reservation. I enjoyed her company. However, I didn't sense any real chemistry between us. Or, now 40 years later, perhaps I should admit I was too self-absorbed in my own changes and development to allow space for any possible relationship. Whatever the truth of that potential relationship, I knew we complemented each other well. I could be decisive which kept us moving, no matter the consequence, and Penny had grounding and the ability to see issues from different perspectives.

A few weeks and a few parties later, I attended another social gathering and talked with a group of contractors whom I'd met when I first arrived in camp. I had connected with one of them, Ron, who also had been raised in the suburbs of London. Over drinks, we all stood around and talked about planned vacations that needed to be arranged well in advance due to Saudi Arabian government regulations.

"I'm thinking of driving a Blazer back from England in August," I said.

Without a moment's hesitation, Ron burst in. "Oh great. I'm coming with you. That sounds like fun."

I felt a little awkward as I didn't know how well Ron and Penny knew each other so I quickly added, "I already have one companion for the trip; you know Penny from my department? So three of us would be on the journey. Does that work for you?" I hoped he would agree as I felt a threesome would create a better camaraderie, and could allow any of us to find some space if we needed to withdraw for a while. I reckoned we would have plenty of room in the Blazer to take all of our gear.

Ron enthusiastically answered, "That sounds excellent! I'll arrange for my vacation at the same time as you. Oh man, this'll be great." He was soon lost in a daydream about the trip.

I took another sip of my well-iced drink. "I'll check with Penny before I confirm plans. I hope she'll not object to another companion." Ron walked off to refill his drink and for the rest of the evening, he kept up a string of questions about the journey, such as will cash or travelers checks be better and how long would I drive each day. I should probably have listened to him and thought more about his queries. A few of them remained unresolved until we were on the road and needed answers.

In the end, we had a group of three. A fourth companion would have overwhelmed our comfortable drive. I would have had to refuse any other adventurers who wanted to join our party. I knew Penny well from almost daily interactions in the office and I knew Ron from many social gatherings. They seemed to be comfortable with each other so I had confidence we could work through any problems.

Without any effort, I'd found fellow adventurers and after a few communication problems, I'd purchased the vehicle. It hadn't been detailed, careful planning, everything seemed to fall into place.

Penny grew up on the south coast of England. Soon after she started work, she apparently decided she wanted to experience more than just England before she settled down in a career. She had applied to Aramco for a job about the same time as myself, but her application was approved more quickly than mine. Since she had arrived, she'd taken a few day trips around the eastern province of Saudi Arabia, but hadn't travelled further afield. To me, she seemed more comfortable in smaller groups than larger gatherings. She wasn't a regular attendee at parties. I was more likely to see her in smaller groups where we played board or card games, and conversations were quieter and more intimate. She had admitted to me she was quite content to wrap up cozily with a good book and be carried away by a good tale. Knowing a small amount about her, I was left wondering. *Now, this isn't the Penny I know in the office. This one has an adventurous spirit and an interest in what is going on around her. She will be a good member of the trio.*

Over the course of our journey's two-week duration, we navigated a route that passed through eleven countries as we crossed from Western Europe to the Middle East. At times, I felt Penny wanted to crawl into a ball and not be noticed, especially by the men in certain places. Her tall, slim figure and shoulder-length fair hair gave her an elegance that didn't go unobserved. She couldn't fold herself small enough to hide in a corner, despite her blind determination and exasperation.

Ron worked for an Aramco contractor and he was located in a different office building to myself, so I rarely saw him while I was at work. During a couple of social gatherings, we both found we shared similar backgrounds and attitudes, and our senses of humor aligned well, too. He could be assertive and, at times, bordered on being pompous, but I never felt uncomfortable around him. He told me what he thought, and he never took umbrage if I chose to ignore him. Ron stood decidedly shorter than my lanky 6' 3"; his fuller frame gave him a solid presence that, at times, gave all three of us the firm grounding we needed. We weren't looking for confrontations with anyone, but we sometimes needed to stand firm and, at such times, Ron was our anchor. When needed, Ron could be vocally forceful which, with his physical presence, proved to be useful on a few occasions.

Penny and I had met when I initially arrived a year before for my new job with Aramco. She had only been in Saudi Arabia for a few months when I joined the group. Fortunately, I had been interviewed by our boss Keith in London. When I arrived at Dhahran airport, the mass of bustling people and the feeling of confusion in the humid heat felt alien and disconcerting to me. Thankfully, Keith met me at the airport; it felt reassuring to have a familiar face to greet me.

Penny and Keith helped me settle in and navigate the challenges of transportation, which was my first real test due to an unusual circumstance. At the time, the camp's population exceeded the housing capacity and I had to be temporarily housed in the local city of Dammam. Each day, I joined dozens of workers in filthy overalls on one of the workers' buses that carried them to camp for their shift in the yards and machine shops. At work, I shared an office with a New Zealander, Bob. With support from Penny, Bob, and Keith, I established a routine quickly. When I had questions or frustrations, Penny or Bob would listen and advise me of the best ways to handle unexpected scenarios, such as my apartment not having hot water for a couple of days or buses failing to arrive on weekends.

After several weeks, a room in a shared house became available in camp, and I happily joined two other guys in the house. One, Jason, worked as an aircraft mechanic on the company's fleet of aircraft. The other, Ian, was a hydrologist, which meant we rarely saw him as he frequently travelled out in the desert with surveying teams. At that time, Penny lived in a comparable house with several other young English women in another part of camp, and Ron was housed off-camp in a hotel in Al-Khobar. About two months later, I moved into what had been termed an "*efficiency*," a basic single unit, about 300 square feet, with a kitchen, lounge, bedroom, and bathroom.

By that time, I had met quite a number of people and camp life had become a little more familiar to me. About one thousand American families lived in camp along with a similar number of bachelor status ex-pats from Britain, U.S., Europe, Australia and New Zealand. A friend, Eric, pointed out to me years later what had amazed him about this entire group. He said he felt most Aramco ex-pats displayed common characteristics such as well-educated, adventurous, willing to face the unknown, and adaptable when faced with the unexpected. I completely agreed with his assessment, it was an exceptional group of interesting and interested people. I felt the four years I spent in the Aramco community and the experiences I had in Dhahran shaped my life in positive and significant ways. In those four years, I started running and racing, I even ran my first marathon with expert help from Eric, an excellent runner, who trained and raced with the Arizona State track team. I learned to sail, water ski, ride a dirt motor bike, became a thespian—I never exhibited any real talent—played some reasonably good squash and tennis, and travelled to several unusual destinations in the Middle East including Yemen and Iran. I also learned basic Arabic—I especially loved writing in Arabic script. Apart from that, I enjoyed work, day to day activities, and the inevitable social gatherings. Much of the activities took place outdoors where the temperature frequently exceeded 100 degrees and, at times, the humidity could be uncomfortably high, too. Luckily for me, my body's ability to tolerate heat aligned with my tolerance to pain. I could be aware of them, but they rarely caused me to stop an activity. I wasn't alone in my ability to have fun in the sun. It was a lively and engaged community where few sat in their air-conditioned homes complaining about the heat; most were out enjoying themselves being active and involved.

I left England as an adventurous, but uncertain and insecure wall-flower, and four years later, I had evolved into a confident, capable, and slightly more mature human being, ready to engage with life more fully.

After my first year with Aramco, I had become familiar with some

Saudi Arabian customs and practices. Would this understanding be useful in other Arabic countries that our journey would cross or would we need to adapt to different expectations/customs in each country?

CHAPTER 3
PREPARATIONS

الله شاء إن   الله شاء إن   الله شاء إن   الله شاء إن   الله شاء إن   الله شاء إن

I flew home for a five week vacation and to see my mother and stepfather Fred. They had been married for a couple of years and had established a comfortable routine together. My own father had died two months after I turned 21, seven years earlier. I had a turbulent relationship with my father—both of us were stubborn and I was young. The combination caused me to withdraw from him after he repeatedly told me how disappointed he was in me.

When I was 21, I faced several disturbing challenges. Apart from my father's death that devastated me, I had fractured my spine in a rock climbing accident that left me in constant pain, and I had been through a difficult emotional period. In addition, that was the last year of my undergraduate degree in college. I just managed to graduate, with the lowest possible passing grade. I've always suspected my departmental head awarded me a degree because he felt sorry for me, rather than my having earned it through hard work.

For quite a number of years before, I'd been a rather rebellious teenager and my belligerent attitudes had continued throughout college. The year my father died had been a major wake up call for me. I began to realize the world didn't revolve around me. Mother and I had several horrendous fights as we tried to rebuild our relationship, while we each negotiated the raw emotions of grief, fear, and uncertainty. Out of those encounters, we forged a new form of peace and mutual nurturing. To my surprise, I realized a few years later I'd assumed the role of my mother's protector—I'd taken my father's place to a limited degree. In the six years after my father's death, the thought of working abroad had crossed my mind. I hadn't fully engaged with the idea because I felt I needed to be around to support my mother. However, when she decided to marry her gentleman friend Fred, I recognized my opportunity to leave England had arrived. I felt she no longer needed me, even though the reality of that need probably only existed in my head. About 15 months after mother's marriage to Fred, I had applied for and accepted the job in Saudi Arabia. My mother found my idea of working abroad, especially in the Saudi Arabian desert, to be utterly mystifying. She heard my words about spending just a single year in the desert to save money for a deposit for a house. That was her grounding—Barry would be home after just one year.

After my first year, I'd flown home to England on vacation, instead of returning to home for good. I had planned to pick up the Blazer, and attempt to make a rational argument to Mother about my plan to drive over 5,000 miles across two continents. In hindsight, I realize I had zero chance of succeeding in my efforts to persuade her driving from London to the Persian Gulf made good sense. She had taken several vacation tours to Europe and thought that rated as adventurous enough. I thought if I could persuade her it was a good idea, then I might actually believe it myself.

Soon after I settled at home, in preparation for the upcoming drive, I contacted the English shipping agents. They informed me that my new vehicle would clear customs the following day and I could pick it up any time after that. Two days later, I took the train down to Southampton and had a taxi driver negotiate his way to a quiet parking lot in the back of the docks. I found a couple of slightly irritable clerks working their way through huge stacks of paper in a small office in a corner of the lot. I inquired about picking up my imported vehicle and confirmed I had ordered a black Chevrolet Blazer from New York. The younger clerk immediately knew all about the black behemoth, which dominated the center of their parking lot. They both stopped shuffling papers and looked at me with expressions that asked the question, *"How on earth did he buy that amazing vehicle?"* The one and only Blazer parked in the middle of the lot, could it really be mine? A sense of nervousness, excitement and awe hit me all at once. The reality of what I planned to undertake over the next few weeks hit me as my mind began to spin; it felt both powerful and quite daunting.

Many forms and documents from multiple government departments needed to be completed and signed. The head clerk led me through all of the paperwork, between phone calls and other dock officials stopping by to ask questions. Luckily, all of these official processes included issuing me with temporary registration plates for the vehicle. They would pass for legitimate license plates for the drive to Saudi Arabia. After an hour or so, we finished the official paperwork. Emotions fluttered between awestruck to delighted to panic-stricken and back again. I owned a big black Chevrolet Blazer; I really did own it. It looked so impressive among the other imported cars that appeared tiny and insignificant in comparison. Trying and failing to look nonchalant, I made my way through rows of imported cars to my Blazer. I pushed the key into the lock, and it turned easily. It may have appeared that my chest puffed out with pride as I opened the door, but in reality my knees began to knock due to a bout of undeniable anxiety. I quickly realized I had only ever been a passenger in several Blazers in my first year in Dhahran, I had never actually driven a Blazer. The fact I now owned a left-hand drive vehicle added to my apprehension because I had to drive on English roads where people drove on the left-hand side of the street. Why did we Brits have to be so damn different? Or to be totally unbiased, how come most of the rest of the world got it so wrong when it came to which side of the road to drive on?

The engine started on the first turn. I slipped it into gear and released the clutch. I started on my way. I soon found I could negotiate the narrow English roads much easier than I had feared. I also quickly discovered the Blazer's presence drew people's attention. They stopped and watched as the large black Blazer purred down the road. The drive from the south coast to the suburbs of northern London took me about three or four hours. As expected, when I arrived home, my mother again questioned why I'd bought such an enormous vehicle. No reasonable answer that she would understand came to mind. A generational void lay suspended between her understanding of what was sensible and my understanding of what would be exciting. No points of commonality existed and, thus, I failed to answer her question.

However, now that I think about her inability to accept my decision about the vehicle I had bought, I wonder how much of her dislike of the Blazer related to the color rather than the size. Black wasn't a common color for cars in England in the 1970s. Three categories of vehicles in London were primarily black: police cars, London taxis, and hearses. Unfortunately, with the size, my Blazer probably reminded her of a hearse, and she still felt traumatized by following the hearse at Dad's funeral, just seven years before.

Over the next week or so, I felt more comfortable driving in the crowded and narrow streets of London. I ran various errands during that period and still have clear memories of several. I had arranged to pick up a couple of boxes from the parents of a friend in Dhahran. One morning, I headed to East London to find the parents' house. After I reached their neighborhood, I pulled up to a red traffic light. While waiting, I looked over at the vehicle, which had stopped alongside me. A young couple stared at me with incredulous looks on their faces. We all wound down our windows and I quickly blurted out, "I'm amazed to see another new Blazer here in London. Wow!"

The other driver stammered, "Man, we hadn't realized how rare these would be here. Are they not normally imported to England? Yours is the first we've seen since we arrived two days ago. How come you have one, too?"

"I think they are only imported individually—not as a standard practice. I had mine shipped here as I'm heading to Saudi Arabia in about ten days' time."

"Really? We thought bringing this one here, for the duration of our work assignment, would be enough of an adventure. Saudi Arabia? Good luck with that one. What are the chances we would be stopped here, next to each other? This is freaky!"

The light turned green and I made a turn, never to see another Blazer in England ever again.

On occasions over the next few weeks, my stepfather Fred would join me for trips around the area. People stopping to stare at the black monster continuously amused him as we negotiated familiar sections of north London. As we drove along, he said he felt so high off the road that he imagined he was a member of the royalty. To my amusement on occasions he even gave people a little royal wave as we passed.

"Good morning, my royal subjects," he whispered as we passed them.

He loved being the passenger as I drove around the area. I had a different relationship with Fred than my own father. Remember, I had been a rebellious youth. I must have been a real pain much of the time. Fred came from a generation that was old-fashioned to me, but with a sense of pride that I found surprisingly enviable. He felt people should be trusted and taken at face value. A classic example of his trust took place several years later. My mother and he visited a nursery to look for a couple of garden plants. In the middle of the nursery, they passed a table that had a sign, *Please take one*," next to a bowl. They had seen a couple of other people look in the bowl and turn away from it rather hurriedly. Fred looked in the bowl and to his surprise, a small pile of ten pound notes lay in the bowl. Ten pounds could have paid for an evening out at a good restaurant for the two of them. He took one, to which Mother said he should put it back as someone must be playing a trick on people. He refused to put it back in the bowl. After they had paid for the plants and headed to their car, a TV personality stopped them for an interview. Thus, Fred got his 15 minutes of fame on the British version of *"Candid Camera"* in a skit that showed most people passed on a give-away when they saw it appeared to have actual value. Not Fred; he trusted the sign and never really questioned it. He had his quirks that made him an enjoyable addition to our family; also, he added ten pounds to his wallet and one evening he took Mother out for dinner.

My sister, Linda, and her husband, Ed, had two small children at the time. My little nephew Andrew liked cars and he wanted to see his uncle's new toy. I went for a visit for a few days, which gave their neighborhood the entertainment of wondering who owned this huge vehicle that appeared around town. I still have a clear vision in my mind of when Andrew and his sister, Elizabeth, had recovered from their shock regarding the Blazer's size. Ed had then lifted them both up onto the hood. They appeared to have sat in the middle of a large shiny black expanse and their faces shone with a mixture of pure joy and excitement. All too soon, I needed to return to London. Elizabeth and Andrew looked extremely sad and told me I could go, but they wanted me to leave the Blazer with them.

The one other major purchase I had arranged prior to my vacation in England had been a sail boat. I had decided to buy a single-handed craft called a Laser, which would fit on the roof rack of the Blazer. My English friends Mike and Anna, who lived down on the south coast of England, had put the idea in my head. Being avid sailors themselves, they convinced me to buy a boat to take back. I had familiarized myself with the great sailing beach that Aramco employees could use. It lay on the shores of a beautiful sheltered bay where shallow crystal-clear waters stretched over beds of multi-colored corals, and the winds blew consistently for much of the year. Given such a venue, my decision to buy the boat took no real thought. I arranged to visit Mike and Anna over a weekend to pick up the boat, which they had purchased for me, and more importantly, for me to take a lesson. I realized I had never sailed on my own before. It turned out to be a brief lesson after the weather deteriorated, and I remembered how cold the waters of the English Channel could be. Mike and I had problems securing the boat on the roof rack until he volunteered a spare tire, which fit snugly under the bow of the boat. We strapped and tied the boat down and thought it should survive the journey. However the arrangement resulted in one significant problem. I couldn't open the back of the truck or open the hood without untying several sections of rope. I recognized it could have been worse, and soon enough it would become so.

Two days before I departed, I went to open the tailgate, but the lock failed to work. No matter what I tried, it wouldn't open. In desperation I drove to the one garage in northern London that claimed to deal with Chevrolet vehicles. They looked at the lock, but said they only had spare parts for older models.

On the day of departure, I confronted the task of loading the sailboat onto the roof rack on my own. It had been straight-forward when I took it off after I returned from Mike and Anna's. However, to get it back on top of the roof rack, on my own, took some effort and a few choice swear words. The sailboat did create a number of complications with loading and interesting challenges at later border crossings, but I still considered it to have been an excellent purchase. Eventually, I had it strapped down tightly, and I loaded my own gear into the back of the Blazer. To get my gear into the back presented additional challenges since the tailgate wouldn't open. The Blazer had only two doors, which meant I had to clamber around the passenger seat, and lift the object over the backseat. I then climbed over the backseat to get into the luggage area so I could pack the object where I wanted it. I felt grateful for being young, agile and not too easily frustrated. Despite my accepting attitude, I admit at times I wished the tailgate lock could have sensed a little of my suppressed rage. The lock remained broken for the duration of the trip back to Dhahran, which made unloading and re-loading tiresome.

Back in London, I never thought I would need to unload and repack all of our cargo later. What possible reason could necessitate that?

CHAPTER 4
UNTO EUROPE

الله شاء إن   الله شاء إن   الله شاء إن   الله شاء إن   الله شاء إن   الله شاء إن   الله شاء إن

My mother's facial expression indicated more than a touch of trepidation as I said my farewells. She'd made it clear to me that she found this whole journey to be perturbing and beyond her comprehension. I could only promise to write a letter when we arrived back in Dhahran. The trip would take about two weeks, and the letter could take as long to be sent back to London. I believe my mother held her breath for a month with her fears painting dire circumstances in her imagination. At the same time, she stayed present in my mind as the days passed. Occasionally, I wished she would leave me alone, even though the reality of her presence resided only in my head; but when times turned uncertain or difficult, I will admit I found a level of comfort in her virtual concern.

I'd told her many people had driven the route and that we could always be assured of assistance, if we ever needed it. In truth, I knew once we left Austria we would be on our own, without much hope of finding English speaking help. This comprised about 80% of the entire journey. I'd been forewarned of this potential problem by my buddy, Hughie, and others. Additionally, to say many people had ever driven the route could only be considered a stretch too—less than ten of my friends from Aramco had made the journey and maybe a couple of hundred people ever did it. Routes could have varied, generally most people drove through France, Germany, Austria, Yugoslavia, Greece, Turkey, Syria, Jordan and Saudi Arabia. Some people may have touched Switzerland, Italy, Albania, Bulgaria, Lebanon or Iraq. It all depended on the political map of Europe and the Middle East, at the time of their journey. The map changed constantly.

I departed my mother's house early in the morning, drove through central London, and headed south toward the English Channel. Penny's parents lived in Worthing, a coastal resort town that was a few miles to the west of Brighton where I lived for a number of years during and following college. I knew the route down to the coast and then drove across to Worthing.

Upon my arrival, Penny opened the front door with a cheerful, "Hallo, Barry. I hope you found the address alright."

"Yes, no problem. Your directions guided me straight here."

"Barry, this is my mum and dad." She turned to her parents, who stood a little behind her. "This is Barry. We'll be taking the trip together." I felt rather uncertain as to what they thought when I arrived. I had no idea how Penny convinced them this journey would be a fine adventure, or if they felt as mystified as my own mother. I sensed a level of nervous tension between the three of them as her parents stood arm in arm, wondering what to do next.

After we all murmured greetings, Penny's mum resorted to the standard English response to any difficult situation. She asked me, "Would you like a nice cup of tea while you sort everything out?" How wonderfully English I thought to myself.

I declined her offer of tea as Penny and her dad led me into the back room.

There, Penny introduced me to her stack of gear that needed to be packed into the back of the Blazer. It looked smaller than I had feared. My sense of relief lasted only a moment, until I realized I couldn't see one obvious item. I had, in a moment of reckless enthusiasm months before, promised to take her bicycle too. Suddenly, my mental image of the space still in the back of the Blazer shrank, especially when I added Ron's gear which would come later.

In my mind, I quickly pictured how to pack her gear into the Blazer and said, "Well, I think that should fit alright. However, we have one small problem; the tailgate failed the other day, and everything needs to be loaded through the front passenger door."

Her father frowned. "Couldn't you get it fixed?"

"I tried. I went to the one Chevy dealership in London. They didn't have parts for this latest model. I'll admit it's frustrating. I just hope we don't have to unload everything at any time."

He nodded, "I hope you're right about that."

Penny looked up from a box she had just taped shut. "I'm sure we'll be fine. Let's start loading."

Her father looked at me with an expression that seemed to say, *Well, young man, if you're taking my daughter on this wild trip, step up and show us what sort of man you actually are. Get loading.*

Penny and I managed to pack her gear, with a little assistance from her dad. Lastly, we tackled the bike. It took all three of us to maneuver it. We grunted, we pushed it, we mumbled, and maneuvered it, and eventually it fit on top of everything else. It felt reasonably secure.

Penny's mother had a look on her face similar to my mother's expression when we completed the packing and were ready to depart. The look spanned multiple emotions: fear, wonder, happiness, anxiety and inquisition—who is this guy? In contrast, her father appeared to be a little more into the anticipation of the adventure and paths less trodden. After waving good-bye, we drove east toward the famous White Cliffs of Dover. The initial miles of our drive progressed easily enough as the weekend traffic moved smoothly with fewer trucks to slow it down.

After a short distance, Penny looked over and said, "This is going to sound silly. I'm surprised so many people are stopping to stare as we pass. I know Blazers are unusual and rather large for English roads."

I interrupted her thought. "You're absolutely correct. It felt strange to me at first. I've been driving here for the last couple of weeks, and I'm used to it now." I went on to explain about my step-father Fred who had imagined himself to be royalty. Penny smiled as she slouched a little, attempting to relax in preparation for the longest drive she had ever experienced.

We arrived at the docks at Dover in plenty of time for our scheduled hovercraft crossing of the English Channel. Neither of us had ever been on a hovercraft before, and we wondered how it would compare to a standard ferry.

One of the dock hands walked over to me and pointed to a line off to the edge the parking area. "Oh, mate, this load's a little tall. Can you park over there?"

"Sure. Do you think I'll be able to get on alright?"

"We'll get you on, mate. It will just need a bit of a shove."

I looked over to where he had pointed. "That open line on the side?"

"Right. We'll load you last." He headed off to direct other drivers, while I repositioned the Blazer into the special line.

After all of the other cars had boarded successfully, they told me to drive slowly up the steep ramp that led to the car deck of the hovercraft. I had no doubt about their concerns—the top of the opening looked incredibly low. As my front tires hit the main deck, the chief deck hand waved at me furiously as he screamed at me. I believe he told me, "Stop," but his words were lost in all of the intense background noise of the hovercraft's engines being started.

The combined height of the Blazer and boat wouldn't squeeze under the entrance. In my mind, I compared myself to a limbo dancer who failed to get under the bar at the first height. I was glad to be last and not be watched by all the other drivers, limbo dancers, behind me. The deck hands had a quick discussion, and while one came to shout something at me that I couldn't comprehend, two others headed toward my front wheels. To my alarm, the front of the Blazer dropped several inches—they had let pressure out of my two front tires. They told me to back down the ramp and come up it at an angle. Penny and I held our breaths as we came up the ramp for a second attempt. Thankfully, we just squeezed under the bar, our limbo team of deckhands exploded with applause and celebrated by high-fiving anybody in sight. We parked at the end of a line of cars before we ventured up to the passenger cabin. It looked surprisingly large and appeared to be unexpectedly similar to a passenger lounge on one of the standard ferries. The hovercraft's overall size startled both of us as it carried 40 or 50 vehicles as well as about 250 passengers.

We sat and looked out of the lounge windows while dock workers prepared our craft for departure. My legs began to twitch and I felt my temperature rise, as an intensity gripped the lounge with all of the huge turbine engines being started and wound up. Their deafening noise made conversation impossible so we had to resort to lip reading and hand signals. In my frustration with our inability to easily talk, I wondered if this state would continue for the entire crossing. As the engines hit a crescendo, I felt my body tensing and I sat more upright. The huge craft started to shake violently. I thought we would move forward, but when movement came we went straight up. My confusion continued until my rational mind kicked in—the hovercraft needed a cushion of air to float on. Even after this shift in my thinking, I watched a nearby wall as we rose and was shocked to realize the skirt on the craft was about five or six feet tall. I scratched my right cheek nervously as my mind wrestled with thoughts around mathematics, physics, and engineering. I was impressed the turbines could lift the weight of the craft. From brochure pictures I had seen, I knew the skirt would now be straightened which allowed the hovercraft to float on a cushion of air, despite its size and weight. I relaxed a little and looked over at Penny who also had given up trying to talk; she simply smiled back at me. The continual shaking and intense noise gained a degree of normalcy as we started to slowly move forward. We made a gentle left turn on the concrete slipway to face the sea. Gradually we increased speed, and without any discernible difference, we slipped from the concrete apron onto the water. The craft gained speed and soon skimmed across the sea at about 60 miles an hour. The vibration and sound subsided, or had we been numbed into not noticing them as much? I wondered if such hovercrafts had been used by NASA to train the original space shuttle astronauts who experienced severe vibration and noise at the time of launch.

As we sat watching the sea rush past the misted windows, I thought about the Aramco camp that would be our final destination. I knew Mother and Fred had reservations about my return to Saudi Arabia. Being away from them allowed me to drop my defensiveness and really think about why I had decided to go back when I knew it wasn't an ideal situation. Life around our camp was secure, enjoyable, and often amusing. Unfortunately, my mother could not conceive our remarkable reality; she could only paint interior pictures of grim, sweltering and filthy conditions. It wasn't for a lack of my trying to explain my situation. Her biases would not allow her to accept that life was quite workable and pleasant—not ideal, however, it was much better than just tolerable. I admitted life in Saudi Arabia required a mental shift. When I left camp to head into any of the local towns, I was never in danger, but I needed to be aware of my circumstances.

As we skimmed across the water, the turbines had been turned down, which allowed for some conversation. I turned towards Penny and shared some of my thoughts with her. "Do you have the feeling we, ex-pats, need to be especially careful about our circumstances when we visit Al Khobar? The downtown market is only five or seven miles from camp, but we are then beyond the protection of Aramco security, and downtown the local police hold jurisdiction."

She looked away from the window with a thoughtful expression on her face. "Sometimes. To be honest, I tend to be really careful when I'm down in Al Khobar, and I try to not go too often."

I nodded. "I avoid going too frequently and try to be aware of my surroundings at all times. As we should expect, we have to comply with cultural norms. Men shouldn't wear shorts and women have to have their shoulders and upper arms covered. In addition to the local police, we need to be careful of the religious police—the Matawa. They are, not surprisingly, more zealous than the civil police on certain matters like clothing and behavior."

Several years later, toward the end of my stay in Saudi Arabia, I had grown quite an unruly mass of long hair. This caught the attention of a few religious police and several of their friends while I walked through downtown Al Khobar one afternoon. Unfortunately, this incident happened during a religious holiday when traditional customs required Muslim men to have had serious haircuts or even shave themselves completely. I could see the Matawa were probably talking about me as they huddled together with furtive glances in my direction. They suddenly turned and ran toward me. Thankfully, by that time, I had taken up long distance running despite the heat. With my long legs, I quickly dropped the group that surged after me with rusty scissors and knives in hand, apparently intent on giving me a trim. I didn't want to discover the quality of their barbering skills firsthand.

Our progress across the English Channel continued smoothly, but I did have brief moments of angst when we suddenly transitioned from skimming across what appeared to be shallow water to flying over sand banks and back again. That just didn't feel normal. When I looked out of the windows, I had the impression I was on a speeding boat. Then, to have that "boat" suddenly hurtle over a sand bar without any disastrous mishap played strange games with my expectations. In truth, we skimmed along on a cushion of air that made no distinction between water, sand or concrete. I sat back and told Penny what I had just realized.

She smiled with a knowing expression "Oh. That was what just went through your head. It would explain the puzzled expression you had."

I glanced around the lounge, while my thoughts contemplated how the mind actually worked. I realized ideas flashed into my conscious and all too soon newer ones were created and vied to hold my attention. Intrigued by how my mind reacted to what I had witnessed with the sand bars, I considered how my mind pre-assigned concepts to an experience and then what happened to my mind when something different to those pre-conceived concepts occurred. Thinking about my inner thought processes was new to me—my poor education had never opened my eyes to such amazingly puzzling ideas. A new way to see and experience the world had become visible to me. My heart beat a little faster than normal as thoughts raced in my mind. I wanted to understand my own mind and how it worked. In Saudi Arabia, I had found different ways to learn about and challenge my physical body. Now my mind and thoughts had been thrown into a stack, marked *"For my deeper understanding."*

After about 30 minutes of gliding across the open sea, we slowed as we approached the French coastline, and with the decrease in speed the vibration began to build again. We effortlessly glided off the sea and up the concrete slipway. The engines' noise began to soften as we gradually descended to sit firmly on the concrete with no air cushion. We returned to the Blazer which looked a little pathetic with its front tires deflated to about half pressure. After most vehicles had driven off without any concern, I advanced toward the opening at the other end of the hovercraft and the ramp to freedom. I wondered how much effort it would take to off-load us. I stopped near a deckhand and indicated my concern for the amount of clearance for the boat on the roof rack. The French deckhand gave it a cursory glance and a quick confirming wave before he turned away to take another drag on his foul Gauloise cigarette—such a contrast to the engaged limbo deck hands on the English side of the Channel. I took a quick look at the amount of room above and found the opening at the other end of the hovercraft had a couple of extra feet of height, so I had no reason for worry.

I drove out of the docks and looked for the first gas station so that I could re-inflate my front tires. It felt good to have all of the tires back up to full pressure. The Blazer looked like it had been returned to an even keel. I joined the stream of tourist traffic as it left the port. We noticed many French locals took a second look at the large black vehicle, but at least we could then drive on the correct side of the road as I had the steering wheel on the left.

I had worked out roughly how far I wanted to cover each day. I didn't have a plan that had to be followed exactly, which allowed time for unexpected events. However, we needed to stay somewhat on schedule because Penny and I had to meet Ron in Istanbul in six days.

Our initial plans had needed to change at the last minute. Ron originally planned to leave London with me to pick up Penny, but he hadn't managed to obtain his Saudi Arabian re-entry visa in time. Despite the fact that his company submitted the necessary paperwork and his passport to the Saudi embassy in plenty of time, the embassy failed to issue the visa on the promised date. As I drove away from London, Ron's passport still remained lost in the Saudi Arabian embassy's paperwork process. When this became apparent, the embassy gave Ron a new date when the visa would be ready, and we estimated that gave him enough time to fly to Istanbul, where we could meet him. This enforced a certain time schedule on Penny and me for the first half of the journey. To drive to Istanbul by the arranged date didn't present us with any obvious problems, but it left us with little time for unexpected delays.

We soon settled into the drive across France. I headed south-east toward the German border, which meant I could avoid the traffic around Paris. It was a familiar route to me as I had previously taken this same route to several climbing vacations in Austria and Italy. No freeways existed back then, so we drove along the main roads that wove between the larger cities of northern France. As we left one provincial town, St. Quentin, I turned to Penny and said, "You know I do enjoy driving across northern France, but sometimes the local road rules can be disconcerting. In fact at times they can make me feel rather tense."

Penny brushed some dirt off her tailored slacks before she turned her attention back to me and inquired, "How come?"

"Certain districts or towns have local laws regarding who has priority at junctions. In parts of France, drivers who enter a main road from a side road have the right of way over those already on the main road. So, I need to constantly worry about every car I see as I never know who has the priority at any time."

She paused for a couple of seconds while she thought about this local law before replying, "Oh, that makes sense of something I saw a few miles back. I assumed a driver was reckless when he appeared to come barreling out of a country lane onto the main road without a glance. So my thought that he was stupid may've been incorrect; you mean, he might have had the right of way?"

"Quite possibly—it all depends on the law in those parts," I said, I had seen several similar types of incidents over the years.

She laughed, saying, "I feel so much happier now knowing you'll be doing all the driving." She took a keener interest in other cars for a period of time.

Later, when we were about halfway across northern France, I saw a small French car in my rearview mirror as it made dangerous maneuvers to overtake several cars behind me. He settled in to follow me closely while he looked for opportunities to pass me too.

I quickly glanced toward Penny. "Hey, watch this car behind me. He's anxious to overtake me, and I suspect I know why."

She immediately responded in a tone that challenged how I could read other driver's intentions. "OK. Why is he going to overtake you, now?"

"He wants to turn right shortly. I've seen others do the same."

"No. That doesn't make any sense."

After a short distance, I noticed him pull out. "Here he goes. Let's see what he does."

He barely drew in front of me and then threw the car to the right. I stood on the brakes hard to avoid him. He disappeared down a side road.

Penny looked over at me with a look of righteous indignation. "That fool could have gotten us all killed!"

My simple response, "Welcome to driving in rural France." For an unexplainable reason, the locals in certain areas played a form of chicken when they needed to turn right off a main road. I had talked with friends who experienced the same behavior. We came to realize that, for safety sake, we needed to keep constant vigilance on the rear view mirror, to watch for potential kamikaze drivers, intent on turning right immediately after they passed our vehicles.

Penny and I decided to stop early for dinner in Reims as we found a good selection of restaurants in our guidebook. We thought we should take advantage of decent restaurants, as food options in countries later on our route might be a little more spartan. After we found a small bistro, we ordered dinner and chatted about our first day on the road. I admitted, "I'm a little tired after today's travels. I don't want to take time to explore Reims. However, I do remember the city has two noteworthy characteristics."

Penny replied, "Not exploring Reims is fine with me. I also feel a little drained from our first day." She sipped on her glass of wine and looked back at me. "Oh, and what's so noteworthy about Reims?"

I pointed to the couple of paintings on the walls. "As the art work shows, Reims is a center of champagne production. For many years, champagne has added significantly to the city's coffers, especially from tourists who come to taste and buy cases of the stuff. This explains the huge acreages of vineyards which extend in all directions of the countryside that surrounds the city."

She looked puzzled. "How do you know this?"

"I've talked to locals on my earlier trips through the region. Not surprisingly, they're proud of their champagne."

"Interesting." She thought about this for a minute before enquiring, "What was the second thing?"

"Ah, yes. Secondly, a German general signed their unconditional surrender to the Allies at the close of the European theater of World War II on May 7th 1945 here at Reims."

She smiled, but with a frown. "You actually know the date, as well. You must have been a Second World War buff when you were a kid."

"I will admit books and magazines on that World War were about the only thing I read growing up. I was such a poor reader, it took me ages to finish even the smallest book."

Penny thought for a while. "That's so sad. I love reading. It gives me so much pleasure. I can get lost in a book for hours and hours. I'm not sure what I would do with myself if I didn't read."

"Ha. I'm so different to that."

After dinner, we drove on for another hour or so. For some time, Penny was lost in thought. Suddenly she shook her head, turned towards me, and said, "Over dinner, we mentioned the war. I have always wondered why my parents rarely talk about it and never with any real passion. Do you find the same in your household?"

"That's an interesting question. My folks didn't like to talk about it much either. I'm not absolutely certain what my father did in the war. He worked as a telephone engineer, repairing phone lines and exchanges in London each day after all the bombing. It must have been horrifying work. He wouldn't talk about it. I sense he had strong feelings about it which he chose to keep buried, and he'd never open up about that time."

She grimaced. "That's similar to me. My father was in the army and, to be honest, I'm not sure I can tell you where he served. I just sense he has hardened feelings about Germany and France that I can't explain."

I looked over at her, nodding. "Yes, I have the same feeling about my parents. They certainly have a negative attitude towards both France and Germany. I don't think seeing Charles De Gaulle on the TV news promoting himself as a great leader helped their feelings."

Penny agreed. "I know what you mean. Hitler and Germany were the aggressors—they needed to be stopped. Later, France had to be liberated by the Brits and the Yanks. I suppose we may have picked up on those bad attitudes ourselves."

"I can't deny it. I know I have. The world would be in a far different state if it hadn't been for us, Brits, standing our ground for the first half of the war. We certainly do owe a great deal to both the U.S. and the Soviets. It took all three of us to defeat Germany and Japan. I hope we never see another war like that one, it was ugly. Even if we win, and we did in WWII, the aftereffects and consequences are so incredibly complicated and potentially troublesome. Their influence ripples out for decades, like now, we have the Cold War."

"I agree with you. War isn't the answer. I'm not sure my brain can handle much more of this subject right now. I need to sleep. Are we stopping soon?"

For our first night, we camped near the French city of Metz. When I first packed the back of the Blazer, I had considered the need to pull out gear for overnights. As everything needed to be pulled over the backseat and out of the passenger door, I was happy to extract what we needed in only a few searches of the pile of gear in the back. I erected a tent at an official campsite which had been laid out among the trees in a small forest. We sat around and talked as the last vestiges of summer daylight gave way to darkness. The campsite had bathrooms which we used before we retired to our sleeping bags. Penny slept in the tent while I found a patch of grass for my bag. I suspected this campsite might feel like quite a luxurious venue in comparison to circumstances we would meet in days to come.

CHAPTER 5

OLD FAMILIAR PLACES

الله شاء ان   الله شاء ان   الله شاء ان   الله شاء ان   الله شاء ان   الله شاء ان   الله شاء ان

The following morning, we drove through the last section of France before we crossed into Germany, just north of Strasbourg. I always felt a little startled when I crossed this border—the German guards all carried automatic machine guns. At that point in time, terrorism in Europe didn't represent much of a threat and so, to me, such weapons appeared excessive. Ah, we can only yearn for the good old days.

However, now that I think about it, this was 1977, and Germany was still divided into West Germany and East Germany. The Berlin Wall still defiantly divided that city. In later years, Berlin would once again become the German capital. But, in the 1970s, all German borders were heavily armed, even those on the French side. Tension existed in West Germany, as the Soviet Union controlled East Germany and all countries allied to the Warsaw Pact—Poland, Hungary, Czechoslovakia, Romania, Albania, Bulgaria and Yugoslavia. Considering the generally peaceful conditions throughout Western Europe, this heavily armed border was the one point where I could witness that the Cold War still continued.

As I settled into the German autobahns and the accompanying different set of road signs, I took some time to think about the differences between countries recovering from the War in western Europe and the oppressed countries of eastern Europe. Such thoughts led me back to the conversation Penny and I had on the hovercraft. I wanted to talk about my impressions of life on and around the Aramco camp with Penny. I hadn't felt comfortable discussing this subject with my mother and Fred as they had rather negative attitudes toward most points east of Austria. It would have justified their feeling that I made a bad decision to return to Saudi Arabia and stay for a few more years. I was more willing to talk through my thoughts with Penny, as we shared some common experiences.

I started, "I think it would be wrong to give the impression life in camp could be seen as a light-hearted combination of work, partying, and whimsical nonsense, which sometimes may be true. However, occasionally, I've detected a darker and somewhat disquieting side to life in camp and in Saudi Arabia generally."

Intrigued by my train of thought, Penny simply responded, "Tell me more."

I scratched the stubble that had grown on my cheeks and considered the matter further. But I was distracted by a need to pay particular attention to my driving and navigating. In certain sections, roundabouts terminated long stretches of the autobahns. I carefully drove around each of them so that I made sure to exit onto the correct new autobahn. Generally I headed east and later to the south. To make navigational mistakes on these roundabouts could be troublesome as sometimes the first exit could be an hour's drive down the next stretch of the autobahn. I didn't want to deal with a potential 2-hour detour to return to the roundabout where the original mistake occurred. These huge roundabouts allowed me to drive around them without the need to take my foot off the accelerator—they each covered acres of ground. In fact, a couple of times I forgot I still circled around one of these large roundabouts as I felt the curve was just another normal stretch of autobahn.

After we joined the next portion of autobahn and I resettled in with a group of cars that drove at a similar speed to myself, I continued, "Once I established a routine living in camp, I began to feel life was rather surreal and strange. Eventually, I managed to define what felt uncomfortable—a combination of two factors played into the feeling. To me, camp represented both what I thought life may be like on an army base and life as it was presented on the 1960s TV soap opera 'Peyton Place.'"

Penny searched through her small bag for some tissues. "So, why those two things?"

"I compared the Aramco camp to an army base because when something needed to be fixed or dealt with, a phone call brought out a repair crew. It left little need for personal or domestic responsibility. It felt fine at first but when I considered the lack of ability of those sent out to do the work, it soon began to drive me crazy. Then, it also felt like 'Peyton Place' because, as happened in that soap opera, everyone knew everybody else's personal business."

I would note that after I'd lived in camp four years, these two negative factors significantly swayed my decision to quit as I needed a rather more traditional community to live in, one where I managed my life and my environment.

As she listened to my comments about life in the Aramco camp, Penny pulled snacks out of a bag of supplies to look for a package of cookies we had bought earlier. After she found them, she looked at me and quizzically enquired, "So, why did you decide to stay on?"

I shifted in my seat and took a little time to think before I found the answer to her question. "What an interesting question. I suppose the truth is I find living in Saudi Arabia challenges me in ways that I like. I'm becoming more confident and assertive. I'm willing to face difficulties rather than cower from them. So, currently, the positives of life in camp out-weigh the negatives."

As we drove south, I hardly gave the map a thought because I felt totally confident of our route through France and Germany, before heading toward Austria. While in college and for a number of years afterwards, I spent several weeks each summer climbing in the Austrian and Italian Alps with a large group of friends. Probably the biggest difference between those previous journeys and this one had been that I didn't fear the Blazer could potentially break down at any point, unlike my earlier English cars. No disguised disparaging comment is implied in that last sentence regarding the reliability of English cars; more a comment about the age and resulting reliability of the English cars I could afford at that earlier point in time.

On the last of those climbing vacations, I had been undecided about the trip and only made arrangements to take my own car at the last minute. When I was with a gathering of climbing friends, I checked to find any others who still needed a ride to the Alps. Two Welsh sisters, whom I knew vaguely, said they would love to come with me as they hadn't made any travel arrangements. We departed a day or two behind the main group. The sisters planned to stay in tents that their college friends had taken and so they brought no tent of their own for the journey. I said my tent would be large enough for the three of us and we could share it for the couple of nights on the road. I soon discovered my invitation had been a serious error of judgment. We crawled into the tent after the first long day of driving. Before I could settle and feel comfortable, one of the sisters started gently snoring. Then the other started. I, unfortunately, was jammed in the middle, between these two noise makers. Once their snoring had started, I found sleep to be completely impossible. They varied in volume, they harmonized for a while, changed to agonizing discord, stopped, and then restarted. By morning, I was exhausted having hardly slept and faced a long day on the road most unhappily. On the second night, their chorus became my nightmare and, by midnight, I headed to a quiet grove of trees about a quarter mile from the tent. They both earned the right to be described as incredible, but for all the wrong reasons for a 28-year-old lad. When we reached Austria, I erected my tent, gave it over to the sisters and went to crash in a buddy's tent for the duration of the vacation.

Thus, I felt quite comfortable to put the tent up for Penny and retire to sleep alongside the car. Let me restate one detail; yes, I acknowledged she was an attractive young lady, and I saw us as just good friends and companions for this journey. As to whether this reflected the reality of the situation or my 28-year-old lack of understanding about relationships is open to debate.

Germany allowed for hours of relatively easy driving as frequent sign-posts kept us informed of our progress along the autobahns, and they had no speed limits. In fact, the lack of speed restrictions caused the only significant problem, I constantly needed to keep a close eye on the rear-view mirror. Anything that may have been a tiny dot, miles behind, could quickly become a Mercedes or Porsche with their angry drivers flashing their lights as they hurtled up to sit right on my tail. Therefore, I felt it necessary to look more backwards than forwards at times.

We progressed steadily along the autobahns without incident since the local laws had no strange provisions that gave traffic entering the autobahns priority, as we had found in provincial areas of France. The miles and the hours passed. North of Munich, I decided to call a slightly earlier end to the day's driving. I wanted to find a quiet place to camp before we reached the outskirts as I knew Munich could take several hours to circumnavigate. I wanted to avoid unnecessarily long tiring days so early in the trip.

Thankfully, the area apparently saw many tourists as we found plenty of sign-posts for campgrounds at autobahn off-ramps. We chose one randomly. The campground looked clean and efficiently run, as one expected in Germany. We ventured to a local small town for dinner. The one restaurant boasted a rather Bavarian menu; it was basically fried red meat and potatoes in any of twelve slight variations. We survived and regretted the heaviest meal of the entire 15-day drive. We skipped breakfast in the morning as we still felt full and somewhat fearful of what selection of fried sausages they considered to be breakfast. Instead, we quickly found a café for two coffees.

I resumed our drive to the south on the autobahn. As the caffeine hadn't kicked in yet, I yawned and stretched. "I don't know how you feel about these autobahns. To me they feel rather sterile and uniform. This is Germany, so I suppose that's what I should expect."

Penny smiled. "There's no denying we're in Germany. The towns are so clean, and all the buildings are impeccably maintained."

I asked her, "Have you noticed how the people have an abruptness about them? They're friendly, but I feel it wouldn't take too much for them to become critical and severe."

"I think I can see that, now you say it. I certainly sensed a difference in the disposition of them versus the French who were friendly and rather laissez faire."

"Wow. You're awake. A French based description for the French people. My coffee's not working yet."

Penny chuckled and turned to take a look at an isolated farm that was tucked in an open area of flat ground, surrounded by huge swaths of forest. The farm house and barn had exposed beams and roof lines that had bent under the strain of centuries of harvests and numerous generations of inhabitants.

Penny posed a question that I had been considering. "I wonder how long that farm has been there?"

"Yes, I was wondering that too. It must have been amazing the day when this autobahn was forced through the forests and along the edge of their fields."

"I wonder if they tried to stop its construction."

"I can't imagine they were too happy to have their peace and quiet destroyed forever. Or did they see it as an improvement as they would be able to reach town far more quickly than their old route along the trail through the woods?"

"Maybe. I just can't imagine the local authorities would listen to a single farm owner." She looked around. "And I don't see an entrance or exit ramp along this stretch of the autobahn."

I thought about the farm for a few minutes. "I suspect you're right. Local authorities probably have the power to ignore a single farmer." We drove in silence for a couple of miles.

Thinking about the farmer and his rights left me in a rather sour mood. My mind gravitated back to thinking about living in Dhahran. "Returning to yesterday's conversation, I sometimes feel we're reasonably well protected in camp from a more insidious and authoritarian side to living in Arabia. However, it does exist even in camp in certain ways. Do you see it too? Or am I being overly sensitive?"

Penny thought about it for a brief time before replying, "I'm not sure I saw it as darker, but, I suppose, as westerners in Saudi Arabia, we need to be constantly vigilant. As you lived off camp for a short time, you may have had experiences which swayed your thoughts on the matter."

Nodding, I added, "In the local cities like Al Khobar and Dammam, the darker side becomes quite apparent to ex-pats who keep their eyes open to their surroundings. The issue is simply that non-Muslim westerners sometimes are seen as infidels, which means we can be regarded as less than camel droppings. Let me be clear, the vast majority of Saudis see us as human beings and treat us with respect. It's that, on occasions, if there's a dispute between a Saudi and a westerner, then the westerner will lose the disagreement simply because he's an infidel—it has nothing to do with the merits of their versions of the dispute. In such incidents, the Saudi would more than likely be compensated by the westerner. That is unless the Saudi holds a more universal understanding of responsibility, which happens more often among the few Saudis who live in camp or those who've been educated abroad."

Penny handed me a water bottle and thought about what I said. She continued, "It seems you've experienced aspects of local life that I, so far, haven't witnessed. I'm not denying what you say, but it hasn't been my experience so far. You say it happened in camp too."

Straightaway, I recalled an unfortunate incident. "One example comes to mind immediately and it actually happened in camp one afternoon after work. A friend, Richard, stopped in a line of traffic outside the post office while he waited for people to cross the road. A young Saudi guy's car had been parked on the side of the road. He returned to his car, started it, and drove out of the space without any regard for anything around him. Within only a few feet, he slammed straight into Richard's car which was still halted in traffic. The claim for repairs went before a local judge. The plaintiff simply stated 'He's an infidel and needs to pay for my damages.' The judge agreed immediately, and Richard paid for the Saudi's new front fender, despite his being stationary when the Saudi hit him."

Penny looked a little shocked by the story and thought about it while she stared out the windscreen. A brief rain squall turned the dust on the windscreen into a murky film. The wipers removed the initial drops of rain and dust from the windscreen and broke through Penny's musings. She let out a long breath and uttered. "Whew, we just never know, do we? It reminds me of a silly story I've heard a few times. If a westerner hits any scrawny camel and the Saudi claims to be compensated, then the camel suddenly becomes the most prized stud camel in the entire country and worth a fortune."

I laughed. "Hey, that's true. I've also heard that. I wonder what grain of truth started that tale."

Looking back on that time, I wouldn't say these types of prejudicial events occurred often. However, a higher potential for such an occurrence existed as soon as I left camp. In any dispute, local authorities would judge me to be at fault simply based on the color of my skin, as it indicated I was an infidel. I do admit that a sense of being seen as inferior, less than, and vulnerable haunted my thoughts at times.

Do such concerns sound familiar, considering more recent events here in the US? Several come to mind: the disgraceful internment camps on the southern border for refugees, the deportation of parents after their children have been ripped out of their care, denial of due process for asylum seekers, and the legitimate claims of groups such as Black Lives Matter? I wouldn't claim my sense of insecurity and feeling like a second-class citizen compared in any way to the fear experienced by African Americans, Latinos, and other people of color here, today; but it gave me a glimpse into the horrors that can be their daily lives. From my Saudi experiences of occasionally feeling judged, helpless, or fearful in such circumstances, based on societally ingrained and religiously supported bias, I have no doubt such feelings are truly dreadful, undermining, degrading, stifling and all-consuming. They can distort and pollute how people see others, even if the others belong to the same group. I question whether human beings, no matter the color of their skin, their religion, their sexual orientation, or any other distinction should ever be exposed to these types of feelings and fears within any civilized society. I feel if any society has become truly civilized, then the answer would be an unequivocal, "No," in all cases.

I said to Penny, "One would imagine if these types of prejudicial, and in our minds, unjust incidents occurred more frequently, we all had the ability to simply quit Aramco and leave the country at any time."

She looked at me puzzled, briefly, before she understood my real meaning. "Oh, yes, you're right. We cannot simply leave Saudi Arabia, can we? Whenever we want to fly out of the kingdom, we need to apply for an exit visa. It can take several weeks to obtain an exit visa from the government, despite having Aramco acting on our behalf in these matters."

I agreed. "At first, I wondered why the exit visas took so long to be issued. Now I suspect it takes weeks to research every foreigner who wishes to leave the country, to ensure they don't have an unresolved dispute with any local Saudi. If any matter is still outstanding, then the exit visa will be denied. Recently, I heard of a Brit at the British Aircraft Corporation at the airport who had his exit visa turned down."

Our conversations continued to cover different subjects that focused on life and friends in Saudi. Our talks, as well as food and drink breaks, kept us awake and energized during the hours of driving. I certainly appreciated that I had a companion for the journey. Taking that drive alone would have been arduous, physically and mentally. I would have felt content with my own company and not in need of constant distractions. However, the daily and ever increasing sense of uncertainty and the constant need for awareness would have taken a far larger toll on my psychological self without Penny's company. I felt confident driving through Germany, but what lay ahead felt heavier and more daunting with each day that passed. I hadn't expected this overpowering sensation, and we had experienced no problems, thus far.

Penny broke my train of thought. "Do you want any water or anything to eat? We have been on the road for a while, and I don't want you wasting away."

"I could probably do with a little water to start. Thanks."

She handed me a bottled water after she unscrewed the cap. I took a good long drink and passed it back to her before I asked, "So. Here's an obvious question for you. We both have to be careful when we venture to Al Khobar or Dammam, and you are far more restricted than I am as you're female. How do you feel in that situation?"

She took some time to think. "Well, at first, I found the need to cover my shoulders and upper arms when I left camp to be annoying. I bought a couple of lightweight shawls which do the job. So, now,

I don't really think about it; I carry one in my bag, so I'm always prepared."

"What about driving? As all females are prohibited from driving, you have to take the bus or get a lift from someone. Doesn't that bug you?"

Penny smiled before she replied, "Well, to be honest, I'm not fond of driving, and am quite happy to have others drive. I do appreciate you're doing all of it now."

"Thanks." I looked over at her and realized that was one of the first times she had really opened up to me. I wondered if I had ever done so myself. I took a minute to think about that before continuing, "Now we both sense women in Saudi Arabia appear to not be valued or respected. I'm sure there are some who are, but I suspect they're a real minority. So, how is it for you, a western woman, living and working in Saudi Arabia?

"Wow, what a question? You know, I try not to think about it too much, because I know I can't do anything about it. I recognize I'm treated well in the Aramco camp, and I'm protected from what many Saudi women experience. From what I've seen, many are treated like second-class citizens, but what can we do about it? I knew it would probably be like this before I came. I don't turn a blind eye to the problem. I just don't know what I can do."

"How did you know about the issue before you left England?" I inquired.

"I had two friends from school who had taken jobs with an oil company in Libya. They were the ones who suggested I work in the desert to save money. Unfortunately, no openings were available in Libya when I looked, so I decided to try Aramco when I saw their advertisement."

"If you had gone to Libya, you wouldn't be on this crazy trip now." I jested.

"You've got that right. And so far, this is fine with me."

We chuckled and fell silent, while we contemplated the choices we had taken that brought us to this time and place.

Many miles later, we departed the autobahns, transitioned to winding main roads that started to ascend toward higher elevations.

The Bavarian Alps are smaller than the main Alps, but storms that occasionally crossed the area could present drivers with difficulties at any time of the year. We climbed through deeply forested valleys and sporadic rain showers quickly changed to snow flurries. As we gained elevation, pine trees soon lost their dark green under frozen accumulations of wet snow. Clouds hung heavy and dark as we wove our way along roads that zig-zagged up mountainsides, through tunnels, and over passes.

I turned to Penny. "Well, this may be the only time this vehicle will ever see snow."

"Yes. You had better use those wiper blades while you can. They may be rather idle in the years ahead."

I countered. "Oh. We do see a few inches of rain each year around camp."

Penny laughed. "Okay. Yes, we do get a few minor deluges—however, if they happen at night we could miss them entirely for one complete year. So enjoy using your wipers while you can."

I looked across at her. "And I'm pleased to have the heavy duty tires which will handle whatever snow accumulates. I think we'll be fine once we can negotiate our way out of this valley and, hopefully, find some clearer skies."

We crossed into Austria and the scenery became even more familiar to me. We saw no more fast-moving autobahns; Austrian main roads could easily be slowed by trucks and tourist coaches. The route took us around the outskirts of Salzburg, which looked like the quintessential Austrian city nestled in a valley below gentle slopes that arched up toward the mountain tops. We bypassed the city, as I had done many times before. It would be another 30 years before I actually walked in the city's streets. We continued south, winding our way through beautiful valleys, many of them dotted with villages, which looked as if they had been plucked from the pastel colored pages of a childhood reading book. Thankfully, the weather cleared and brightened, giving us great views of the surrounding mountains, a few of which I had climbed in years gone by. On this trip, the drive itself would be the "*mountain*" that I needed to "*climb*."

Over these initial days, Penny and I had fallen into a routine. We found a bakery or similar type of store for a quick breakfast, then we would start to drive at about 8:00. For lunch, we generally bought a small block of cheese, bread and fruit from a delicatessen. We would try to find somewhere quiet to take a break and enjoy our lunch. When nature called, we headed to a café or when things became urgent, then it could be necessary to find a copse of trees or a farmland hedge. As we slept on the side of the road and didn't stay in hotels, we washed ourselves in restaurant bathrooms and used deodorant. I will admit looking after our hair did become a challenge, especially for me, as I had amassed a rather long and unruly head of hair. Early each evening we started to look for a suitable place to camp for the night. On occasion, we stopped in the corner of a farmer's field, which meant we couldn't put up the tent. Under this condition, Penny took the back seat of the Blazer and I slept alongside it in my sleeping bag. Thankfully, the weather most nights felt balmy and warm. I had decided to make the trip purposefully in August as the weather could be dry and settled for longer periods.

As we drove through sections of the Austrian Tyrol, it felt strange to not take one of the smaller side roads that led to the camping sites which I'd used as base camps when I climbed in the mountains. Occasionally, my mind wandered down memory lane as I relived those wonderful fun-filled days. I probably bored poor Penny with my endless tales of climbing, or withdrew into internal states of rapturous reflection. Instead of turning, we drove in a southerly direction and headed for the unknown. Up until this time, I had only ever driven as far as central Austria, via France and Germany. Southern Austria and Yugoslavia were new areas to me with unknown conditions.

So I did feel a small twinge of nervousness as we headed toward the Yugoslavian border. The country broke into five independent states in later years, but at the time we approached its northern border Tito still ruled the entire country with an iron fist.

I hadn't been through the most southern section of Austria before and had not anticipated how slow the roads would be. Also, the few communities along the road weren't prepared to feed a pair of travelers. As a result, when light began to fade, Penny and I still searched for any decent dinner option. Eventually we decided to cross the border into Yugoslavia and hoped we would find a restaurant within a few miles of the crossing.

After only three days of driving, our path now crossed to the section of the journey where language, communication, and obtaining help could be challenging. Luckily, we hadn't needed any assistance as yet, and communication hadn't stopped us from attaining what we wanted. Hopefully, dinner in Yugoslavia would be a simple affair after which we would look for a quiet spot to enjoy a good night's sleep.

CHAPTER 6
NEW TERRITORY

الله ه شاء إن   الله ه شاء إن   الله ه شاء إن   الله ه شاء إن   الله ه شاء إن   الله ه شاء إن   الله ه شاء إن

The Yugoslavian border guards appeared gruff and curt. Of the six whom I saw, a single rather bland neutral expression resembled the nearest thing to a smile. Despite the guards' manner, the formalities of the border crossing were eventually completed in a disorganized fashion. One guard stamped papers and checked our passports, then after a period of waiting, another guard repeated the whole process. After a short delay, we gained entry into Yugoslavia. I stopped to change my French francs and German deutschmarks into the local currency at the bureau de change on the border. The Yugoslav bank notes and coins looked so foreign, I couldn't understand the printed script. I had no idea of the worth of any note or coin—20 dollars or 2 cents. I stuffed them all into a back pocket before we departed.

Before we left England, I had wondered about the condition of Yugoslavian roads. Thankfully, it turned out to be about the same as most of the European roads we had seen so far. Occasional pot holes plagued stretches, but the Blazer took them in stride. As our route followed a major road, we found it to be well marked with white lines, designating lanes. I felt content with our progress and our prospects as we continued south.

After about ten miles, we came to the first town. Neither of us could see any signs to indicate the name of the small town. A few people meandered along the sides of the road in the glow of the occasional illuminated street light. As the dusk light faded, time felt later than our watches showed, emphasizing our hunger that gnawed into our thoughts. I slowed to a temporary stop so we could check out potential options. We watched a few locals head into one particular business which had a couple of tables outside.

I felt hungry and, hopefully, I said, "That place looks like it could be a restaurant. Do you want to give it a try?"

Penny tried to sound reassuring, "OK. I hope you're right. I must admit I've been hungry for a while. Let's give it a try." In the weak street light, I could see a small glimmer of uncertainty in her eyes. When she noticed I had a concerned look on my face, she sat up straighter, lifted her shoulders, and shook her head to allow her hair to fall more naturally. A more determined expression crossed her face as she looked back at me and said, "Let's go! Sitting here isn't getting us fed." I smiled. That was more like the travelling companion I needed.

I parked on the side of the road and, after I locked the Blazer, we crossed the road. I hoped we would find something that resembled a menu near the entrance. The exterior wall exhibited no indication of the type of business; multiple layers of ancient faded paint flaked off it. When we reached the entrance, I took a hold of the crude iron handle on the door, looked at Penny, and pulled the door open. We entered and I thought we had been transported back to a 1930s vintage working men's club. The interior looked like a small hall dotted with tables and chairs with people hunched over plates of food and glasses of various liquid refreshments. Uniformity dominated the entire sight; the tables, the chairs, the people's clothing and the people's skin all blended in with the color of the dirt that covered the floor. The din of conversation slowly died as people turned to look at we two strangers who stared back at them with a degree of apprehension. Only the cloud of dense cigarette smoke lurking toward the rafters took no interest in us and didn't look our way.

We noticed a serving hatch that opened into a kitchen, located in the far wall; a menu chalked on a board hung high above the counter. A small sense of normalcy crept into me as we skirted the tables and headed toward the menu. As we did so, a level of conversation became audible from the locals again. Unexpectedly, a sense of total despair hit me. Tiredness, hunger, and a menu board written in Slavic script—it all suddenly felt utterly impossible. Had Mother been right to say that I must be crazy to entertain this journey? I tried to dismiss her doubts while we both tried to ignore the penetrating stares from the locals—had we been wrong to come into their dining hall? Could travelers come into this place? We could see nothing to give us any indication. Many weather-beaten round faces looked at us. Nearly all the men wore flat caps and the women wore head scarves—their uniformity bordered on the eerie. All of their facial expressions displayed a combination of inquisitiveness, suspicion, and discomfort. Penny and I could relate to the discomfort, however, I don't recall sensing we were in any possible danger. Where else could we find a simple evening meal? Doubt and hunger made a troubling partnership, I felt Penny and I definitely sailed under their joint pennant in that moment.

I tried to ask the man behind the counter, "Do you speak English?" He sullenly looked straight through me.

Forcing a smile, I tried my simple German. "Sprechen zie Deutsch?" At least, that raised a little acknowledgement from the man but nothing else.

My attempts at French failed pathetically and resulted in no response. Even in Arabia, I could normally find someone around who could translate so I could communicate with local people. Despondently we stood and looked at each other, the local Yugoslavian man and the two British folks, words and language failed us all. However, hunger spoke a common language and apparently the proprietor had been confronted with such a problem before. His thin stature, untidy greasy hair, and rather vacant way of looking at us indicated a beaten down man who simply accepted his lot in life—he exuded no real vitality. The man surprised both of us with the last thing we would have expected from him. He suddenly launched into a well-rehearsed version of charades in which we assumed he mimed and indicated the various options on the menu. Occasionally, he tried to mimic the sounds of farm animals. However, this only confused us as either he had never been near a farm, didn't recognize tone deafness to be a problem, or the creatures had been extinct for centuries. In response to his antics, we started to point and give thumbs up enthusiastically when we thought we understood an item that we wanted.

After a few minutes of this foolery, all of the locals had turned back to their meals and friends. The proprietor rang our order up on the cash register and told us the amount we owed him. We looked at him with puzzled looks on our faces. He smiled when he realized the problem and wrote the amount down on a scrap of paper, in Slavic, which presented us with an equally difficult problem. So I pulled out the wad of notes and coins I received at the border. I offered the handful of money to him, I knew what I exchanged had been worth less than a few English pounds. The proprietor took a bunch of notes and coins that he tossed into the register and returned the rest to me. Penny and I found an unoccupied table on the edge of the hall. We examined our remaining money and tried to fathom its value while we waited for the food.

Penny enquired, "Do you have any idea how much this meal is costing us?"

"Not really. Based on the simple theory that more colorful and less wrinkled notes probably have higher value than the well dog-eared less colorful notes and how much I exchanged at the border, I think the meal was pretty cheap."

She grinned. "Now, I know why you never became an economist."

We both laughed and began to relax after the long day. What eventually arrived on our table didn't have much similarity to what we thought we'd selected. We didn't care, we wanted to satisfy our hunger and anything that looked and smelt like food would work. To describe what arrived as a gastronomic mystery tour may sound harsh, but it accurately portrayed our meal. Most of the dishes swam in various gravies or sauces which made identification of the contents more challenging. A couple of them did have bones, so we hoped they contained various forms of meat. I particularly enjoyed a few of the dishes that intrigued my taste buds; the cook apparently liked to use plenty of herbs and some spices. After we sampled several of the dishes, we no longer felt ravenous—such a relief. It actually did feel good to me to simply sit in a basic wooden chair with my feet relaxed on the floor for an hour. We finished most of the dishes and departed before the dreaded ever-growing cigarette smoke cloud could descend any lower. Relief washed over me when the foul cloud didn't waft after us. I felt the smoke had a presence that could have dictated it to follow us, if it decided to do so.

After a few more miles, we found a quiet group of trees in the corner of a large farm field. I felt it was past the time for an end to the day's driving, I was ready for sleep. As the evening temperature felt warm, both of us rolled out our sleeping bags under the stars, alongside the car. Soon we transitioned to skipping across the stars on our way to dreamland.

The next day's drive confirmed a suspicion I begun to sense at the border. The cloud in the restaurant had been due to cigarettes, but similarly, I felt a dark cloud hung over the entire country. In comparison, Austria had been light, alpine, and animated, an energy and purpose lifted the people. In Yugoslavia, people thoughtlessly went through the motions because the system required them to do so. Additionally, the roads reflected a similar type of drudgery. The majority of traffic comprised large diesel trucks that hauled food or goods to and from the factories. Little driving appeared to be done for pleasure or convenience.

About 80 miles from the border, we came to our first Yugoslavian city, Zagreb, where we skirted the more modern, industrial outer regions as we headed to the older central section of the city. We were curious about its architecture. Grand baroque-style buildings dominated the center, their immensity and grandeur broken by wide-open plazas and tree-lined parks where I assumed poets and lovers may have once ambled. Our visit was quite simple, we needed to exchange a few traveler's checks into local currency. I hoped we would then have enough money for gas and food for the rest of the time we would be in the country. As we entered a larger bank, I sensed a rather ancient, surreal air blanketing the interior, adding unwanted years to its crumbling facade. Its worn, cracked marble floors told stories from centuries past, while its dark wooden paneled walls and wrought iron chandeliers added a weightiness to the atmosphere. Both staff and the few customers moved wearily by the light of a few inadequate light bulbs. It may have been the nearest I have ever come to walking into Harry Potter's Gringotts Bank—at least Gringotts appeared to be able to afford better lighting.

As we progressed further south, occasional major towns or cities stood out as the most striking features on the landscape. They could be seen from many miles away because huge complexes of high rise apartments, each about 20 stories, encircled their perimeters. If the uniformity of their unimaginative architecture didn't look monotonous enough, their dull gray, brown, and swamp-green colors completed their totally uninspired appearance. The people on the streets also appeared to be drab in both their clothing and their general disposition. After we had been in the country for a short period, it appeared to me that Tito's Communist government must have made every effort to drown individualism and spirit. Tito ruled harshly. This appeared to be the case in more densely populated areas, but in the countryside, occasional lighter indications of individuality could still be seen. The paint colors on occasional farmhouses displayed choices other than earth tones, a few women wore more brightly colored items of clothing, and once in a while people gathered to share a story or even a joke. This was not the case in the built-up areas where we saw constant signs that indicated repression had won the day.

Later, the subject of road conditions came up in our conversations—no freeways had been built at that time. I commented, "I think driving the length of Yugoslavia is testing my patience. To overtake the slower, pollution-belching trucks on certain sections can be frustratingly difficult. Many of these trucks crawl up anything that resembles a grade and seem to be challenged by even a downhill."

Penny looked intently at me for a second. "Are you okay? I know we've made decent progress so far, but I'm wondering if you need to take more breaks?"

"No. I'm actually feeling pretty good. I just may need to vent a little if I get stuck behind another belching monster for too long."

"You go right ahead, whenever you need. I had wondered how

the roads would be here and they look alright. But I'm not doing the driving."

"I wasn't too concerned about the Yugoslavian roads as Hughie never warned me about them. He said cutting across the mountains in central Turkey was the main area to worry about. Thankfully, I had decided to take the Turkish coast to avoid the mountains. It will be interesting to see how that coastal highway is."

A thoughtful look crossed Penny's face. "Hmm. Did you have a chance in London to check out how the Turkish coast road looks?"

"No. All I could find were a couple of maps and documents that confirmed a road does wind along much of the coast. There are stretches where the maps showed no roads, but we can cut around those sections. We hopefully will find our way." I made an effort to not let my mind worry about future sections of the journey, instead I returned to our current location. "You know, I've noticed one redeeming characteristic about driving the length of the Yugoslavia. I've seen gas stations in the strangest and most remote locations. I presume the government dictated gas stations would be regularly spaced along the main roads, and I'm thankful for the consistent availability."

Penny pulled out a bag of cookies, which she opened and offered to me. At the same time, she responded. "I hadn't thought about the gas stations. I've actually been surprised by the lack of stores along these main highways. We always need to take small diversions off the main roads, into villages or towns, to buy food and other supplies. Eating has become less attractive as the quality of the choices in the cafés and restaurants isn't as good as what we had in western Europe. I've also noticed the selection of stuff in stores and cafés is limited without much variation." Penny and I tended to buy food from small markets where we had a better chance of recognizing the labels of food items.

I agreed, "Yes, selection is an issue. I do sometimes have to stop and wonder how old some of the produce may be. I generally avoid items that are covered with a measurable depth of dust and dirt." Expiration dates still waited to be introduced at a later time.

Penny checked our bag of supplies. "Well, it's time to start looking for another market now. I must admit I do enjoy finding quiet places to stop to have our picnic lunches and take a short break from constantly moving."

"Me too. I wonder what we'll find for today's gourmet extravaganza."

She looked at me. "I'm hoping for anything that's fresh."

When we stopped, we resorted to what had become a routine. We found a bakery or store that had fresh bread to buy a couple of bread rolls or whatever looked freshest. If we could find some local cheese, we often tried it as we felt there was a chance it wouldn't be ancient and potentially full of unintended mold. Normally, we could find some reasonable looking apples, which we bought in larger quantities as they made good snacks later while driving.

Miles turned into tens of miles, tens turned into hundreds, and by this stage, hundreds turned into a thousand miles. Our consistent progress ensured we successfully met my daily mileage estimates. We had driven about a quarter of the journey and, thankfully, managed to do it without any significant problems. We felt fine but welcomed the end to our fourth day on the road.

We decided to call a halt to the day after darkness had fallen. I became frustrated as I couldn't find any convenient fields or quiet side roads where we could hide away for the night. After checking out several potential places, I found a small flat area alongside the main road. A line of tall trees formed a boundary about ten feet back from the road. The volume of traffic reduced significantly with the onset of dusk, so I thought this spot would be a perfect oasis for the night. I pulled the Blazer in close to the trees.

"I think I'm done for the day. Do you feel we will be alright here on the side of this road?" I sleepily enquired.

Penny who had been napping for the last few miles agreed. "Sure. I hope all of the truck drivers are home with their families for the night. I sense I'll sleep well—being a passenger and sitting for such long stretches is tiring."

Penny settled into the back seat while I found a patch of softer grass in front of the car where I snuggled into my sleeping bag. Soon I dropped into a deep sleep as sweet dreams beckoned me to let go of the stress of driving. At about 1:00 in the morning, a regular series of speeding heavy trucks which shook everything within a short distance of the road started to roll down the main road. They appeared to be specifically timed to allow me to just fall asleep before the next one thundered down the road. Thankfully, this torture only went on until about 3:00. I then enjoyed a good couple of hours of undisturbed sleep, and I awoke refreshed at about 5:15. However, as soon as I awoke, I knew something felt awry. I opened my eyes and nothing could have prepared me to find two older women standing about ten feet from me, staring down at me with rather bland expressions on their faces. I nodded a polite, "Good Morning" gesture, but it gained absolutely no response. They wore drab long coats, head scarves with a little color, and practical flat-heeled shoes. I took a look around to see if I could work out why the two happened to be standing there. I felt certain the joy of staring at a disheveled guy in his sleeping bag probably didn't rate highly on their list of things to do. However, I didn't know how limited the entertainment options could be in those parts.

To my dismay, I found another six or more people passively standing there eyeing me. I looked away from the road and found a small village lay a short distance beyond the line of trees. My sleepy mind began to focus. I realized I only wore my underpants, as all the rest of my clothes had been bundled into a pillow. I set about the utterly impossible task of putting on my jeans while jammed in a tight nylon sleeping bag. This rather awkward situation also caused me a little embarrassment which resulted in my sweating. That made the task even more impossible. By the time I managed to dress sufficiently to look decent and depart my cocoon, a rusty bus drove up to take these workers off to their factory. In the light of day, I realized I had inadvertently parked in the village's bus stop. I certainly had a tale to tell, and I wondered how many similar tales would be told at dinner tables by the village people later that evening.

I opened the driver's door to the Blazer and said, "Hey, Penny, guess what happened to me, just now?"

Penny sleepily peeked her head out of her sleeping bag to check her watch. "Oh, my goodness. It's only 5:40. What's wrong with you? I'm going to sleep for another hour or so. Tell me your story later."

I quietly closed the door. While she slept, I re-secured the lines that held the boat on the roof rack after I checked the oil and water levels of the Blazer's engine. I was set for another day in Yugoslavia. Later, I told her about my encounter with the workers who had to wait for their bus while I struggled out of my sleeping bag. She giggled so much that she didn't feel the need for any coffee or tea to wake up.

We continued south through industrial regions, farming areas, cities, and we were fortunate to drive along the coastline in places. We felt blessed to view beautiful sandy beaches which sheltered between small rocky points that jutted out into the warm, inviting waters. Groves of cedars and pines formed backdrops to these untouched beaches. They all gently blended in with the sun-drenched azure blue waters of the Adriatic Sea.

It appalls me how many of these beautiful natural beaches have since been overtaken by massive development programs. Where groves of old growth trees stood and witnessed our passing, now, huge resorts, hotels, and condominiums preside. Is the difference for the better? Who is to say? I have realized it simply is a fact of life that the only thing that can ever be guaranteed is everything is subject to change. I cannot stop change, but I can attempt to influence the direction and outcome of the change. When I was in my late 20s, I thought I had a choice as to whether I tried to influence or discuss change. However, now I am older, I feel it's our right and, in many circumstances, it's our obligation to discuss or challenge change. Change can be promoted by both those with selfish agendas and those who haven't thought through all the consequences of a proposed change. When that happens, I cannot complain about the consequences of change if I didn't voice my concerns during the initial stages. Sometimes, it feels as if change is presented as a fait accompli, because so much ground work has already occurred. Perhaps, I have become jaded; just because a proponent of a change says studies and approvals have be completed, I now would hope they would produce the physical proof and people would not just accept their spoken word. If there's no transparency or the opportunity for discussion regarding changes, then I believe such proposed changes should be opposed.

While I had prepared for the trip back in England, I thought we could cut across Albania from the southern part of Yugoslavia to drop down into Greece. It appeared the roads could be better. However, I had been unable to gain the necessary documentation for Albania during my stay in London. So we took the winding, slower roads through south eastern Yugoslavia into Greece, and ultimately along the warm Mediterranean coast. Our option did sound more idyllic, but we needed to pick up our third member, Ron, in two days in Istanbul. So we didn't have much time to spare.

Navigating around Albania caused us to drive through Skopje, a city that had been devastated by an earthquake, just 14 years before. Much of the city still showed signs of reconstruction and recovery. As we cut through an area, close to the center, I noticed one unusual development. Several large concrete domes rose in an organized mound, on top of which sections of wooden scaffolding precariously perched. The scaffolding gave the site the appearance of crude and rough workmanship, while the cascading domes demonstrated engineering and precision.

I have since learned this structure was the beginnings of what became the Church of St. Clement of Ohrid. This cathedral church was started in 1972 and was finally consecrated in 1990. I have now seen photographs of both the completed church complex and the interior; they are breathtaking.

While I stopped to take a photograph of the structure, I whimsically asked, "Hey, Penny, do you think they are constructing that structure or knocking it down?" I didn't know then what I know now. I only recently discovered what a beautiful church it had become.

Penny glanced at the structure inquisitively for a few seconds. "Well, to be honest, that question could be applied to many buildings in this city."

I looked around where I had parked. "You're right. I can't recall seeing a single block where there hasn't been scaffolding or rebuilding. I'm sure a lot of older buildings are being reinforced to make them safe, too."

"I wonder how long will it take to stabilize all of the buildings."

"Possibly, decades, if ever." I mused.

I had watched the TV coverage of the 1984 Winter Olympics games, hosted by the Yugoslavian city, Sarajevo. As the program showed panoramas of other Yugoslav cities, I was struck by the views across Skopje showing both the spires and domes of Orthodox Christian churches and the minarets of Muslim mosques piercing the clear frosty blue sky. Mantles of snow covered the city's roof tops. Both the Christian and Muslim communities apparently lived peacefully as neighbors at that time. Their harmony was demonstrated by the construction of a fountain, a gift from the local Islamic community, in front of the main entrance to the Church of St. Clement of Ohrid. Since the break-up of Yugoslavia, the region has suffered through a major war, after which Skopje became the capital of Macedonia. As a result, tensions between the two communities have risen, leading to a fragile co-existence that could be easily destabilized.

We planned to cross from the southern part of Yugoslavia into Greece, and head directly to Thessaloniki to purchase tourist gas coupons, which would halve the price of gas. We crossed the border without much trouble or delay on a small main road that wove its way through sun-drenched low hills. However, as soon as we left the border, we found the entire road, then under Greek jurisdiction, had been taken over by a major reconstruction effort. The Greeks didn't keep one half of the road open while they worked on the other half. No, they completely ripped up five miles of road and then slowly rebuilt all lanes of the entire stretch. This left travelers with no option other than to forge their own route through the construction site or through the wild countryside on either side. We made it through a few miles of the reconstruction and felt we had passed the worst terrain when the unspeakable happened.

A soft "*pff*" sound gave us the first clue that life had just thrown a curve ball at us. The last phrase is for all Americans. For British readers, I would rephrase it to be "life had just tossed us a googlie," which basically has the same meaning.

Shortly thereafter, I noticed that the back right side of the Blazer looked slightly lower than it used to be.

"Oh, Crap! I think I just got a puncture."

"I did wonder about that little noise. Do you know how to fix a flat?"

"Oh, this'll be interesting, jacking up the car on a soft, uneven surface. This could delay us quite a few hours. Do you think the British Automobile Association will come to help us?"

"Unfortunately, I don't think they cover this area and, besides, it may take them as long to reach us as it will take for the two us to fix it."

Resigned to our fate, I stopped on a reasonably solid stretch of road gravel off to one side, a quick inspection confirmed we indeed had a flat tire. It had been less disturbing blaming flat tires on limbo dancing deckhands who purposefully deflated them, but we now stood out in the wilds of northern Greece without a hovercraft or any deckhands in sight. I wondered what could possibly have punctured a truck grade tire.

I swore at the broken tailgate lock as Penny and I set about the laborious task of unloading much of the luggage from the back of the Blazer through the front passenger door. The situation necessitated it, the spare tire had been stowed in the luggage area behind the rear seat. Eventually, I gained enough room to unfasten the spare wheel. An unpleasant period of grunting and swearing followed, while I maneuvered the 100-pound wheel and tire over the back seat, around the passenger seat, and out onto the road. After that, changing the wheel was relatively simple; however, it still took some sweating and growling. Penny gave me encouragement and a few timely slugs of water. Then we packed everything into the back again, except the punctured wheel which I dumped behind the front seats as it would be pulled out as soon as we found a gas station to repair it.

It didn't take us too long to navigate our way through the last sections of the road reconstruction. I'll admit the rebuilt road looked as good as any I saw in England. After six or seven miles, we found a reasonably-sized village with a gas station. I pulled in and the owner wandered over to see what we wanted. I pointed to the flat tire in the back; he shook his head and pointed to his tire collection. He only repaired and sold tires for cars, but I needed a shop that repaired truck tires. Luckily, the village straddled several large roads that crossed through a large agricultural area. The surrounding farms created a constant need for large tire repairs. He directed me to a shop a short distance up the street. As soon as I drove up to the forecourt of the workshop, a mob of men and boys poured out of the building to greet us. I showed them the tire, and they hauled it into the workshop. Penny and I sat on a couple of chairs, on the side, to watch the action. Many of the men and boys who greeted us outside, gathered around us—mainly on Penny's side. Several of the boys tried to touch her fair-colored hair which she naturally found annoying. Probably, fair hair was so unusual to Greek children who generally had dark or black hair that they wanted to find out if her hair felt like their own.

In frustration, Penny exclaimed, "What is it with these kids? They are constantly trying to grab my hair."

"You have long fair hair, which they probably don't see that often in these parts. So, the kids may think it will bring them good luck," I offered in response.

Meanwhile, several of the mechanics struggled to take the tire off the rim and when they did, they let out a communal cry of dismay. The mob rushed forward to see, Penny and I were left to wonder what had been discovered. One of the mechanics rolled the tire over to us to show us a road spike buried in the tire. I couldn't believe it punctured the truck grade tire as its sharp end looked about a quarter of an inch square and the other end, which was firmly embedded in the rubber of the tire, measured about half an inch by one inch. The spike had penetrated all the way through the tread to its blunt end. It made an extremely large hole to have in a tire. Through sign language and verbal grunts, the mechanic indicated I needed a new tire before he went to find if he had any in stock. Soon he returned to indicate that they had none, so he sent one of the boys to check with the other tire shops in the area. He also checked his supply of inner tubes, but he soon found he didn't have the correct size. Another mechanic even started to search through the pile of discards from previous repairs that hadn't yet been sent to the dump. He found a correctly-sized discard. Since it had been patched multiple times, he considered it to be beyond further use and tossed it further into the pile. Eventually, the boy came back with the news that he couldn't find any replacement in the entire village. A cloud of gloom descended on the workshop.

"Well, this wasn't how I imagined we would start our time in Greece—surrounded by grease and filthy urchins," I quietly said to Penny; not that anybody else in the workshop understood my words.

She looked over at me with a resigned look on her face. "You did warn me that we could be in for some tough times. I believe your prediction just came true. Do you have any idea how we deal with this situation?"

"I think we should give these guys a little more time. The main mechanics appear to know tires pretty well and they are earnestly thinking about our predicament."

A rather weirdly disconcerting thought struck me, as we sat in the workshop. I realized we depended on the mercy of this group of mechanics. Had I misread their earnest effort and discussions? Here we sat in the hill country of Greece that saw foreigners only once in a while. Nobody knew our location, we couldn't communicate easily with anyone around us, and we had no means to contact anyone at home for assistance. I wondered if the garage crew had any crooked intentions, in which case, life would have become downright difficult. A vision of my mother's expression, while we talked about the trip, floated into my mind, her question about finding assistance echoing in my ears. Had I been foolish? I dragged my thoughts back to the mechanics and the garage to consider what we could realistically do in the situation. Our best tactic appeared to be show appreciation and give encouragement for whatever they wanted to try. Thankfully, despite the lack of direct communication, I sensed the mechanics were making a concerted effort to resolve the problem and get us back on the road.

The workshop owner looked at Penny and me with apologetic

facial expressions and body gestures that I surmised were supposed to assure us that his mechanics were good workers. He felt so badly about not being able to repair or replace the tire promptly that he resorted to his apparently normal strategy under such circumstances, a bottle of ouzo, Greek hard liquor. He poured glasses for Penny, me, and himself. He then spoke excitedly to the mechanics who appeared surprised by his suggestion, but they seemed willing to try. One mechanic struggled up the pile of discards to retrieve the already well-patched inner tube, which he had earlier thrown further up the pile. Meanwhile the other mechanic started to dig the road spike out of the tire. He gave me the spike for a keepsake—I still have it in a box to this day. I'm always amazed by the amount of damage it caused when I look at it, especially considering it went through the tire tread, at its thickest and the tire had been a heavy-duty truck grade.

The greasy group of boys continued to hover around Penny. They found her fair hair too intriguing and constantly tried to touch it, despite her fierce looks and occasional growls. She turned toward me. "These little horrors are so annoying! How can we make them go away?"

I turned back to her and saw her expression was dark. Her eyes shone with pent up frustration. If she could have run away, I suspected she would have done so, but where could she go? I offered, "Penny, I admit they're causing me a lot of frustration, too. I cannot imagine how you're handling all of their touching. You probably will get more peace in the back of the Blazer. You may need to hide in your sleeping bag."

"Yes. I had thought about that too. Will you be alright if I go and hide?"

"I think I just need to be patient and see what the mechanics decide to do."

Finally, in total despair, she retired to the back seat of the Blazer, locked the doors and buried herself in her sleeping bag. The boys then took up siege around the back of the Blazer, leaving a few local older men, the shop owner, myself, and the bottle of ouzo to watch over the mechanics.

The liquor continued to flow while the main mechanic made several attempts to seal the well-patched inner tube. At the same time, his associate attempted to glue a chunk of tire rubber into the hole in the outer tire. I was fascinated to watch how he creatively tackled the problem, it took much patience and in-depth knowledge about tires to perform this surgery. The group of local men watched and cheered both mechanics' triumphs. After a couple of hours and too much ouzo, both the tire and the inner tube appeared to be serviceable. The mechanics placed the inner tube and tire back on the rim. Finally, the mechanics gave the re-assembled wheel a thorough test and it successfully held air. I felt so relieved to have a full set of tires again, but at the same time, I couldn't let go of a feeling of uncertainty about that tire. I decided to relegate it to be the spare tire. Then, with many helping hands, we loaded it into the space behind the front passenger seat. I paid our bill with English currency, which pleased the owner so much that I wondered what I may have missed. After a rather uncomfortable four or five-hour diversion, we thankfully continued on our way.

However, it only took me a few seconds to realize that the ouzo and I found ourselves in absolutely no state to drive. By then, evening had already started to darken the skies. Penny said she could sustain herself on the snacks we had in the car. I pulled off the road before I retired to my sleeping bag in a rocky ditch. I had become an incapable wreck with the stress of the afternoon and too much ouzo. I passed out soon enough and slept well. I awoke with a nasty hangover. I deserved it, but at least we now had four good tires on the Blazer and hopefully a good one as a spare. We planned to head to Thessaloniki to buy gas coupons and a new supply of essentials and snacks. I looked forward to a quiet uneventful morning.

We drove a few miles before I found a large open area, where I stopped. I wanted to repack the back of the Blazer so that the spare tire was stowed properly. A little hard labor helped to clear my head a fraction, but it was far from feeling fine when we returned to the road. My hope for a quiet morning lasted only a few miles. I noticed the gas gauge had dropped to below a quarter of the tank.

I mumbled, "Just what I needed. I'm not sure we have enough gas to drive all the way to Thessaloniki. I'll probably need to stop, if we come across a gas station."

Penny stared across the low barren hills, day dreaming. After a few seconds, she replied, "Oh, right, I'll keep an eye out."

Before the trip, Hughie warned me that gas had two official prices in Greece, a local's price and a tourist price, which worked out to be about double the local's price. Tourists and travelers could obtain the local price if they bought gas coupons in any of the larger banks. That had been the primary reason to head to Thessaloniki—it would be the first city on our route with banks that sold the gas coupons. I reckoned I would be a couple of gallons short for driving to the bank, so I decided to stop in a village to buy a small amount at the tourist price.

We found a pretty old village with cottages built in a period that had been long lost in the echoes of time, with flowering vines that climbed the outer walls of many of the enclosed gardens. It looked like an idyllic setting—a perfect opportunity to buy gas. I pulled into the tiny service station at the end of the village. As I walked around the back of the car to the gas tank, a large man rushed out of the office and started to unscrew the cap. Despite the hangover, I recalled fuel was sold in liters, not gallons, in Greece. A choice of grade didn't exist. The pump exhibited a simple choice; petrol or diesel.

He grabbed the gas pump nozzle, jammed it into the gas tank pipe, and started filling. He said one word "Full?"

I heard it not so much as a question, but more as a question with an assumed answer. I immediately countered with, "Ten."

To which he reaffirmed, "Full."

I waved all of my fingers and thumbs at him to indicate ten. He simply leaned his 300 plus pounds of weight determinedly onto the pump nozzle from which petrol already poured into my tank. I didn't feel I could handle an altercation on top of a headache and hangover. However, life happens when it happens with no concern for one's state. The pump had already passed ten liters. I suspected he realized as I came from the direction of the Yugoslav border, I probably had an empty tank and, more importantly, I had no gas coupons, needing me to pay the tourist gas price. Indeed, the Blazer's 35-gallon tank contained little gas and primarily air. I grabbed his hand that pressed the nozzle into the tank and inflicted enough pain that he momentarily took his weight off it. Luckily, as I pulled the nozzle out of the tank, he let go of the trigger, and we didn't have a petrol spill around us both. He reluctantly put the pump nozzle back in its holder on the pump. To my relief, he managed to pump in a little over 30 liters, much less than the 170 he could have done if he'd managed to fill the entire tank. I paid the bill begrudgingly before we returned to the road for the drive into Thessaloniki.

Penny had busied herself while we were in the gas station, looking at a map to see what sights maybe on our route. She looked up as I sat back in my seat. "That sounded a little problematic."

"Bloody crook! I suspect he knew I didn't have gas coupons and tried to fill the entire tank. I had to almost fight him to stop him."

"I didn't think I would be much help to you, so I stayed here."

"Very wise decision."

"Well done! You probably weren't at your best to deal with a scoundrel like that."

"Thanks."

My anger at the gas station owner softened and my headache lessened as we wound our way down through the hills. We enjoyed exquisite views of the coastline that appeared to have come from the easel of a gifted watercolor artist. An abundance of flowers and trees displayed a delightful array of pinks, peaches and pale yellows that transformed the umber hillsides into a palette of pastel tones. The morning sun's rays were softened by the mist drifting in the valleys that meandered down to the warming Mediterranean seashore.

Penny watched a hovercraft depart the French coast while I re-inflated my two front tires.

The shell of the Church of St Clement of Ohrid in Skopje, Yugoslavia.

The Blue Mosque, surrounded by rose gardens in Istanbul, Turkey.

The front façade of the Library of Celsus being reconstructed in Ephesus, Turkey.

Ron and Penny shared some amusement as we toured Ephesus, Turkey.

Rows of stone seating in the Aspendos Amphitheater, Antalya, Turkey.

*Kizkalesi Castle, built to protect the southern
Turkish coast from passing Crusaders.*

Beehive Mud Brick houses in the northern Syrian desert.

The photographs that have been included in the book, as well as additional ones, are available in color on my website at: www.bdhwrites.com.

CHAPTER 7
WEST MEETS EAST

Thessaloniki met my expectation, it was an idyllic, pretty city that overlooked the gentle waters of the Mediterranean Sea. The main downtown area was modern, by Greek standards. I parked in a shaded square near the center of the city and after a quick search, we found a large bank with a sign indicating that they sold gas discount coupons.

I pushed on the large ornate handle on one of the main doors. It didn't move so I tried the other door and that one appeared to be locked too. "That can't be. They should be open by now." I checked my watch. "It's almost noon."

Penny stood by the railing on the side of the steps that led up to the main entrance. She leaned over the railing to look in a window but turned back with a concerned expression. "It doesn't look like there's any light on inside. They can't work in the dark."

"Today hasn't turned out as I had hoped. Greece welcomed us with a flat tire, then a gas station owner tried to rob me, and now the banks are closed despite it being hours after the sign indicates they should open. Have I upset the Greek gods?"

Penny glanced at me "I can't speak for the Greek gods. You could have upset a couple in your drunken slumbers last night. By the way, how's the hangover doing?"

"It's down to a gentle throbbing. Let's go and try to find an open bank that sells these bloody coupons."

We searched for other banks, but couldn't find any that sold the coupons. It appeared that only the bank, which we initially tried, handled the gas coupons in the city. With a cloud hanging over us, we trudged down to the harbor to look for a café for lunch. A small taverna had a quiet terrace overlooking the water. A few potted trees gave us a little welcome shade, while we discussed what to do about the gas coupons.

Penny asked, "So what are you going to do if we can't get the coupons?"

"If we can't buy these damn coupons here, then I'll need to pay the tourist rate for petrol. But, that means we'll first need to go to a bank to exchange additional traveler's checks into Greek drachmas."

Soon after, our waiter came to take our order—thankfully the menu had been in Greek with English explanations. As he took our selections, I realized he spoke reasonably good English. I enquired about banking hours and he assured us all banks should be open before noon. He suggested we try the large bank again later. On our return to the car, we stopped at the bank and the still-locked doors prevented our entry.

I started to rant. "What the hell is up with these people? Do they not have clocks?"

Penny pulled my shirt to catch my eye. "Shhh. I think I heard a voice after you tried the door."

Indeed, after I rattled the doors, we could hear a couple of voices on the inside. We waited and soon a young woman, dressed in a business suit and heels, opened the doors. I looked at the woman and asked, "Are you open for business? Your doors were locked."

The woman ushered us inside. "Yes. We are always open for business." She offered absolutely no reason for the doors being locked, despite our questions. It appeared to be normal to her.

After the frustration of gaining entry to the bank, we discovered the gas discount coupons themselves could only be considered a rip off. They could only be bought in such large denominations that one coupon would have bought enough gas for me to drive all the way back to England and return to Greece. I decided to forget the coupons and buy as little gas as necessary to cross into Turkey, at the Greek tourist rate. I thanked the woman as we turned to leave. She followed us across to the main entrance where she bade us a good day. The door shut behind us and within a second, we heard the resounding thud of a bolt being closed to firmly lock the doors.

As we headed back to the car, we found several market stalls lining quiet side streets. We wandered around the market buying snacks and fresh fruit that delighted our senses. The selection felt a welcome relief after the lack of food options in Yugoslavia.

Penny picked over a pile of gorgeous peaches that smelled amazingly. She said, "If I buy all the fruit I want to buy, I'm not sure we'll have room for Ron in the car."

"Oh, right. I want to see you try."

"Perhaps, another day, if Ron teases me too much."

"Okay. I'll warn him that if he misbehaves, then he'll be replaced with fruit."

I was surprised how much I had missed not having good, fresh produce while in Yugoslavia, even though we had only been in the country for about two days. We soon carried more than an adequate supply of enticing food in our arms and, once again, we prepared to return to the road.

As I settled into the car, I commented, "I must admit I feel better, especially knowing we are at last on the Greek coastline. We have another 30 hours before Ron's flight is due to land."

Penny questioned my math. "Don't you mean 26 hours to get to Istanbul airport?"

"That's true. All this driving is addling my brain."

"Well, you have been sitting on your backside a lot lately."

"Oh, cruel words." We laughed as I pulled out onto a main road.

Once we had left Thessaloniki, the road ran alongside the Mediterranean for much of the route. The warm sunny conditions made the drive extremely pleasant with the windows wound down, allowing a beautiful breeze to gently waft through our hair. Along the way, restaurant signs displayed a wonderful variety of great quality food and the wondrous joys of fresh fish. We felt like we had landed in gourmet heaven, where the vastness of potential selections created the major problem. However, in most restaurants where we stopped, the wait for someone to take our orders could be an interminable amount of time, which added an unfortunate frustration to the experience. Everywhere in Greece, a lack of timeliness or organization ruled the day. Events rarely occurred when they were scheduled or expected—some just never happened, and always without any explanation. When we visited the bank, we apparently had been lucky as on some business days, the bank simply never opened its doors, in spite of their claim to be open for business.

Several years later, I was thankful to have this understanding about scheduling in the country. I had arranged with a group of running buddies from Aramco to run the original marathon from the plains of Marathon to Athens. A day or two before I flew out of Houston, where I lived at the time, I received a letter that informed me an emergency general election for the Greek parliament had been called for the Sunday on which the race had originally been scheduled. As a result, the race date had been shifted to the following Tuesday morning. Luckily, my flight arrangements allowed for this rescheduling, but it must have caused many runners major issues. I thought back to the drive through the country. *Why does this not surprise me? At least they sent the letter with the details of the change.* That had been a major improvement on what I had come to expect from my experiences during the drive through Greece.

Penny and I stopped overnight several miles before we reached the Turkish border. Early the next morning, we drove the last few miles to where we found trucks and vans crowded into the congested crossing, such a difference from the border where we entered Greece 36 hours before. A long line of trucks waited to cross from the Greek side, but we managed to avoid this back-up as I drove a passenger vehicle, which was treated much differently to a commercial vehicle. The Turkish guards lackadaisically gave the car a quick look over. They took no real interest in us.

I was relieved to be in Turkey at last. I looked over at Penny. "Well, I'm glad to have that border behind us. Now, all we need is to find Ron and then onto several ancient ruins. I've heard the road across the middle of the country to Ankara can be tough, as traffic can be thick and the road's condition is bad in places. So I decided to take the coastal road, which will give us access to Troy, Ephesus and Antalya."

Penny wondered, "I hope the route won't be too slow."

I agreed with her, wishing she hadn't said it out loud as I had my own concern about the speed along this section of my planned route and had been trying to ignore it.

As we cruised through the coastal agricultural areas, I noticed many farm workers pedaled their bikes along the road. A number of them had large boxes of produce balanced behind the saddle. I turned to Penny. "It looks like some of those men have perilous tasks riding with such heavy loads. I presume they're off to market." She smiled in agreement before I continued. "Thinking about bikes and their purpose, I reckon your idea to take a bike back to camp is a good one. Are you planning on riding back and forth to work each day or using it for exercise?"

She looked inquisitively at a field where rows of small plants with ripening fruit grew, as if she wanted to guess what type of fruit they may be. Having failed to identify them, she turned to reply, "Hopefully, a little of both. On really humid days, it may be easier to walk, whereas on days when it's really hot, it may feel pleasant to pedal along quietly and generate a little artificial breeze."

As I took a turn onto a larger main road that continued along the coast, I looked over at her and agreed. "Yes, I've heard a few others say it can be refreshing to take an easy bike ride."

Penny switched the topic around saying, "I honestly don't know how you can run with the lunchtime crew. How far do you all go? Is it ever too hot?"

I paused while I passed a slow moving tractor and then said, "We always head out at lunch, no matter how hot it is. If it's particularly hot, we take diversions across people's lawns when they have the sprinklers running. I've been surprised how rejuvenating it feels. You could try it too when you are out on your bike. Generally, we do a standard course of about three and a half miles. Then afterwards, we take a quick dip in the swimming pool to drop our body temperatures to something close to human again. I must admit I never imagined I would take up running at any point in my life, especially while living in the desert. But I absolutely love it."

She looked intrigued and responded with the obvious question. "So, why did you start running?"

Out the corner of my eye, I caught sight of a hawk as it flew over the fields searching for a meal. I pointed it out to Penny. We took a moment to watch its graceful flight before it sailed out of sight and I replied, "Once I moved onto camp, I played squash frequently, but I realized I had gained weight. This surprised me as I thought I ate healthy meals. I met a doctor at a social gathering and I complained about it to him. He recommended a change in my diet—reduce my intake of red meat—and start a cardiovascular exercise regime. As I work around Bob, Hughie, and Greg, I saw the obvious choice for cardio would be to join their daily running outings around camp. Even though they all looked super fit and were probably fast runners, I went out with them for a trial run one lunchtime. I was hooked by the end of that first lunch-time run. All of the mountaineering I enjoyed as a youth and in college gave me good leg strength and I had a surprisingly high level of natural endurance which proved to be what I needed to develop as a runner, despite my gangly height."

It intrigued me to reflect on how I became a runner. I recognized how my activities as a youth had been foundational in my quickly becoming a competent runner. I saw how my playing tennis, canoeing, climbing, hiking, playing squash, and mountaineering had contributed to my developing physical confidence. But, it took one vault in gym class to move me from suspecting 'I could' to knowing 'I would'. These reflections about my previous activities sent my mind spinning through thoughts that I had never before considered. As we continued along the sun-drenched coastal road, elements of my upbringing formed a chain of stepping-stones in my mind through my physical development. The validity of that chain of activities still makes sense to me, even today.

I let my arm rest on the open window as we cruised along. I felt at peace and relaxed for a short time. I quietly sighed and started talking about these memories. "Looking back, I do acknowledge one school gym teacher was a significant influence in making me feel physically confident and in becoming active. For my first few years of high school, I had a tall gangly frame without any discernible amount of muscle. I had little body strength and detested gym because the thought of getting hurt scared me. Then a new young gym teacher who had been in the Air Force joined the staff. He carried himself like a man who knew what he wanted of us. He joined us and actually participated in the class workouts. Listening to his encouragement gave me the guts, one day, to let go of my fears and to really give a vault over a box a serious attempt."

When I paused for a few seconds to think, Penny wanted more. "So, did you make it over and were you invited to join the Olympic team?"

"Let's say yes and no. I won't say I made it over with any elegance, however, I did stand on my two feet on the far side of that box, realizing then I could and would do better. I never imagined one semi-successful vault would turn out to be so transformative for me. As I worked harder in gym, I gained confidence in my physical self."

Penny reflected about her own schooling. "Wow. I can't say I had a good experience like that. I wish I had, but I didn't. I was happy to give up gym as soon as I could. So, what happened for you after that one vault?"

I slumped down in my seat as I reminisced about my life. "A year or so later, another teacher wanted to start a rock-climbing and mountaineering club which I decided to join as it forced me to face physical challenges I would have never considered a couple of years previously. However, my long thin frame didn't adapt well to the exertions of climbing vertical rock. After about five years of climbing, I had become a moderately competent rock climber, but then gravity proved its superiority in the matter after I took a life-changing fifteen-foot fall. It may not sound far, but fifteen feet was an awful long distance to be in the grips of gravity, before it slammed me, lower back first, down onto a rocky trail. Several years of unrelenting and agonizing back pain followed. As you can see, I eventually did recuperate."

Penny grabbed my arm to stop me. I turned toward her; her eyelids flittered nervously as she stared into my eyes. "I don't think I've ever heard that before. Barry, are you alright, now?"

I realized that I had moved on with my life and didn't focus on it much anymore. "You know, I honestly don't allow it to restrict me. It's always in the back of my mind, and I do need to consider it in all physical activities. I'm thankful to probably be as active as most people who have never had back issues. I celebrated my ability to still walk by relegating rock climbing to my memories and I focused on general mountaineering. The many miles of arduous mountain hiking and clambering gave me the endurance, leg strength and the determination to later train as a long distance runner."

She sat quietly and mused, "That's quite a story. I'm not sure I'd have had the inner courage to do that."

I responded, "It's surprising what any of us is capable of doing when we feel motivated."

Looking back now on that period of my life, the transition from being an almost-crippled climber to becoming a road racer has blessed me with two wonderful gifts that I have come to recognize more deeply in later life. No matter how much others might have wanted to help me or guide me through such dark times, only one person could overcome those hardships—it was me. And, after all the climbing and running, I thought my most important asset was my physical self. However, as I trained to become a serious road racer, I realized my physical self could be seen as the least important piece. I sensed my psychological self and emotional self were more important, but most important was my spirit, my belief. What I held in my heart was what I needed to be the strongest. If I could persuade my beliefs and train my mind that I could endure more pain and discomfort, then the physical side would tap into depths of strength that I had never before acknowledged. It was the strength I found in my heart that carried me through all of my mountaineering and road racing.

Along the journey back to Dhahran, I learned I could always rely on this strength that lay in my heart.

As we drove through a small Turkish farming community, I took time to think about both my growing up and how I developed into a young adult. After a few minutes, Penny broke my train of thought when she looked a little sheepishly at me and said, "You do realize a few single females arrange their lunch-time walks back to their houses so they cross paths with your group of sweating runners, dressed in the least amount of clothing possible?"

I knew about these encounters. I tried not to smirk when I responded, "Oh yes, some of them aren't too subtle about their 'chance' encounters with us. Also, I suspect almost as many married women arrange their schedules accordingly too. Surprisingly, the one place we are guaranteed to hear a bunch of wolf whistles is when we pass the construction area over at the university. Yemeni and Pakistani laborers really love to watch us pass by also, and they aren't shy when they want to show their appreciation!"

We chuckled at the image, but were soon absorbed by the rugged beauty of the terrain. The rich ochre tones of the earth and rocks that extended out in all directions contrasted dramatically, and perfectly, with the multiple shades of azure blue of the sea as the breeze swept small waves toward the sandy beaches. It would have been wonderful to park and relax in the shallow warm waters for an hour or two. Sadly, we had to deny ourselves such a luxury. Time and distance demanded our constant vigilance as Ron would expect us to meet him at Istanbul Airport.

After a few more hours of easy banter and driving along the sun-drenched coastal highway, the road left the sea, heading slightly inland. It didn't take too long before we reached the outskirts of Istanbul. We marveled at the incredible sight of the towering minarets of the Blue Mosque that pierced the brilliant blue sky, even though the mosque still stood miles from where we perched on a ridge that overlooked the vast city. Before I left England, I had gone to the library to research where I would find the airport in this large, sprawling metropolis. The atlas gave me an idea—the north western suburbs, but I couldn't determine a more definitive location. We headed in that direction, but found no sign of an international airport. As we didn't speak Turkish, we tried to solicit directions by mimicking planes to people on the street. Unfortunately, our attempts to imitate planes by running around with our arms held out like wings while making loud disgusting noises simply confused local people. By noon, the situation started to become extremely frustrating, especially when we realized Ron's flight should arrive at 2:30.

Exasperated, I looked over at Penny. "How can we have made it all this way and now not be able to find the airport?" I could feel my mother look over my shoulder with an all-knowing look on her face.

Penny was also frustrated. "I can't believe it's so difficult to find. We've seen no signs for it, anywhere. This is the last thing we need."

Eventually, in desperation we happened to look up to the heavens for guidance and I saw our answer.

"Alright!! There's our solution!" I triumphantly cried.

Penny looked incredulously at me. "You must've lost your mind. What are you talking about?"

I pointed ahead of us at a commercial airliner as it made its descent. We headed in the same direction, hoping it hadn't changed course after we lost sight of it. Then another plane screamed low over us, we knew we must be getting close. After a few more miles, we found the wire fence that surrounded the runways. Relieved, we drove through the airport entrance with only one hour to spare.

The airport didn't present us with any last-minute obstacles. We parked reasonably close to the single international terminal; thankfully, it displayed large signs in both Turkish and English. Penny and I walked to the exit from customs, scanning passengers as they rushed forward to meet family and friends. We amused ourselves for a little time guessing from which cities the exiting passengers had departed.

Then, to our relief, we recognized a familiar face, relaxed and happy to see us. Ron greeted us. "It's great to see you guys. Has it been a good drive so far? I'm really sad to have missed the first week of the trip. You know, we had no control over the Saudi Arabian Embassy—they had my passport. The important thing is I'm here now and so excited to join the gang."

As we approached the Blazer that stood out in the mass of smaller cars in the parking lot, Ron looked disapprovingly at it. "Well, I think you could have, at least, washed it before you came to collect me. I've just flown all the way from London to meet you."

Smiling, I said, "If you're going to worry about it, I'll buy a bucket and sponge in the market. You can work on it later."

Penny joined in the banter. "He's only been here for five minutes and already we see his cheeky sense of humor. Ron, you may be surprised by the hassle we went through just to find this airport to meet you."

Ron put his arms around both Penny and myself saying, "I'm so damn happy to be here with you two. The last week in London hasn't been easy for me either, but more on that later. Let's get going."

We gave him a quick synopsis of the drive to Turkey while we stowed his small amount of luggage and then started to navigate our way toward the center of Istanbul. We headed toward the Blue Mosque through neighborhoods where animals, people, bicycles, and vehicles negotiated for space on the crowded narrow roadways. Buses and trucks belched exhaust fumes everywhere. In the parts of the city where the breeze from the Bosporus River couldn't reach, a heavy, humid atmosphere hung, stifling, despite the clear sunny skies that covered the city.

Ron told us the details of his delayed week in London, while he waited for the Saudi Arabian Embassy to issue his entrance visa. "When I talked to you last, in London, I had been told the visa would be issued on the Tuesday after you both left. Well, that scheduled date came and went without any sign of the visa. I began to panic as the embassy still had my passport which I needed to leave England."

As Ron talked, we drove slowly through open markets where stalls, stocked with colorful produce and wares, lined the edge of the roadways, making driving a challenge. He continued. "My company realized the urgency of my situation. They rang the Foreign Office and explained the predicament to them. The Government official assured them that they could handle the situation. The next day, I went to the Foreign Office and they issued a temporary passport for me, which is what I used to fly here today. When my company retrieves my real passport, with the visa, from the Saudi Arabian Embassy, they will rush it over to the Foreign Office. They then will add it to the next day's Diplomatic Pouch that is headed for Amman in Jordan. So, I'm afraid we'll now need to head into central Amman to find the British Embassy. I can trade passports and we'll then be in great shape."

Penny reacted to the tale of Ron's hassles in London. "That sounds much more stressful than our week simply driving a couple of thousand miles across Western Europe." I simply grunted agreement as I wove a tight course between multiple obstacles.

As we drove through residential areas, we occasionally could see into the gardens of larger private houses, many of which had six-foot high walls that surrounded the property. The gardens looked sumptuous and gorgeously colorful. It highlighted the economic divide—those who had money looked demonstratively rich while the vast majority of the Turkish population lived meagre, hard lives. This majority lived in small older houses or more modern apartments that could only be described as basic with no frills. For many such families, multiple generations lived together in a few crowded rooms.

Once we figured out that we had reached the city center, I moved away from the main roads with the hope that I could find a more tranquil area along a residential street. I then added, "Speaking for myself, I look forward to a few relaxing days as we cruise around the Turkish coast. But, before that, we can allow ourselves to take a few hours to explore Istanbul. I hear the main market is fun so let's take a wander through there after the Mosque."

When I believed we had reached the correct area of the city, I found a quiet backstreet where I felt safe to park the Blazer. This was the first time I looked back at the Blazer with some hesitancy as we walked away.

I hope my Blazer will still be sitting here with the Laser on the roof rack when we return. I know there's more money tied up in this vehicle than many people in these parts make in an entire year.

These thoughts colored how I saw the local Turkish people. I had no real understanding of their daily lives or their struggles. I could only observe these people, but I felt I was seeing them from a removed distance, even though we walked side by side along passageways. My 28 years of life as a privileged white male tainted how I saw all of the people whom I could reach out and touch in that moment. I felt awkward and a little guilty for suspecting people who lived in the area. To add to my confusion and mixed feelings, my mother's concerned voice rang clearly in the midst of my thoughts. I was filled with excitement, fear, amazement, suspicion, wonder, and curiosity. My stomach churned, my shoulders tensed, and my mind spun. The unease I felt physically, along with my mixed emotions, my own rational thoughts, and Mother's voice made me feel extremely uncomfortable. But as I started to walk into the locals' world, my need for control began to fall away because I realized I actually had almost none. I suddenly began to feel vibrantly and amazingly alive.

Damn the discomfort. Instead, let me celebrate the blueness of the sky, take in every breath as if it was my last, allow the aromas to dance and entrance me, sense our trio's joyful camaraderie, conduct the surrounding cacophony of noise into an uplifting choral crescendo, feel the sun's embrace, taste the experience, I am living my life, the life I chose with all of its unknowns, and I love it.

Allowing myself to drop the walls of protection that my upbringing had built around me, I found fear about the Blazer was washed aside in my engagement with the life that teemed around me. I would be the one to establish the protections that I needed, not those that my past imposed on me.

With a lighter step, we had to only walk a couple of blocks to reach the Blue Mosque, an amazing structure. Tiled mosaics and stylized calligraphy covered the walls. The external windows displayed a large variety of ornate stained glass, much of it created in intricate patterns. Huge arching columns supported the towering domed roofs. The floor comprised a mixture of carved marble interwoven with more intricate mosaic stonework. I felt especially drawn to the mosque when I started to recognize Arabic words and phrases in the calligraphy, which had been integrated with mosaic patterns and repeating borders. The mosque's name isn't without reason as much of the interior decorations displayed various shades of blue. After we explored the inside of the mosque, we wandered through the surrounding extensive rose gardens where we enjoyed the traditional external architecture, with its rising levels of domed roofs and beautifully decorated minarets that looked incredibly high.

Later in the afternoon, we walked into the main bazaar area of the city for a quick exploration. Noisy activity, insistent talking, loud yelling, and general bustle hit us like a wave, almost stopping in our tracks. Carts, bicycles and pedestrians wove around each other with amazing speed and apparent mutual understanding while successfully avoiding the occasional car or truck that tried to navigate through the narrow streets. The bicycles provided the best entertainment as many substituted for carts. Most had small luggage racks behind the saddle which their riders had loaded with boxes of goods—sometimes the stacked boxes rose to over six feet above them. The riders would tie the stacks onto the racks with strands of spindly old string. Then the men would push the bikes rather than try to ride them. We watched near calamities as tilting stacks tottered. They caused us much amusement as such incidents occurred quite frequently, offering us a constant source of merriment as we walked.

In places, we found small engineering shops spread along the pavement in front of tiny stores. The owners had no apparent concern for the safety of people who walked by. Lathes turned metal pieces within inches of the shoppers as they trudged home with their purchases. Everything that one may ever need to buy could be found on stalls in the streets or in small stores which flowed out over any nearby pavement. Merchants bartered over sacks of spices and grains with people shopping for home use and with other merchants who would return to outlying smaller markets. Other vendors sold a wide variety of snacks and Turkish coffees from different regions. Metalworkers beat out pots and pans which were in constant demand. Many pans were used over open fires that couldn't be easily controlled causing the pans to fail after a short period. In one section, we saw tanners as they cured and worked on dyed hides. Much of the processing of these hides took place in back alleys where people would not be exposed to the chemicals they used. We noticed a slightly rancid aroma hung in the air that we assumed was caused by the large vats of chemicals and dyes that lay out of sight. Inevitably, and thankfully infrequently, we came across slaughterhouses, right there on the side of the street. For a few hours, we happily wandered through this environment that pulsated with activity, motion, noise, people, and life simply being lived. Eventually, we forced ourselves to walk back to the Blazer.

As we meandered back toward the car, we noted that all taxis appeared to be 1940s and 1950s vintage Cadillacs. Istanbul seemed to be their retirement venue—if anyone owns a vintage Cadillac and wants a spare part, I suggest they check out Istanbul. If they don't have it in stock, they can probably find one of those street-side engineering shops to make it.

Before we returned to the road, I decided to check all of the lines that held the boat on the roof rack. The wear had begun to show, especially on the two front lines. We decided it might be easier to find a store that sold rope in a smaller urban community than the heart of the city. Rope had been one item we couldn't recall seeing for sale in the bazaar—not that we could have found any particular part of the market, if we could remember a stall that sold rope.

Before starting, we took a quick look at a map which showed the main cities and towns across Turkey with all of the intersecting main roads. We decided to stop the following day at a town called Izmir to look for rope. We had two possible routes out of Istanbul as we needed to cross the bay that lay directly to the South.

Ron sensed his first opportunity to help with navigation and offered, "While in London, I mentioned to an associate that we'd be driving down to Troy from Istanbul. They said to take the ferry across the Sea of Marmara as this section of the coastal road is highly populated and slow."

Penny was fascinated by two bicycle riders as they balanced a large piece of furniture on their two bikes. She watched them turn a corner before adding, "A quiet ferry ride sounds perfect after an afternoon in the bazaar."

Happily, I concurred, "Well, I guess that resolves how we're leaving town. Do you have an idea how long the crossing will be?"

Ron thought for a few seconds. "I think they said it was an hour or two."

As we reached the side of the bay, we saw a couple of ferries and, from their position, guessed where the ferry terminal was located. As we approached the terminal, we saw signs along the road side. I thought, *Why couldn't they have done the same for the main airport?* The bay crossing took about 90 minutes without any problems loading the Blazer and boat on the ferry's open deck. We stood on the upper deck, enjoying the warm breeze while quietly observing the city of Istanbul that has, for centuries, been known as the gateway between East and West.

After we docked close to Bursa, we drove off the ferry and headed straight through town. The road had just a narrow single lane in each direction as it wove along the coast through agricultural areas. Alongside the road, small farms grew quite a variety of produce. Some grew grain, some raised animals, others grew crops, and many had orchards of olive or fruit trees. We found it to be an idyllic setting for a relaxed drive, but progress could only be described as slow. I soon began to wonder about the wisdom of my intention to drive around most of the Turkish coastline. All other friends who had done the journey cut straight across the middle of the country to the capital Ankara and then dropped down to the Syrian border. I estimated it might take me twice the time on the coastal route. My mother's voice started to question the validity of that assumption. I knew roads ran along most of the coastline, but I had no details of their condition. I found it difficult to argue with my mother's doubting voice and decided to simply focus on the driving.

Our day continued as we wanted to cover most of the distance to Troy and it took more time than I had hoped. Night had fallen by the time we set about the task of finding a camp for the night. From this point on, our sleeping arrangements remained the same. Penny retired to the back seat of the car, while Ron and I found comfortable spots to lay out our sleeping bags on some nearby, flat ground. We thereafter never erected or considered the tent again.

As we started to relax from the busy day, I turned to Ron to explain, "Penny and I have had many fun moments on the trip so far. But it feels really good to have the three of us all together as we had planned so many months ago. Penny has a determined and strong personality which has helped us through a few incidents when doubt set in. I'm really glad everything worked out for you to make the Istanbul flight. Now, welcome to the joys of sleeping under the stars on hard rocky ground."

Ron rolled toward me in his clean sleeping bag. "I am so grateful I could join you both today. I've dreamt about this journey for months and it's great to be here at last. Good night."

I turned over and tried to better estimate how long it would take us to reach the Syrian border. Ron soon fell fast asleep, enjoying his first night alongside the road.

CHAPTER 8

ANCIENT WORLDS

الله شاء إن   الله شاء إن   الله شاء إن   الله شاء إن   الله شاء إن   الله شاء إن   الله شاء إن

We arose early and found a small café in a village for tea and a breakfast pastry. The last few miles to Troy passed along quiet roads that probably hadn't seen masses of people since the downfall of this ancient city. Parking at the entrance to the site presented us with no problems as we had been preceded by only four other cars and no tourist buses. We paid the entrance fee before we meandered into a time warp. Troy flourished from roughly 3,000 BC until about 500 AD. Archeologists have excavated much of the ancient city's tell, an artificial mound formed by the accumulated remains of prior eras of the city's existence, and have found over nine distinct periods as the city rejuvenated itself to meet ever-evolving societal and commercial needs.

We walked along paved roadways between the remnants of what had been the structures of this ancient city. Some walls stood barely inches high while others rose a few feet. Occasionally the bases of columns could be seen making long lines alongside pathways in sections of the ruins. Everywhere, we saw piles of broken pillars, segments of walls, decorative carvings, and fragments of arches that had fallen as the city decayed and surrendered its spectacular splendor into the withering hands of time. In many parts, the crumbling structures had smashed the paved roadways with such violent force that the pavement had reared up or been crushed completely. It made walking quite difficult in places. Sections had been cordoned off so that groups of archeologists could sift through the ruined pieces as they tried to reconstruct portions of structures.

The sections where reconstruction had been completed were revealing, as they either confirmed or denied how each of us had envisaged the city to have looked. I must admit I could have stared at the piles of light brown rubble for hours as I attempted to put the pieces back together in my mind. I could be such a nerd—the thought of doing three dimensional jigsaws in my mind actually appealed to me. No wonder I felt comfortable thinking of Penny as only a traveling companion and not potentially something more.

Penny and Ron also wandered through the ruins in a state of mesmerized fascination. We stopped to look at the infrequent information boards where artist renditions portrayed how they believed the city may have looked. The artistic beauty in the frescos and borders painted on many buildings looked so finely detailed. I found the art of the city to be quite remarkable. Penny apparently had similar thoughts. "It's unbelievable that artists could produce these beautiful frescos with such crude brushes and basic paints. They must've made the city feel rather sophisticated and cultured."

Ron added, "Yeah, but they certainly were advanced and cultured for their time. The variety of subject matter is impressive. I've seen a lot of variation from flowering vines woven through wooden trellises, to geometric patterns that repeat hypnotically, and many types of animals portrayed in enclosures as well as out on open mountainsides."

She replied, "I wish more of the frescos had survived because they add so much to the feel of the place." She wandered toward a set of marble steps that now led to nowhere.

I caught Ron's sleeve. "Take a look at this. It seems the city planners wanted to remind the populace of community commitments like military service. Here are frescos that portray armies marching or preparing for battle to defend the city. It appears to be an interesting way to keep the masses mindful of their civic obligations, but without actually saying so."

He grimaced a little and thought for a few seconds. "No matter its intent, we have to acknowledge all of these beautiful masterpieces had been painted with the utmost skill."

"Indeed."

Much of this paintwork had been lost from the surface of the rubble pieces. However, enough pieces of stonework retained a faded touch of the frescos that we could see the modern-day artists' renditions on the information boards didn't overstate the quality of the ancient work.

As time passed, more tourists arrived and groups started to hover around certain areas of the site. We latched onto a couple of groups as their guides appeared to be quite amusing or really enthusiastic about what they described. Even when they spoke in foreign languages, their facial and body movements expressed meaning, which we found useful. We were especially grateful to find English speaking guides.

After a couple of hours, we had toured much of the site and overstretched our imaginations. We decided to depart before the main influx of foreigners started to arrive after their leisurely breakfasts in their comfortable hotels. I will admit to a slight twinge of jealousy—it was only the slightest twinge. One day, it may feel good to enjoy this ancient site after a cook prepared a tasty breakfast and someone else drove the tour bus. Back then, such a thought felt like nothing more than a pipe dream. The honest truth is I'm glad the trip happened as it did—I wouldn't change a detail, even the scarier ones.

The next section of the drive took us through remote farming and fishing communities where local residents treated us with a degree of suspicion. They had seen plenty of tourist buses, but saw few tourists in private vehicles. As we progressed south, the appearance of the countryside that surrounded the road held our attention as it changed from mile to mile. One side of a ridge may have been barren and rocky while the other side often contrasted to it markedly, it being deeply forested with a rich carpet of ferns and vegetation. The warm weather along with the forever changing landscape made the slow drive remarkably pleasant but, at the same time, the slowness was frustrating.

In the mid-day sun, we found Izmir to be a picturesque fishing village with a large harbor overflowing with fishing boats. We drove along the side of the harbor as we looked for any store that might sell rope. At the far end, we found a small stone cottage on the harbor's edge. It had been transformed into a hardware store for the local fishermen. Perfect, we thought and I parked outside.

As soon as we had taken our first couple of steps inside the old cottage, we stopped for a few seconds to allow our eyes to adjust to the dark interior. Luckily, we had stayed close to the door at first. In the light from the still-open door, we could see the few aisles didn't appear to be straight and piles of goods that hadn't fit on the shelves littered the floor in places. The owner sat behind the counter located along the back wall. He gave us a cursory glance before he went back to what he had been doing. We searched around for rope and found a few spools lodged under other goods. After I extracted one spool that contained the type of rope I needed, I took it over to the owner to ask for ten meters. He didn't seem too interested to help me. I grumbled under my breath and persisted as I needed to buy some new rope.

Ron spotted a meter measuring stick in a corner. "Ah, that is precisely what we need. I'll fetch it over so we can measure the amount you want."

Meanwhile, Penny had searched the counter. "Barry, here's a pair of shears you can use to cut the length you need."

We measured off ten meters in front of the owner so he could see our accuracy. I cut the rope before we tried our crude version of sign language to pose the question of how much would it cost, while we reiterated the rope measured ten meters in length. The owner glanced over at us with a rather sour look on his face and wouldn't answer, even though he appeared to understand the question. We coiled the rope up in a manner that hopefully indicated we intended taking it with us. We again gestured the question 'how much' and Ron even pulled out his wallet to indicate willingness to pay for it. Frustrated, I became the ugly tourist. My vocal tone, in comments to Penny and Ron, sounded irritated and I spoke louder. However, we could only communicate with the owner through gestures and I couldn't gesture more loudly.

The owner grabbed one side of the coil to pull it out of my grasp. I immediately thought this guy must be related to the Greek gas station owner who had intended filling my gas tank. I found myself in another altercation with a local over a purchase, but at least I was clear-headed on this occasion. Eventually, I lost the struggle and the store keeper took the coil. He turned around and, to our absolute amazement, he tossed it onto a set of scales. He sold rope by weight, not by length!? After he weighed the coil, he turned around with a mischievous smile on his face and told us the price. When we saw his smile, we realized he had been fooling around with us—foreign tourists. Thankfully, the two small windows in the store were in the back wall, behind the counter, which allowed us to see well enough to deal with paying him. We indicated that he should write the price down, which he happily did. We matched the symbols in his price with the symbols on the bank notes and eventually paid him. He gave us a big wave as we turned around to try to find the exit in the dark. We tripped over several piles as we blindly stumbled our way out of the store. At the entrance, I glanced back at the owner; he had a smile on his face that suggested he would tell a wry story about tourists trying to buy rope by length to his friends later.

This particular small incident has always stayed in the forefront of my memories because it has a few profound lessons about life. Just because I normally took certain actions to achieve mundane tasks, often without thinking, it didn't mean other people would do likewise. It was unreasonable to expect others to do the same as me to accomplish similar tasks. Second, as I was the foreigner, I needed to solicit the assistance of locals—not dictate their actions in response to my needs. To talk more loudly or angrily wasn't an effective way to solicit help. Humbleness became an important lesson I learned a little later in life, and this encounter began that important part of my maturation.

As we continued our drive toward Ephesus, I commented, "It feels so unreal to be driving through this rugged beautiful terrain on such uncrowded roads, not concerned with other drivers and what they are doing. All the time, knowing driving around Saudi Arabia will be so different to this."

Ron immediately connected with my train of thought. "You have that so right, Barry. Every morning, a bunch of we contractors take a small bus from the hotel in Al Khobar to the Aramco camp for work. I witness so many examples of impatient and bad driving every day."

As we dropped down from a higher plateau, Penny joined the conversation. "That appears to be the reason why so many locals say *Inshallah* as they drive. I believe it means 'God Willing' and probably many drivers barely survive their commutes because Allah willed it to be so."

Ron looked away from an abandoned farmhouse that had caught his eye and smiled in agreement. "*Inshallah* is the only possible reason many of them manage to cross the junction close to the airport entrance. We go through that junction every workday and often we have to close our eyes and wonder. In many ways, it does make a good case for their belief that Muslims have a connection to God. It can only be due to Allah having their best interests at heart that so many survive the daily commute."

Penny countered, "I'm not sure Allah has them in mind. Their assumed closeness to him seems to give many of them permission to act badly, and that's not only when they're driving. But, I do agree many of them are pretty bad drivers."

I glanced back at her. "Penny, can you give an example of what you are thinking, when you say they act badly?"

A frown crossed her face as she twisted to face the other side of the car, thinking. "Well, there was the work crew who came to our house to fix our faucet, and they drank half of our Sid supply. And I heard about a house, down the block from mine, where a friend saw a local guy steal several girls' underwear off a washing line. That's the sort of thing."

I negotiated a couple of sharp bends before I responded. "You're right. They were acting badly. Did they report the theft to security?"

In the rearview mirror, I saw her shrug and raise her eyebrows. "What would have been the point?"

"Sadly, we know there are rules for we infidels and rules for the locals." I took a drink of water before adding, "And, their driving certainly leaves much to be desired. I've only been through the airport junction in the evening. Ron, is it as bad in the morning?"

"Ha! Is there a better or a worse time? It's potentially dangerous at any hour. An example occurred a few weeks back when we'd stopped in the slow lane at the airport junction traffic light. Despite it still being early in the morning, the two lanes between us and the central median had three vehicles abreast as they gunned their engines, and a fourth actually straddled the concrete median. Then to our right on the shoulder and desert, a couple of others jockeyed for positions."

Suddenly, sunlight on the umber-colored ground that ran alongside the road transformed the interior of the car into a tapestry of rich earthy tones. The temporary beauty of the colors caught my eye for a few seconds and challenged my interest in Ron's account, but soon I had to know what happened. "How many vehicles got across the junction in one piece?"

Ron answered immediately, "All of them, with a whole lot of *Inshallah*'s. Our bus driver knew to take it slowly and to keep to his lane. I have to admit I wouldn't want his job!"

I chuckled to myself. "Isn't it ironic that we are talking about this subject while we drive this vehicle back to Dhahran so I can, at my leisure, join these crazy folks on the roads around Al Khobar?"

We all smiled as we turned our attentions to the forested valley into which the road had just wound. The road crept higher as it wove through the trees and headed up toward yet another ridge line. Our attempts to guess what the landscape would be on the far side provided us with a few moments of distraction as our drive down the Turkish coast continued.

In the late afternoon, the weather became partially cloudy, and it began to feel humid. This didn't deter us as we had a second ancient site to explore that day. Ephesus had been built about 150 miles south of Troy's location and it had been built roughly two thousand years later. The Greeks built the city in about 1000 BC. It went through multiple revivals before it was finally abandoned in the 15th century AD. It, too, covered a significant area with low ruins, huge piles of carved pieces and shattered rubble. The city had been built of a white and gray colored rock, whereas Troy had been built of a light brown stone. We toured the remnants of palaces, temples, houses, amphitheaters, and other structures. Several front facades of temples stood tall, re-constructed by archeologists. Most of these structures had been destroyed by earthquakes, fires or marauding invaders. The structures' size, design, decoration, and the beauty of their finely chiseled motifs took my breath away. I noted the roadways looked to be in better shape than some of those we had seen in Troy, allowing us to meander the ruins more quickly. The ruins covered a larger area, which we tried to explore, but time wouldn't allow us the luxury of staying longer so we decided to depart despite having probably missed many amazing sights.

As we walked back to the car, I posed a question: "By the looks of what we have seen so far, the coastal route around Turkey is even slower than I feared. To stay reasonably close to our anticipated schedule, would it be alright if we make this a long day and try to reach Antalya tonight?"

Penny yawned before replying, "I've no problem with that. Pretty soon, I'll be asleep in the back seat."

Ron added, "It works for me as I really want to see the Roman Amphitheater near Antalya. If a longer day today will give us additional time at the amphitheater, I'm all for it."

We stopped for dinner and gas after we left the Ephesus ruins and then wound our way inland. Soon we drove through long stretches of open wild country. We crossed open moors, rocky ridges, forests, and open grassland. The drive went on forever. One noticeable consistent detail struck me about this section of the drive—a total lack of human existence or any sign of their presence, nothing. We felt totally alone, mile after mile. At times we each pondered our own thoughts, but it didn't take much to start a conversation because in that environment of aloneness, silence became a deafening, unwelcome fourth member of our group.

Ron had been lost in thought for a few minutes with a funny expression on his face. He turned to Penny and me. "I cannot believe how unpopulated this area is. The road is the only sign that any humans have ever been here before us. We've seen no farms, buildings, walls, fences, or even derelict, abandoned structures." He scratched his head briefly before continuing, " Now, thinking about structures, I want to ask you two, have you seen the apartment building on the Al Khobar road with the sloping upper floors?"

I responded, "You mean the recently completed peach-colored one, on the right as you head toward the sea?"

Penny sat up straight and jumped in, "Really? I must keep an eye out for it."

I added, "Such a simple mistake that should've been addressed."

Ron prompted me, "Oh, do tell. It never made sense to me."

I shifted around in my seat so that I felt comfortable and began. "They built the fourth floor in their normal backwards fashion. One should construct the reinforced concrete pillars first, then fill in the wall sections with cinder or concrete blocks. However, that would've taken skills those local builders hadn't learned. So they built the two opposite end walls with the blocks first and formed the reinforced concrete pillars at both ends of these two sections of block wall. On the fourth floor, the front block wall had one or two additional rows of blocks, which made the front wall higher than the building's back wall."

Ron stopped me. "Are you telling me they didn't notice?"

Penny laughed heartily at the visual she had conjured in her mind. I continued, "As to whether the builders ever noticed their mistake, I've no idea. And, indeed, no effort was made to correct the error. The upper six stories now have floors that have a gentle downwards slope toward the back of the building."

Penny sounded amazed. "You mean they never did anything to correct the problem?"

I confirmed her thought. "No. They did absolutely nothing. If they later realized it, but didn't want to demolish whatever they had built above the fourth floor, they could have added additional rows to the back wall so all floors above where they made the correction would be horizontal again. But, no, they even missed that opportunity. So now if you look at the longer side wall of the apartment block, the vertical lines of the entire structure have a kink in them. It's impossible to ignore once you've noticed it!"

Penny said, "I really need to spend more time down in Al Khobar as there's always something weird to see."

Laughing, I added, "You know learning Arabic helps me see other strange things down there."

I looked over at Ron as he raised his eyebrows, "Like what?"

"Most of the stores have the name of the business written on large signage across the front of them. Their names are in large Arabic script and some stores have smaller names or information in English, like 'Al Aziz Market, in Arabic—TV, Stereo and Radio, in English.' But after a while, I realized some stores' names in Arabic script were straightforward transliteration of English words or names, like 'Burger Joint'."

Ron inquired, "You mean, if you read the Arabic script, it would sound like 'Burger Joint'?"

"Yep. Or pretty close, depending on how good the sign maker's English happened to be."

Laughing, Penny added. "Oh, that's really strange, I've never heard that before." She paused to take a sip of water. "You know, I do get annoyed by how badly the English and American newspapers and magazines are censored. I look at them occasionally in the one store that sells them."

Ron agreed. "Yes. I was just thinking the same. I wonder how many black markers they use each day. It's amazing—they censor every single copy by hand. No wonder we can only buy newspapers that are about a week old."

Penny replied, "It seems like each person who censors the papers has different standards. Some black out references to alcohol, others to sex, and others censor out all references to women. You know, this reminds me how badly censored the western movies are that are shown at the movie house in camp. A Hollywood film editor would be appalled by the sudden scene shifts that result from their extreme censoring. Some movies that are supposed to be two hours long make it onto the screen in a butchered 55-minute version."

Ron laughed. "I gave up on the movies after just a couple—they were so bad. Even worse are the magazines' pictures in the downtown store. Some are censored to black out all females' legs, others have all sections of pictures that have any breasts—covered or exposed—blacked out, and others have any sign of women's bare skin censored. A couple of times, when I had time, I opened multiple copies of the same magazine, eventually I could reconstitute the entire picture. It's just a farce."

I added, "I admit that I also find their attempts at censorship to be so inept, it borders on being ridiculous. May I remind you two that we're heading back to the land of this farcical censorship. Wajid Zain!—Very Good!" Penny and Ron groaned their agreement.

The discussion of crazy things we had observed around Al Khobar continued for a while. After half an hour or so, we all fell quiet for a few miles. A little later, Ron looked over his shoulder and nodded to confirm what I had suspected; Penny had settled down for a long deep slumber.

Soon enough, day turned into night. A beautifully clear sky with a full moon blessed our passage. We had crossed a high plateau by this time and dropped down to the small coastal road where again we found no sign of human presence. As the miles crept by, our path continued along torturously winding roads which followed the cliff tops overlooking the Mediterranean. We passed through groves of pine trees grouped tightly along the sides of the road.

One factor made that night's drive tantalizing—the stark contrast of the lighting. The sky's blackness contrasted dramatically with the blazing silver beauty of the full moon that hung suspended low over the water. I sensed being in a solo spotlight, which followed our slow progress across a stage, but without the blinding intensity of a real spotlight. The moon's luminescence gave our world a magical touch of absolute black and silver—no other colors could have existed. The sea's gently undulating waves consisted of nothing but pure liquid silver. Ron and I became spellbound by the scene's alluring beauty. Groupings of trees were set against the dazzling sea that made them stand out as stark two-dimensional black cut-outs and islands transformed into featureless black shapes that floated in the silvery sea.

This enticing vista consumed my attention. I took energy to draw my focus to anything else. The winding road forced me to drive at a snail's pace, which was good, as my distracted driving occasionally deviated onto the shoulder, which ran close to the cliff top.

I drove slowly through this entrancing landscape. We hadn't seen any sign of humans for ages. I hadn't heard Penny utter anything with each beautiful new sight. I turned around momentarily and saw she was still sound asleep. Ron and I used hand signals to determine if we should wake her, but then in an instant all of our thoughts froze.

In that moment, Ron stared straight out of the windshield, he let out a strange utterance, "Wow. What on earth?"

I quickly looked at him and sensed an immediate need to look at what had grabbed his attention. I looked straight ahead of the car and involuntarily uttered, "Jeez. That's bizarre."

A lone figure stood in the middle of the road. By the light from our headlights I could see he intended stopping us. As we pulled up in front of him, he presented a weird sight; he was a lone soldier dressed in full combat gear that may have been considered to be modern at the end of World War I. He wore a dirt brown uniform with canvas gaiters and the style of battle helmet which looked like an upside-down soup plate, straight out of the Battle of the Somme, 1916. Encountering a soldier in the road caused us a degree of trepidation, but the rifle over his shoulder with its bayonet attached concerned us much more.

Ron and I grabbed our passports as the soldier started to walk toward my door. I rolled down the window so he could see us more clearly. Despite the warm breeze, I sensed a cold shiver snaked down my spine and the hairs on my neck stood out. Each step of the soldier's steel-capped boots on the road produced a sharp click, which was immediately consumed by the silence of the still dark night. Had the click ever existed? Or had my mind created it to normalize this bizarre situation?

When he saw our passports, the soldier realized our foreign status and spent a couple of minutes inspecting our passport photographs. Apparently, he couldn't read many of the details in the passport booklets as he flicked from one passport to another in frustration. Eventually, he searched each of them and found our entry stamps as they had been printed in Turkish, and he appeared satisfied.

After attempts at English, French, and a few Turkish words from a guide book had all failed, we found he understood a few words of German and, thankfully, he could work with my pidgin Arabic. So with a mix of German, Arabic, and a fair amount of hand gestures, he indicated he wanted to check the contents of the vehicle. He'd noticed Penny's sleeping figure in the back seat and gestured she needed to get out too. The soldier positioned himself opposite the passenger door so the moon shone from behind him and he could keep an eye on this third person. While Ron got out, I turned to awaken Penny. As she tried to wake up, I told her we'd been ordered to get out of the Blazer for a search. The bright moonlight probably felt harsh on her waking eyes, so she chose to not open them until she took her first step onto the gravel alongside where we'd stopped. When she opened her eyes, I imagined her first visual impression was the black silhouette of a combat-ready soldier with a rifle and bayonet poised in his grasp; this apparently triggered frightening messages in her half-asleep mind. She let out an amazingly piercing shriek that probably woke the dead, and if the sea had been made of glass, it would have been shattered into billions of tiny stars. All four of us stood frozen, and wondered if our hearing had been permanently damaged, or if God would appear on a cloud to witness an unforeseen event. Whatever nervous feelings I had felt encountering the soldier were replaced by waves of icy chills that ran down my back. Gradually, normalcy began to trickle back into our perceptions—not that being searched by a World War I relic on a moonlit road corresponded with my understanding of normal. Our elevated heart rates slipped lower with each passing minute.

The soldier took a quick look inside the Blazer and was soon content to let us continue on our way. He tried to explain his mission; we eventually decided he had been on patrol looking for smugglers who apparently used that strip of coastline where little traffic occurred at night. As we drove away, we realized any smugglers who thought of operating that night deserved to be caught because their boats could be clearly seen from many miles away in that spotlight of a moon.

We negotiated a few more miles to a point where the road wound inland. When we felt we had left the smugglers' territory, we found a quiet resting place for the night. Time had moved well past midnight and I felt shattered. Snuggling into my sleeping bag, I wondered if my heart rate would ever again drop below 100. Even though Penny may have not intended it, she surely had gotten three guys' hearts racing.

Despite the late end to the previous day, we arose early, anxious to see the new morning and drove into Antalya to find a café for breakfast. We intended visiting the Roman Amphitheater on the outskirts of town before we continued along the coastal road to Mersin and on to Adana. Arriving in the parking lot next to the amphitheater, we were surprised to find nobody else parked, despite it being a few minutes after 9:00. The sign by the entrance made everything clear. The amphitheater was closed on Mondays and we quickly ascertained that we had arrived on a Monday. Days of the week had lost all their meaning for Penny and I as we had been on the road for over a week. Luckily, Ron could still determine the day and couldn't deny it was Monday.

"They've gotta' be kidding!" exclaimed Ron.

I looked at the sign again. "Can you believe it? It's really closed today. Damn!"

Ron exploded in frustration. "Do you mean we came all this way to simply miss such an amazing amphitheater? Look at this exterior. Wow. Look at the carvings. It's phenomenal! And, to be honest, I can't see any possibility that I'll come this way again."

Penny couldn't believe our misfortune either. "I have to admit it's disappointing. But, what can we do?"

I suggested, "Well, at least we can look at the outside, which appears to have survived its 2,000 year past rather well. It looks surprisingly intact. I wonder why it hasn't decayed as so many other ancient structures have?"

Penny offered, "Well, they don't have the rain and cold as we do back home. That must take its toll over the centuries."

Ron still looked annoyed about the closure, he said, "That's true. And perhaps later invaders didn't destroy this amphitheater to build their own fortresses. This place looks incredible. I wanna' get inside."

We wandered along the length of the front wall, towering above us with intricate carvings and porticos around doorways and openings. When we reached the far end of the front wall, Penny pointed to the trees which lined the parking area. "Is that a path leading up into the hills? It may take us around the upper sections."

Excitedly, Ron almost ran toward the trail. "Hey, you're right. Let's go and explore."

We started along the path where low trees provided welcome shade. It felt good with the sun already dominating the clear open sky. The path turned a corner to follow the side wall as it began to ascend the hill. After only a few yards, we came across a side entrance into the amphitheater that had been fenced off.

"Hold on," cried Ron. "By the looks of the fence, a number of folks have squeezed under it without too much effort. How about we try it, too?"

Penny expressed her doubt. "I don't feel comfortable. How about you, Barry?"

"Breaking into a National Heritage site may be considered illegal in some places. But, if nobody is around..." I held up the bottom of the wire fencing and Ron crawled under it on his hands and knees. Penny followed and despite her being dressed in a nice pair of dark blue slacks and a blouse, she stood up on the far side with only a few flecks of dust on her clothes. I scrambled under the fence quickly without a concern for dust and dirt to join the others.

"Woooo!" was all we could say.

We walked into the empty, silent vastness of the amphitheater. A sense of awe and amazement struck us. Semicircular rows of stone seating rose above us until they became lost against the perimeter wall. Fascinated by different points of the structure, we separated to explore the amphitheater or take in its magnificence from different vantage points. For a while, I sat up on the raised stone seats and tried to imagine what it must have felt like to watch a performance back in the Roman period. The lines created by the rows of semi-circular stone seating that rose up in ever-widening arcs captivated me for several minutes. As I scanned the amphitheater, I was surprised, and also delighted, to see it had relatively few signs of decay, despite its being about 2,000 years old.

I dropped down to the stage to see the vastness from an actor's perspective. My voice felt weak when I thought that the actors had not used microphones; the actors had no other option but to project their voices. I felt humbled and terrified by the thought of acting on that stage with such a huge audience. I have since learned the amphitheater could seat about 20,000 people.

I walked into the backstage area and found Ron exploring the storage and dressing rooms. He was impressed with the stone carvings that decorated the interior walls and trimmed all door frames, no matter the room's intended usage. These carvings comprised small porticos, borders of raised ribbing, emblems of armies, and many depictions of fierce-looking eagles.

When I returned to the bright sunlight, it was significantly warmer despite the short time I had been backstage. Penny had sheltered in the shadows of the outer walls high up on one side. I started to climb up and when I reached her, I realized a cloistered walkway ran around the structure, above the top row of seating. From the cloisters, I could see much of the farmland and local hills that lay beyond the amphitheater's perimeter walls. The farm fields diminished in size as I looked further, every field was covered in patterns of varying shades of green formed by rows of crops. The fields created a beautiful natural quilt that stretched across the open terrain to a line of dark brown hills. As the hills were only a few miles away, their ridgeline formed a horizon which was a defined line, whereas more distant horizons were not distinct. Their muted earthy tones merged into the blueness of the sky. I felt contentedly relaxed as I looked out over the surrounding country noting that not a single cloud dared to interrupt the vast blue expanse of sky.

The three of us enjoyed the amphitheater for about an hour before other tourists found their way under the fence. We decided to depart before any officials turned up to remove us all. It had been an incredible experience having an entire Roman amphitheater to just the three of us for that short period.

We clambered under the fence and back onto the path. As we made our way over to the parking lot, Ron stopped to take a long look at the main front wall.

He frowned thoughtfully before saying, "This magnificent

structure wasn't built by paid workers. The Romans may have paid their own engineers who designed it, but I would imagine slaves formed the majority of the labor force."

Penny walked closer to the wall. "Can you imagine how conditions may have been for slaves working here?"

Ron scratched his black beard as he replied, "Considering how we will be happy to soon retire to the comfort of an air-conditioned car; I would imagine their lives were pretty harsh. It probably was hard manual labor from sun-up to sundown." Sobering thoughts of the slave workers' conditions dampened our feelings of awe as we walked away from the amphitheater.

I struggled to balance both the wonder we had experienced as we quietly explored the structure and the reality of conditions that may have existed when it had been constructed. As I walked forward, I mused out loud, "I wonder how many died or were injured during its construction?"

Penny looked over at me. Her eyes were sad. "Barry, I didn't need to think about that."

"I'm sorry. We can't avoid the fact that two thousand years ago, conditions were dangerous for workers on these huge construction projects." Such thoughts certainly colored our impressions of the amphitheater. When we'd first arrived, our initial reaction had been fascination and awe; but as we left, they'd been transformed to utter amazement, with a touch of humility. Our impressions felt tainted by a recognition of human suffering that only the ghosts of those ancient worker slaves could fully impart to the scene.

We returned to the road. As the miles separated us from our conflicted reaction to the amphitheater, we relaxed and soon were overtaken by the beauty of unspoiled beaches sheltered in small, sun-drenched bays. We passed valleys filled with scrubby undergrowth and bushes which we imagined were the domain of small wild animals and birds. Nature surrounded us. It lay waiting for us to simply take a moment to let go of our distracting thoughts and to see it. The weather and the scenery filled me with joy, peace, and a sense of being grounded as we made our way along the coastal road. The road overlooked sandy beaches and rugged points that dared to jut out into the inviting warm waters of the Mediterranean. However, the drive also caused me to feel frustrated as it was still too slow. The road twisted between the coast and hillier country where we encountered the first humans since we left Antalya—groups of farm workers and small farming communities. These farms were so remote that they probably had been run by the same families for centuries. The occasional farm tractor or herd of sheep didn't help our progress. Hours and miles passed us by, as we slowly inched our way toward the Syrian border, which still lay over a hundred miles away.

I thought about our previous day's conversation and, after a short time, another memory came to mind. I said, "Yesterday, we talked about the apartment building in Al Khobar with sloping floors. I just remembered another entertaining structure that I once saw in one of the quieter neighborhoods of Al Khobar."

Ron was lost in thought as he watched waves claw at a rocky point. Slowly, he turned toward me and, after a few seconds, he inquired, "OK. Where did you see it?"

I thought about it briefly before I said, "I need to go exploring to find it again. If I can, I'll let you know. By the looks of what I saw, I presumed a developer had proposed building a block of luxury apartments on the site. I can only imagine the city planners accepted the apartments proposal and agreed to build pavements and street lighting ahead of the construction. Unfortunately, the developer drew up his plans to fit the exact dimensions of the empty lot. They apparently didn't understand the city planned to construct the pavements and street lights within the lot's boundaries. Luckily, the apartment plans had wide balconies on the outer sides of the building. These conveniently protruded out over the newly completed pavements, which worked out well enough. However, the street lighting presented them with a more serious problem. They resolved it by constructing the balconies so the installed lamp posts poked up through the first two floors' balconies, before the top sections of the street lights arched gracefully out over the road, having just cleared the railings on the second floor's balcony."

While Penny sat in the back seat laughing, Ron responded, "When we are resettled, please try to get a better idea of where that block is.

I have to take a photograph. Speaking of photographs, can you pull over somewhere soon, I just want to grab a shot of this coastline. It's so natural, rugged, and just plain beautiful."

I made a suggestion. "Let's just take a look around this next point because I've been getting glimpses of what appears to be a castle, but I haven't been able to see it clearly yet."

Ron and Penny kept a closer eye on the views ahead of us for a while before they confirmed there was a castle ahead.

"It's out in the sea!" cried Ron.

Penny moved further to the right to get a better view, "Yes, it looks like it is on an island."

Eventually we stopped where we could take photographs of the castle that sat a little offshore on its own small island. We thought it had been built by crusaders, but I have since learned that Kizkalesi Castle was built by a Byzantine king, Alexus I Comnenos, in about 1100 to deter passing crusaders from occupying the area. The castle covered just about every inch of the island, which sat about 400 yards from the beach. Originally, it could be reached by a breakwater that has since been eroded and washed away.

I have realized that taking photographs was an exceptional event while we drove. I took photographs at spectacular sites; but while we were on the road, rarely did we take time to stop to capture a scene. I went for days between when I pulled out my camera, I was focused on driving.

After we'd stopped for a few minutes, we continued through the beautiful terrain with its low unstable cliffs which cascaded down into the sunlit waves. After several hours, we reached the city of Mersin, which had one noticeable feature, an old area of docklands. By the looks of the few rusting cranes, they seldom saw much shipping any more. The docks looked abandoned, left to become derelict. I was struck with a feeling of sadness. This man-made eyesore contrasted so dramatically with the natural beauty that could be seen along every other inch of the coast. I felt ashamed we humans couldn't find money to demolish the docks and allow Mother Nature to take back possession of the coast. Instead, hulking rusty statues and dilapidated, crumbling buildings scarred this strip. My feelings of disgust didn't stay with me for too long because even with my limited understanding of life, I had come to recognize that Mother Nature will prevail. Though she will take time, she will tear down and remold those structures into a place of beauty once again. To humans, it may feel like forever, but, to Mother Nature, it will be a mere blink of an eye.

After we left Mersin, we turned inland to cut across a large promontory and lost the Turkish coast for a while. We crossed large expanses of low scrubby wilderness, interspersed with occasional groups of farms where reliable water springs provided consistent irrigation for the fields. In the mid-afternoon, we reached the city of Adana where we briefly stopped to restock our supplies in the downtown market. I also decided to buy a fresh tank of gas, as Adana was the largest city along that stretch of southern Turkey.

I was surprised how driving along larger main roads, where I could maintain a speed over 40 mph, felt like such a relief. I slumped lower in my seat as the anxiety caused by two days of driving along slow winding roads gradually released its grip on my shoulders. It took another couple of hours to reach the Syrian border, Ron's first encounter with the entertaining challenges of border crossings.

CHAPTER 9

GETTING HOTTER

ال له شاء إن   ال له شاء إن   ال له شاء إن   ال له شاء إن   ال له شاء إن   ال له شاء إن   ال له شاء إن

W e knew we had reached the border when we found a straggling line of trucks along the edge of the road. A short distance ahead I could see barriers and a crowd of people milling around so I parked behind the last truck.

I looked across at Ron. "Welcome to the crazy zone where all normal expectations can be cast to the wind."

He immediately took off his seat belt. "Oh, boy, I can't wait to see this!" He bounded out of the passenger door like an anxious dog ready for its evening romp around the neighborhood.

Penny decided to stay in the car while Ron and I checked out the border. We walked up to the actual crossing point to ascertain how to expedite our passage. A vision of total chaos gave us little hope of a quick crossing. Angry truckers argued with officials while other groups of drivers sat on their haunches engaged in heated debates. Unable to determine any order or pattern to follow, we decided to wait our turn with the Blazer.

When we returned to tell Penny the news, we found a few other trucks had parked behind us, and their drivers had gathered nearby, sitting on their haunches to enjoy a smoke. They all wore the standard garb of truck drivers in that region. Khaki long-sleeved shirts sported large pockets sewn on both sides of the chest; all looked to be a couple of sizes larger than they needed to be. The pants were made of a khaki-colored light cotton material with an elastic or a tie waist and elasticized cuffs at the ankles that made them balloon widely. Despite the heat, they all wore khaki felt hats with a two to three-inch side and a flat top; they fit tightly on the crown of the head. A narrow band on the lower edge displayed a little variety of patterns that were primarily red or green.

As soon as the group of drivers saw Ron and me, they called and waved for us to join them. They all wanted to talk to us, all at the same time. As neither Ron nor I understood a single word of Turkish, we felt verbally overwhelmed by the torrent. If we could have deciphered what one of them, alone, had said, we may have gleaned some idea. However, from all of their insistence and pointing we suspected they were telling us to drive past the parked trucks to the border crossing directly. Bypassing a queue felt rather 'un-British'; however, I followed their instructions and did so.

We entered the sea of arguments and frustration, only to be immediately directed to a dirt patch off to one side. I parked and walked into the small hut which lay a few yards away. I found a desk with a sign written in badly spelled, broken English indicating the office only handled private passenger cars. The official who sat at the desk expended far more energy demonstrating his control than performing any useful duties. As I didn't immediately return to the Blazer, Penny and Ron came to join me in the hut where we waited while papers circulated among desks, but none were ever fully processed. The main official ignored us despite the fact we stood only feet away from where he sat shuffling papers.

Penny scratched her head and whispered, "Do either of you know what's happening here? He knows those are our passports sitting there. He put them on his desk next to his tea and we're waiting right here." When neither Ron nor I had an answer, she exclaimed. "What is wrong with him?"

Ron looked directly at the official and coughed. The official who took his role of being in charge with much zeal simply ignored him.

I decided I needed to once again be un-British, and I said, "Let me try this," as I pulled out a $20 bill and held it out while I pointed at our three passports. The official yelled commands at his subordinates, to add some dramatic effect, as he stamped our documents. We had our completed papers in a few minutes. We then had officially entered Syria. I felt strange having just bribed an official to allow us entry into his country, but I felt really good about it. Move over James Bond, your replacement is here!

We continued southeast in the late afternoon and, after a meal, stopped relatively early as I felt drained and in need of a little down time. The demanding drive along the tight and narrow roads around the Turkish coast and our strange encounter the previous evening with the lone soldier had worn me down. I slept well, despite the rather rocky ground, and we arose to find the northern Syrian desert had already started to bake.

Our next destination, Damascus, felt doable as the road was well constructed, clearly marked, and I could drive at 60 or 70 mph without trouble. However, to the south and west of Damascus lay the Golan Heights which had become well-known in the 1967 Arab/Israeli War. Israel had captured much of the Heights and retained them after the peace accord was signed. They justified their annexation of the area claiming they needed to prevent Hezbollah fighters from hiding on the higher ground to fire rockets and RPG rounds into nearby Israeli villages. This has been a point of contention between Israel and Syria ever since. Being aware that we would be close to the Heights made the three of us a little anxious as we planned to drive through the area that Syria still controlled. Occasionally, we passed army vehicles as well as trucks and cars; all of their occupants stared at us suspiciously.

As we crossed the plains of dusty rocks and drifting sand, we encountered occasional villages. One that lay about half a mile off the road caught our attention. That particular village comprised a group of attached round white-painted huts with conical tops. I could see no signs of windows in the huts and they lacked conventional roofs. Each of the units appeared to be about the same size and they stood in a line, adjoined. Each had round walls that simply rose vertically before they narrowed to a point. Ron asked, "Is that a village or something else?"

Penny took longer to examine the village. "People are around and I see a couple of trucks parked nearby. I saw a group of kids playing near a bunch of goats. So it looks like a village, but those houses are really strange."

I looked around. "I don't see any access roads, so I don't feel right about driving across to take a closer look."

Later, I learned such villages were made of what is known as Beehive Mud Brick Houses. They were an ancient traditional style of housing in northern Syria and were the Arabic equivalent of adobe construction. Bricks of mud and straw were dried in the sun and used to create thick circular walls about 20 feet across. When the walls gained their full height, they bulged out slightly before they tapered up, like a cone, to an apex leaving a small hole at the peak. The hole was left open to allow light into the interior and smoke from cooking fires to escape. A small cover was attached on the outside of the opening to prevent rain from entering the interior. Despite being in a harsh desert area, these houses were occasionally subjected to torrential rainstorms. Small windows were included in the walls, but they were low to the ground, which was why we didn't see them from the road. A single small doorway was positioned on the side that was opposite the prevailing winds. The thick mud and straw walls enabled the inside temperature to remain in the 85 to 90 degree range, even when the outside temperatures soared to about 140 degrees.

We kept driving and later our route took us through a line of low barren rocky hills which looked desolate and uninviting. Unfortunately, along with the desolation, the area lacked gas stations, a serious concern as my gas tank was close to empty. I nervously glanced at the gas gauge every mile and I kept changing the positions of my hands on the steering wheel to wipe sweat off them. The road dropped down the last of a series of hills allowing me to scan the next few miles of road as they stretched out across the open harsh desert. Off in the distance, three small objects caught my eye. On one side of the road I saw what appeared to be two gas pumps and a small hut nearby. Mirages or real? As I drove anxiously across those couple of miles, the pumps became more solid and real.

Before I slowed down to cross over to the pumps, I looked at Ron with a few words of explanation, "I've been looking for a gas station for a while as we're getting rather low."

Ron looked puzzled by the gas station's starkness, "Are you sure this is a gas station? There aren't any giant signs or cars lined up waiting for fuel."

I rationalized the situation. "I will admit it's rather strange. Who knows how gas stations operate out here in the northern stretches of Syria?"

I pulled in between the pumps and the small hut so that filling the tank would be easy. I turned the engine off, wound down my window for circulation, and unfastened my seatbelt to get out of the Blazer. The door to the hut opened and two nervous soldiers walked out with their automatic weapons. This region still lay north of the Golan Heights. Despite not being on the actual Israeli border, I had realized many people especially military personnel displayed an intensity, nervousness and seemed extremely wary of unexpected circumstances. My stopping the Blazer next to the two gas pumps, apparently, was seen as an unexpected circumstance to them.

In almost a whisper, Ron said, "I think this is a military refueling point. I say we should leave, now."

The soldiers walked cautiously toward us, keeping a close eye on the three of us. I turned back to Ron. "Yes, you're right. They don't look too pleased to see us and not anxious to sell us any fuel. We'll leave."

I put my seatbelt back on, ready to return to the roadway. Unfortunately, as my window was open, the two soldiers heard the seatbelt's click. They both instinctively hit the dirt and rolled away from each other as they released the safety catches on their weapons.

The ends of the gun barrels were cold steel rings that surrounded circles of blackness which hid bullets, agents of destruction. They could beckon death in an instant. My alarm spiraled as the two soldiers lay prone in the sand. They held their weapons steady looking for a reason to unleash death's agents. Their fingers tensed against the smoothness of their weapons' triggers. The safety catches were off and I stared down those barrels. Cold sweat soaked my brow, my heart pounded, a clamp gripped my gut, thoughts raced, time stopped, and I froze. *Was this my time to die?* It was both my perception and my reality in that moment.

Thankfully, Ron immediately realized what had just happened. He didn't scream, but forcefully spat out the words, "Hands up, now!" His words jolted me out of my petrified state.

Ron and I raised our hands with such force that we almost punched four dents in the roof of the Blazer. I couldn't see what Penny did because I stared down the barrels of two automatic weapons. I realized the soldiers suspected I had caused the click because it was me who was dead center in their gun sights. Putting our hands up quickly may have saved our lives. One of the soldiers kept us under steady scrutiny, finger on the trigger, while the other who was more behind me stood up slowly and approached my open window. His brown eyes were deadly serious and his movements conveyed an authority that only came from training and repetition. His earlier look of suspicion was replaced by a hardened expression that sought answers to the potentially fatal question—what had caused that click, if it wasn't a gun? I unfastened the seatbelt and refastened it—click. I repeated the action and he looked relieved. Seat belts were an unusual idea to most Syrians back in those days. The click, which sounded normal to Europeans, caused great alarm in the two soldiers. One of them wanted to satisfy his curiosity about the click and tried to question me, but I couldn't understand him. I considered showing him my passport, but realized pulling an item out of my pocket could raise further suspicion. Instead, I spoke to him in English, which confirmed to him that we were foreigners and therefore probably unaware of military refueling stations. He quickly said something to his comrade who still held us in his gun sight. They both put on their safety catches and came closer to look in the car. They could find no other reason for the click.

Before Ron, Penny and I had the opportunity to look at each other or to simply sigh in relief, the two soldiers walked back to the hut with lit cigarettes as if this type of incident was quite normal. I pulled out onto the road and muttered, "I promise I'll never again stop at any place that has gas pumps, but no large advertisements, billboards, nor a line of cars—no matter how empty the gas tank may be."

"I'll keep you to that promise," Ron replied as the hint of a smile began to replace his pale fearful expression. Seeing his expression hit me hard, *Oh. My God! We could have been shot.* My legs started to shake, slightly. My hands felt sweatier than normal. I scratched at itches that probably weren't real. That incident almost broke me. I stared at the road, I drove, I struggled to contain my flailing thoughts and reactions, driving was the one detail that felt real. This was the first time in my life that I looked death in the face, and all I could do afterwards was drive. I couldn't look in the rearview mirror to see the two gas pumps because I feared death's face would be there, bidding me a temporary adieu. I drove, I drove away.

We all felt both shocked and relieved. I couldn't recall a time when I had been through a more severe emotional roller-coaster. I had been propelled from a state of anxiety about an empty gas tank to abject terror sensing I was about to be riddled with bullets and, as quickly, dropped back into a peaceful composure, once the gun safety catches were back in place. However, the resulting adrenaline spike left me feeling uncomfortable and jittery. My muscles twitched involuntarily, stiffness and soreness caressed my shoulders, and a weight sat in the pit of my stomach. I suppose shock was a pretty healthy response to the experience. I felt unnerved for hours afterwards.

I don't recall how much further we drove before we found a real gas station—I felt happy to have a tank full of leaded gas and not a body full of lead. Yes, Mother, I was possibly foolish to stop by those gas pumps. I had probably exercised a degree of bad judgment. If I had been out for a relaxing weekend drive, I may have made another decision. I had been driving for about ten days. I'm not sure if I felt stressed, exhausted, or perfectly fine. I could only describe my condition as a surreal blend of all three. Driving through such desolate terrain with an almost empty gas tank distorted my thinking, and normal rational thought had been nothing more than a pipe dream. To find gas, at that time, had been an essential motivation; it was not a simple rational decision that prompted me to stop by those particular pumps.

Now, in hindsight and after a lifetime of experiences, I know the path I chose in such a stressful situation had consequences, some good and some not so good. I feel that is precisely the same as daily life, not just what happened in northern Syria forty years ago. I can never pre-determine the outcome of my actions, no matter how well considered they are. I had simply put on my seatbelt in the hope I would be safer and as a result was almost killed. In my 28-year-old mind, that started a powerful and profound understanding. Life is fragile and uncertain. Such a realization could be equally true during a wild adventure or during a day-to-day mundane activity—the lesson was simple and true in both scenarios—live life fully, always. For many people, this incident and its potentially tragic outcome would be the justification to not entertain such a journey. To me, it was the proof I was right to do it because I learned I will never know how any of my actions will turn out, despite my intentions. In a matter of seconds, I learned to move beyond any fear regarding death and to live life fully. I believe those who think they have control over their lives, and in doing so, can avoid death or other calamities are living a fiction. To me, those who accept that a lack of control is normal and healthy are living a life that is free of unnecessary fear. I suppose some people aren't comfortable accepting life can throw us curve balls at any time, and they hope holding onto fears will keep them aware, helping them ward off such uncertainties. For me, that doesn't work, as fear tends to immobilize me, right at the time when I may need to take action. As a well-worn cliché from a decade ago said, "Shit happens."

After an hour or so driving south, we reached the city of Aleppo, a city in the middle of a huge expanse of barren sandy desert.

Penny peered out the windscreen at the outline of the city as it shimmered in the distance. "I wonder why a city came to be located here in the middle of a sandy wasteland?"

I ventured, "Maybe long ago, a number of standard caravan routes converged at this point."

Ron said, "Also, there could've been an oasis here at some time."

I said, "That's true. I would think, in time, probably a market may have grown where caravans traded goods from various far-off lands, and that led to a village which eventually grew to a city. Who knows?"

In the rearview mirror I could see Penny had a pensive expression on her face. "You two always seem to have ideas of how things happened or started. I wish I could do that."

Ron turned to her, "You're way too hard on yourself. You obviously have some great skills as you organize the offices for both Keith's and Wyatt's groups. They couldn't function without you."

Penny smiled. "Thanks. I can be hard on myself, at times."

I felt sympathy for Penny's doubting herself. "Also, Ron and I may have had ideas about how Aleppo may have come about. But, more importantly, you were the one who posed the question in the first place. You have an inquisitive nature which is essential in any collaboration. You shouldn't underestimate yourself."

She sat straighter and more lightly replied, "Thanks. I, sometimes, need some cheerleaders on my side."

As I approached a junction, I quickly asked, "Do we need supplies?"

Both of them replied, "Yes."

As I had no concept of the significance of Aleppo in later news stories, I took the side road toward the city as the main highway skirted around the outer edge of the built-up areas. We drove through the main thoroughfares and looked for the center of the city, but without any real interest. It looked like a standard Arabic city with buildings constructed of concrete columns and block walls. Sadly, these became ideal conditions for deadly close quarters combat in later years. It is appalling and unbelievable that, only a few years ago, the vast majority of the entire city had been destroyed with thousands, including significant numbers of innocent civilians, lying dead in the rubble. I remember it as a vibrant city with streets filled with market stalls, people peacefully going about their daily lives and groups of children playing in the sand. I parked near the main mosque to search a few stores for provisions which I hoped were younger than the store itself.

As our journey took place forty years ago, the children I saw then have probably been forced to flee their homes. Some have fled their homeland to distant countries, some possibly have adopted different beliefs, and I'm sure all of them have experienced various tragic events. How many have died, how many joined the military, how many became freedom fighters, and how many became terrorists? Did any come to America and now worry our current U.S. Administration will expel them back to torture and death? Have others survived the terrifying journey of being a fleeing refugee and now live in a foreign land being treated with suspicion, intolerance, and hatred? How many have actually lost someone in their immediate families due to violence, and how few have lived what we in the West would consider a normal happy life? These are the potential outcomes for those children who tied weeds and trash into a makeshift football, or dressed a small twig with a remnant of filthy tattered cloth to become a dolly that a girl could make-believe was her baby. It is horrendous to me how such innocence could so easily be overtaken. It only took a demonstration of what a gun could do, or a bomb could destroy, along with distorted religious beliefs to pivot such innocent, disadvantaged children into monsters of hatred. But, let me be pedantic here, this isn't only a statement about Muslims. This is my condemnation of all people and groups who think weapons of any type, violence, all acts of terrorism, and larger armed forces are the solution to problems between people of different creeds, beliefs, and skin color. I believe this whole-heartedly at all levels of society: national, local and personal.

In the previous paragraph, I used the phrase "*how many*" multiple times to emphasize the numbers of people who have been driven from their homes and neighborhoods to avoid violence—but it isn't only in Syria, it's true in too many countries. Also, I don't want to present this as purely an exercise in numbers, even though the number of refugees, worldwide, is sadly huge. I cannot separate these large numbers from what they represent—human beings. These people suffered situations that are beyond my most horrifying imagination. I believe these people want the same as you and I—a place to rest each night, knowing our children and loved ones are safe, comfortable, and fed. To me, this is the meaning of universal love and I sense the world needs more, much more of it.

For the three of us, after the incident with the gas pumps, the drive down to Damascus felt rather surreal and unsettling. Also, knowing what is still happening in Aleppo, that entire section of the drive across northern Syria feels both unreal and disturbing. However, forty years ago, we did eventually wind our way into Damascus and parked near what appeared to be the main market area. To walk around on solid ground and to breathe the fresh air for a while felt good despite the triple-digit temperatures. I wonder how much of this market area still functions and whether the nearby neighborhoods are still vibrant with life? I am saddened such an authoritarian as Assad has been allowed to arm his military so that they may kill and maim their own Syrian people. I don't think either the Russians or the Iranians can claim total innocence in this matter. And I do wonder how innocent the U.K. and U.S. truly are. Unfortunately, I find the lines between world leadership and bullying to have become blurred of late. To me, the arts of diplomacy and civility need a resurgence.

CHAPTER 10
BEING TOURISTS FOR A WHILE

الله شاء إن   الله شاء إن   الله شاء إن   الله شاء إن   الله شاء إن   الله شاء إن

Penny had heard that one of the oldest churches in the world had been built in Damascus. As we meandered through the markets and alleyways, we decided to try to find it. When we occasionally saw anyone who we thought to be European or might speak reasonable English, we asked them if they knew of such a place. On our fourth try, a man said he knew it and led us through a mile or so of twisting courtyards and alleyways. They formed the main thoroughfares through the older neighborhoods where the houses rose three or four stories high. Houses packed close together, and many were attached with no room for gardens. Most had been painted in pastel colors that primarily fell in the cream to sandy to brown range. None appeared to have air-conditioning and, as a result, most had their windows opened wide to help catch any wisps of breeze that penetrated the passageways. We could see many houses created their own breeze with constantly spinning ceiling fans. Their drone blanketed the area with an ever-present background noise which felt both comforting, but annoying. In places, house balconies protruded out over passageways so far it felt neighbors could shake hands or converse across the alleys. For certain stretches, we couldn't see the sky at all.

Laundry hung on lines from many of the balconies. Small children scampered through the pathways playing imaginative games. At times, wafts of aromatic spices teased our senses. Demanding cries of babies caught our attention. The tension of people in heated arguments stopped us for a second. Women beat the dust out of rugs they had hung over balcony walls. Groups of men in the midst of ardent conversations strode through the passageways wearing traditional attire. Their dress comprised a light-weight flowing robe, which was normally brown with gold trim which was worn over a full-length white tunic. On their feet they wore leather thongs that slapped on the soles of their feet as they walked. A checkered scarf, a *keffiyeh,* covered their heads to stay cool. A heavy cord braid, an *agel,* held it in place.

The sounds of sweeping or scrubbing pervaded everywhere. They were Syrian people simply living their daily lives. In the most fundamental sense, these people were similar to you and me in their daily home environments.

Our guide, who wore non-traditional clothing—western slacks and a casual shirt—even though he said he had been born and raised in Syria, stopped at a doorway between two small stores which we would have bypassed had he not stopped us. A hand-written sign pinned under an ancient carved stone plaque on the wall indicated the Church of Saint Hananiya would open later in the day. As the opening time would need us to idle away about an hour, we thanked the man and briefly explored the local streets, passageways, and stores while we waited.

When we returned, the narrow door that appeared to have been painted many times over the centuries from its multiple flaking layers had been unlocked and stood slightly ajar. We headed down a flight of stairs into the basement of the building. It felt wonderful to be in a cooler temperature for a brief time. Four or five overhead lights led us along a narrow corridor and into a tiny chapel. The stark bareness of the interior surprised me, simple stone walls and a stone ceiling supported by stone arches. The stone's light yellow tones in the artificial electric lights gave a warm ambiance to the space. The altar appeared to be a plain stone slab supported by a single carved column. A narrow piece of damask was draped across the slab. In the center, stood a simple small brass cross. A rather surprised docent looked up from her reading to greet us. Apparently, we would be counted among the small number of visitors who actually found the chapel. Her gray hair, pulled back into a bun, and her simple dark blue dress reminded me of a novice nun. Whether or not she belonged to an order remained a mystery.

The chapel had originally been built almost two thousand years ago, during the Roman period. The docent said this chapel had been purposefully built and hidden in a basement as several of its more ancient predecessors hadn't survived various uprisings, invasions, and general unrest. However, I have since learned this version of the chapel's history had been no more than a myth. The chapel stood on street level originally, but the level of the city had risen about five meters in the subsequent two thousand years. Archeologists believed the chapel had originally been attached to Hananiya's house. When time and age had snatched away the house's former glory, its stone walls had been re-used in the construction of newer structures, leaving the chapel free-standing. In time, it was overtaken by the rising level of the city and now formed part of the foundations for an apartment building.

A few of the icons and aged painted pictures that hung around the walls of the church portrayed God sending Hananiya to convert Saul of Tarsus who later became known as Paul the Apostle. Several of these ancient relics appeared to have been painted on pieces of wood, which had split and twisted. Despite their state, their gold leaf backgrounds gave them a sense of power and awe that couldn't be bypassed.

The small rows of pews could accommodate about twenty people, with barely enough room between the front row and the altar for one member of the clergy to lead a service. We looked at the framed icons that depicted Hananiya's life, as well as a few faded brass plaques which commemorated people who had attended the church or had been buried along the outside of the walls of the structure in millennia past. We asked the docent a few simple questions in English; she could only repeat a few well-rehearsed sentences of explanation in English. After we spent a few minutes trying to decipher inscriptions on brass plates, the three of us departed the calm and coolness of the hidden sanctuary. We stood in the doorway to the street for a few minutes to allow our eyes to re-adjust to the bright sunlight and decided to next head to the main section of the Damascus market areas.

As we walked along the dusty pathways that wove through neighborhoods, Penny, Ron and I watched vendors at their stalls as they tried to entice nearby shoppers, mechanics as they worked on cars and pieces of machinery, business men drinking coffee while arguing over a deal, and metal craftsmen working to make any item they felt would be purchased.

Ron took a few steps across the passageway to check out a stall and when he came back, he said, "It's interesting how boys stay close to their fathers who are running the family business."

I responded, "Yes, I'd noticed that too. I presume the boys will learn the family trade and gain enough knowledge to take over the business when the father decides to stop working. From discussions I've had in the office with Saudis, I've heard young girls stay close to their mothers to learn how to run the household. It apparently isn't a matter of just doing laundry, shopping and cooking—women truly do manage the day-to-day running of the household, everything from budgeting, decision making and planning, but men always have veto power."

Penny apparently heard Ron's and my comments about boys and girls being prepared for adulthood because she looked over at me and, with a smile, said, "I'll admit that I'm glad I grew up in England where I had some options. I can't imagine how young women survive here." She looked directly at me. "And, Barry, I don't think you followed your father's profession, but if you ever decide to change careers, I'd recommend you become a cop, not a play-acting one, a real one."

I instantly understood her reference and took the bait, replying, "Well, you realize if I hadn't pretended to be a policeman at the art show last fall, Ron and I wouldn't have become household names for many families in camp, especially families with young children."

Ron made efforts to distance himself from a number of flies, but they persistently pursued him. He surrendered to them and joined in the banter. "Oh, yes, we are known in too many households. Now,

Barry, I'm not certain I've ever heard how you became an imitation cop, which I believe only started at the art show, last year."

The art show had become a popular annual event on the Aramco camp. A surprisingly large number of talented artists worked for Aramco and lived in camp. When I had toured the art show during my first year, the asking prices on a number of pieces had shocked me. However when I took time to comprehend the skills and talents to produce these pieces of art, I quickly came to realize that most of these items hadn't been over-priced. I remember falling in love with one piece of sculpture, even though I didn't normally like sculpture, but I couldn't justify the $1,000 price tag for it. It may sound strange, but the outline of a fetus in the womb had been cut out of a piece of rusting one-inch boiler-plate steel with a blow torch. Only an extraordinary artist could conceive of such an incredible combination and juxtaposition of subject matter and medium. The preciousness and beauty of a fetus portrayed exquisitely in such a hard and unyielding form forced me to reconsider what I considered to be art. I can still see the piece in my mind and it still evokes a deep sense of awe in me. While I stood looking at that one piece, I was moved and intrigued so much that suddenly art became a vibrant, real concept. That iron sculptor had a reputation in camp and he was invited to create small sculptures as prizes for road races that were being arranged in camp. I was fortunate to join my friends Eric and Hughie, and we won the team race. I still have several of these unique sculptures and I didn't pay a cent for them.

After a while, we wandered into the main market area of Damascus to search for the stores that made wooden board games and those that sold brass goods. As we walked, I told them both how I became a character actor about ten months before. During a party, soon after I had moved onto the Aramco camp, I met an English couple, Patsy and Don. They told me they had been asked to find a few English folks who would be willing to dress up in costume and pretend to be certain well-known English characters for an upcoming art show. The characters would then mingle with the people while they perused the art show as an added small side-attraction. Patsy asked me if I would join the group. Possibly, the alcohol I had imbibed or my sense of the ridiculous forced me to say "Yes."

We continued our tour of the Damascus markets and navigated our way through the vegetable market. Crowds of shoppers, who were making their daily rounds of the stalls, looking for what they needed for the evening meals, split us apart so our conversation faltered for a brief period. When the crowds lessened and we could walk as a group, I described the organizing meeting that Patsy and Don held. Patsy asked us which English characters we thought we should portray. We soon had identified the obvious ones: Henry VIII, Nell Gwyn, and Guy Fawkes. Then someone offered to lend the group a genuine London policeman's helmet which he had grabbed off a policeman's head during a riot in central London. The helmet's new owner didn't feel comfortable pretending to be a cop. At 6' 3," I stood taller than any other person in the meeting, thus people thought I would be the best substitute. After a little coaxing, I agreed. As I had been an inept klutz for most of my life, a sense of possible embarrassment had become a normal state of being for me; trying to avoid it bordered on being pointless as such humiliation apparently sought me out.

I felt strange admitting to Penny and Ron that I had quickly become surprisingly comfortable as I wandered through the art show crowds, murmuring, "Hallo, hallo, hallo." This was with a small accompanying knees bend, a quintessential pairing of greeting and action that all British TV and movie coppers incorporated into their characterizations, back in the 1960s and 70s. As I had been so new in camp, at that time, many people didn't recognize me and asked if I was a real policeman brought in from London, just for the event. The mocked-up uniform fashioned from my own limited wardrobe and borrowed pieces, along with the genuine helmet, made me appear reasonably convincing. The art show enabled me to get to know many people in camp because for weeks after the show, I would be stopped by total strangers with comments like, "Hey, are you the policemen from the art show? Hi. My name is so-and-so." Thus my social connections in camp had expanded quickly.

As our meander through the extensive Damascus bazaar

continued, we took mental note of the locations of its different sections as well as mosques or office buildings. In each section of the bazaar, all stalls sold primarily one type of commodity—grains, vegetables, hardware, etc.. With this information, we hoped to be able to return to the sections that interested us, when we were tired of exploring and ready to make some purchases. Both Penny and Ron wanted to look for several small presents that they could take back to England on their next vacations. They both spent time checking out the metal workers' stalls that had a wide selection of copper bowls, ash trays, wall decorations and anything else which could be beaten out of copper, brass or any other soft metal. However, we found it difficult to focus on their artistry with their work benches right alongside their stalls with items for sale. Their pounding hammers transformed the raw pieces of metals into beautifully crafted final products. However, the narrow streets and passageways gave the sound little chance to escape. It simply reverberated and hung like an audible presence. Dampened cloth hung over the stalls, intended to shade and cool shoppers from the few rays of sunlight that managed to penetrate down to street level. Unfortunately, it more effectively contained the hammering and beating sounds.

I had wanted to buy a backgammon board in Damascus as I had heard the local craftsmen demonstrated exceptional skills. We found all the stores that made and sold board games. Each of the stores comprised four distinct areas: the workshop, the store, a lounge, and a kitchen. As we entered each store, the owner directed us to where examples of their polished game boards filled display cases. If it looked likely we might be interested in making a purchase, we would be invited into the lounge for tea. We soon discovered the tea had been brewed hours before and stored in old thermos's that had lost their insulation. When we started to haggle over the price of a particular board, then we might be invited to tour the workshop to better understand how beautifully their craftsmen created the boards. I was fascinated to watch thin sticks of different colored wood glued lengthwise into rods that had a diamond shape in cross-section, with a consistent pattern of all the various colored sticks throughout each rod's length. When these rods had completely dried, the craftsman would cut the rod into diamond shaped slivers that would later be inlaid into boxes to form the pattern of the backgammon boards. Aging master craftsmen and younger apprentices focused on their incredibly painstaking work that took time, patience, and skill, gained over many years of practice.

I found the store I preferred and selected the board I wanted to buy. The owner invited us to tour the workshop where half a dozen craftsmen bent over their benches and machines. They chatted constantly as they worked, lifting the mood of the workshop where natural light only reached the benches of the master craftsman. We sat down in the lounge with the owner to haggle over the price of the board I had chosen. Ron and Penny added words of encouragement, suggesting different ways to haggle the price down. After about three cups of cooling tea, I had bartered the asking price down by about 20% and agreed to pay in British pounds. I was delighted with the board I bought and accepted the fact that I had probably paid twice what a local person might have paid for it. That backgammon board may not get too much use these days, but it has been with me for the last 40 years along with my memories.

With a backgammon board under my arm, we continued our tour of central Damascus. At various points, we saw large pictures of men in uniform hung on the sides of buildings; we assumed they were members of the President's family and other high-level military leaders.

Penny asked, "Why are these pictures hanging in many parts of the city?"

Ron replied. "They feel rather creepy and intimidating to me."

I joined in. "They feel oppressive to me."

Ron stopped to look at one for a few seconds. "It feels to me like he's keeping an eye on us."

I shivered at the thought. "Oh, that feels even more oppressive than I had thought initially."

Penny quickened her pace, "Let's keep moving, I can feel that one's eyes following me."

Ron spotted one located down a side-street and said, "Huh. I wonder what that guy did wrong to have his picture stuck there. I don't think I'd like to be an army general or a Syrian dictator. In actual fact, I'm still not certain I know what I want to be when I grow up."

I sensed a lighter mood and asked, "You really think you'll actually grow up, one day? That's questionable. You'd agree with me, wouldn't you Penny?"

"I'm not sure. Only time will tell."

Ron tried to look hurt, which just made us smile more broadly. He asked, "So, Penny, what are you going to do with your wealth after you quit Aramco?"

She considered for a few seconds, "Well, I have a dream, but I don't know how much money I'll need to start out. I've been thinking about starting a small-scale clothing business. You know, design some business type clothes for women and have some manufactured. I'm not sure how to market or sell them as yet. There are so many things to think about. It's just an idea, a dream, something I would love to do if I can."

I was intrigued, "So you'd quit being a secretary to start your own business. That takes determination. Good for you."

Ron looked a little envious, "Wow, I'd like to do something like that, too. I can't say I know anything like clothing to start with. All I know are computer systems, and I certainly don't have the capital to start my own company."

I encouraged him to continue, "So, do you have any aspirations in the computer field?"

He happily launched into what was a passion for him, "Yes. I do like computing and I love how it has developed into various disciplines of expertise. However, now, I want to somehow bring these various elements back to communicating with each other to make computer systems much more efficient and really useful."

"Seems like you have some ideas already in your mind," I followed up.

Penny asked, "Do you know other people with similar ideas?"

"Actually, yes. I've realized that a number of people in London are thinking along similar lines. We've talked about this over a couple of pints. We reckon we need to redirect the British Computer Society to orchestrate new protocols and define a list of best-practices. So when I return to London, I'll join the society and try to become a force within it."

Penny couldn't miss an opportunity to rib him, "I'm sure you'll manage to force some changes on the computer society. I love your enthusiasm."

Ron smiled and turned to me, "So, Barry, are you going to become a chauffeur, with all this driving experience?"

"No. I couldn't contemplate such huge responsibilities. Perhaps I'll become a wandering minstrel or a brain surgeon." We chuckled as we walked on. "I reckon I'll work in computing as a manager, some day. I would prefer finding a position in a technical systems group. To me, commercial applications are so boring. You know I think I'm more interested in continuing to work abroad than returning to England. I suppose I'd go back if I had to, if only to figure out where I felt like going next."

Penny responded immediately, "Not me. I love England and I want to go back."

Ron agreed, "Absolutely. Barry, don't you still have family back home?"

I concurred, "Sure, my mother married her second husband two or three years ago and she seems to be well settled. My sister's in the midst of having a family, so she's busy. I can't say I'm that engaged with more extended family. So, I feel reasonably content to visit them every so often."

Penny looked a little pensive, "I also have a pretty small family, and for us, that seems to make us closer. I miss them while I'm working in the Middle East."

We continued through the streets and alleyways for a while before we headed back to the Blazer. We next needed to head south across the border to Jordan where we hoped to swap Ron's temporary passport for his real one which hopefully had been sent in the diplomatic bag to the British Embassy in Amman. Damascus traffic had become more congested with the start of the early evening commute. We determined what felt like a southerly course and headed on a main road in that direction. Traffic flow and one-way streets brought us back to about where we had started within a few minutes. We tried a second variation, which took us on a longer circuit, and about ten minutes later we once again found ourselves back where we had begun. Not to be discouraged, but feeling a little annoyed, we tried a third route. We passed our starting point again about a quarter of an hour later. I had noticed we passed one rather large, busy roundabout on these three circuits, and we decided we may find a clue if we went around it a few times. Having Penny and Ron's eyes to look out for any useful signs gave me a little relief as I needed to focus on the weaving lines of traffic that averaged a good speed while circumnavigating the large roundabout. In the middle of the roundabout stood a series of large, dry and dusty fountains. Who had been the country's President when water last flowed in the fountains and surrounding pools? Oil revenues may have allowed for the building of such grand structures to demonstrate the country's wealth, but budgets hadn't been allocated to maintain them. From what I could see, maintaining these fountains needed to be a continual requirement in the harsh environment of central Damascus.

As we circled the roundabout, the only signs or directions that we found hung on small, broken signposts, written in faded Arabic that none of us could comprehend. They provided us with no help and no hope.

As we made our second circuit, I happened to see what looked like two police cars in a walled compound on one side of the roundabout. On our next circuit, I negotiated my way to the outer lane so I could make the turn and drove through the narrow entrance into the compound. Almost immediately, I had to hit the brakes hard for an unexpectedly quick halt. I found not only two police cars in the rutted dirt compound, but two dozen shiny, official looking police cars sat in the lot and they hadn't really been parked. They had been randomly stopped wherever their drivers felt like stopping, without any concern for others getting around them.

Ron had been frustrated by our failure to navigate out of the city on our own. I could sense in him a need to fix this problem. Even though he spoke absolutely no Arabic, he said, "Let me try to get directions. I presume all the police are in that building next to the far wall of the compound."

I felt awkward being jammed in the entrance to the compound and willingly agreed, "I will stay in the car with Penny, in case I need to move."

He grabbed the door handle to get out of the car when suddenly multiple alarms and sirens started up, and strobe lights flashed in every window of the building. Before we knew it, a stream of policemen wearing immaculate uniforms and caps came pouring down the steps of the building and headed toward the scattered police cars. It didn't take me more than a nanosecond to recognize I had been forced to a halt in a rather precarious position, I was stopped just inside the one and only entrance to the compound. I tried to back out through the narrow entry way which allowed me no view of the traffic that hurtled around the roundabout.

It amazed us to witness the ability of the policemen to maneuver their police cars into two orderly lines. They set all their strobe lights flashing, and their sirens clawed into our collective consciousness as the two lines headed toward the one entrance and us. We sat, transfixed, in the Blazer, barely a few feet inside the one entrance. The six-foot high concrete wall gave me no chance to see anything and whatever Penny could see from the back seat gave me no encouragement.

Ron said, "Let me be your eyes for this one," and jumped out of the car. He darted behind me so I could see him in my wing mirror. He started waving wildly at the traffic that flew around the roundabout. When he turned, yelling, I think he said, "Now. Fast. There's a small gap." He waved for me to go as quickly as I dared. I had to trust a gap would open in the line of traffic and I hit the gas. I shot backwards out of the entrance, praying, and as soon as I could, I made a turn, so I didn't cross too many lanes of speeding traffic. As soon as I had cleared the entrance, the column of flashing, screeching police cars hurtled out of the compound and quickly disappeared into the flow of traffic. Despite my fried nerves, I knew how a cork must have felt as it was forced out of a champagne bottle with all of that effervescent bubbly anxious to get out of the bottle too. It now feels strange to compare myself to an inanimate object, but the comparison of myself to a champagne cork still feels totally valid, even after all these years. When the noise of all the police cars' sirens had faded into the far distance, I tentatively pulled back into the compound and parked in a manner which allowed me to exit easily if I needed to do so again. That time Ron returned from the small building with directions, and they actually turned out to be useful.

Sometimes, we felt safe being in a city where we were surrounded by people, even though communication could be difficult. Those long stretches of open wilderness that lay between cities began to feel daunting and the distance between the cities seemed to become longer. I had started to feel irritable and grumpy. At times, I felt there was nowhere to rest. I'm not sure if my exhaustion became apparent to the other two. I sensed a communal spirit of determination and mutual respect. If one of us was short or frustrated, it didn't take much for the other two to lift them. For me, as the driver, the black ribbon of asphalt drew me onward and, hopefully, away from my mother's doubts that still permeated my thoughts.

We followed the directions and headed in what felt like the wrong direction at first, but we eventually managed to leave central Damascus and drove toward the Jordanian border. As early evening had fallen by the time we left the city, we decided to find a place to sleep soon after we returned to the peace of the desert. A rocky gully, a few yards off the main road, was a perfect place for Ron and me to put down sleeping bags and relax under a beautiful canopy of stars while Penny snuggled in the back seat. It certainly had been quite an interesting day's visit to Syria. We could still breathe the dusty air due to our fast reactions while under potential fire. We had been blessed to see one of the oldest churches in the world, I had a beautiful backgammon board, and we each had some really strange stories to tell our grandchildren.

Today, looking back on that time in Syria and, particularly, the half day we spent in Damascus, I find it difficult to envisage how life in those older neighborhoods and markets has been in these last few war-torn years. I suspect nerves are raw, tension spikes quickly, suspicion is rampant, supplies are restricted, and fewer children scamper along the pathways lost in imaginative games. Division and intimidation probably drive many peoples' motivations and behaviors. This amazing city and its people have been transformed. It may now be as close to hell on earth as any location in the modern day. I fear it shall be decades before the city will be stable again or be safe enough for many refugees to return. What will their conditions be if they do return? Will they still have homes? Will local infrastructure still exist? Will it be maintained if it does exist, and will funds be available to rebuild or repair it? I suspect these people's heads are filled with too many such questions. If they do rebuild their lives in Damascus, it shall be because of three reasons—their guts, their determination, and their will.

I sense life as a refugee in a foreign country may feel unsafe and uncertain, but can it potentially feel better than returning to "home?" What an awful predicament to have to consider while trying to fall asleep each night. I know a parent's most basic desire is to ensure their family, especially their children, feel safe, secure, fed and happy. I believe this to be true for all parents; American, English, Syrian, or any other nationality. It is a basic trait of being a sentient being. I wonder why such desires have a much lower priority than money, or nationalism, in the human world today. I sometimes feel money is some people's goal. To me, money is simply a means to an end—safety and security, not just the end in itself.

To me, this simple basic desire for safety and security has, in part, been lost in our apparent need to protect our American lifestyle. We Americans could lose the understanding that we don't stand alone. If America builds walls, literally or metaphorically, we isolate ourselves and we'll be more insecure. We will be unsafe because outsiders will want to understand why we are reclusive. We'll also be unsafe because being hemmed in will create a scared society within the U.S. which will feel the need to react violently to any small incident. I would suggest if Americans and Europeans want to feel safe and secure at home, then we should work so that Syrians, Afghanis, and all other nationalities also feel safe, secure and respected. I fear we western nations have much to learn about cultural respect before this can be achieved. Peace and stability aren't created by isolation or by selling arms and ammunition to dictators because it's good for the U.S. economy. Such stability will only be created if we find common understandings with other nations, and help them alleviate their own people's suffering with compassion.

Likewise, within America today, for Caucasians to feel safe and secure, I would advocate for African Americans, Hispanics, Native Indians and all other ethnic groups to be able to feel safe, secure and respected, too. I believe we are all one, we are all human, and I hope we can respect our differences—not fear them. Differences of race, religion, gender, sexual orientation and all other distinctions weave color and strength into the fabric of our society. Let us celebrate and honor these differences. I have read that, in the 19th century, white males were considered to be the supreme group of humans, the only ones worthy of being leaders. I am white and male, and I have no doubt such 19th century thinking was utterly wrong. I feel certain if we humans are to overcome 21st century problems, then I would advocate for all humans coming together to confront them in unison. I think the necessary talents can be found in all races and creeds of our kind. From experience, I've found no group is all-supreme, and all groups are capable. Everyone deserves an equal chance.

CHAPTER 11

HOME-STYLE COOKING

الله شاء إن   الله شاء إن   الله شاء إن   الله شاء إن   الله شاء إن   الله شاء إن   الله شاء إن   الله شاء إن

Our path continued south along good stable roads which for periods wove rhythmically between sand dunes that lined both sides of the road. Their golden color contrasted beautifully with the sky's intense blue. I felt relaxed after a good night's sleep. As I encountered little traffic headed toward the Jordanian border, I could take in the beauty of the dunes with each curve of the road which revealed yet another dune.

After about half-an-hour, we saw several huts, many stationary vehicles, and people everywhere. We had reached our next border crossing. On the Syrian side, the standard line of trucks stood patiently waiting; we passed them before we entered the insanity of the border. After a brief check by the Syrian guards, we crossed into the Jordanian border check point. We found each of the senior officials commanded one of a line of huts, and they ruled their piece of jurisdiction as if they wielded power equal to the King of England. Several heated arguments raged between frustrated truck drivers and officials in various offices. We waited until one of the offices became vacant before we entered the official's domain. The official looked quite relieved to deal with our crossing as he had no argument about the goods we declared or their value. It only took about ten minutes to enter Jordan once we found an available official. I felt a sense of relief when I realized we had managed to cross the border without the need for a bribe.

After we entered Jordan, I decided to find a gas station with acres of signage and plenty of cars. It didn't take us too many miles to find a large gas station teeming with dozens of trucks and private cars. We joined the queue for the gas pumps and relaxed, sensing this refueling would be a little less worrisome than yesterday morning's attempt in northern Syria. After we filled the tank, I parked to one side as Penny and Ron wanted to check the gas station's store for anything that would make a reasonable breakfast. I asked them to grab me something so I could check the ropes that held the boat on the roof rack. It didn't take me long, and afterwards I looked over to see if my companions had completed their search of the store. I saw no sign of them, but a young boy, about 7 or 8 years of age, came dancing toward me across the dirt. He grabbed my hand and insistently pulled me toward the road. I could see nothing of interest on the road or on the far side of it, only a standard sand dune. From my limited Arabic and his perpetual chatter, I sensed he really wanted me to follow him. Nowadays, I would never think of doing so. Back 40 years ago, being inquisitive was more accepted.

Penny and Ron had still not left the store, so I crossed the road with the boy. I wondered why such a young boy would be crossing a main road with fast moving traffic on his own. My intrigue about his circumstances rose when he started to head up the sand dune, insisting I followed him. Halfway up, I stopped to look for the others, but they still hadn't returned from their exploration of the shelves for any edible food. The young lad indicated we had almost reached the top, which I could see to be totally bogus. We continued to climb the dune, and to make it tougher, I recognized we were climbing the steeper face of the dune—yes, the windward side of a sand dune isn't as steep as the leeward side and unfortunately the leeward side of this dune faced the road. When we reached the top of the dune, he raced off while urging me to follow. He headed toward the only structure built on the plain that lay beyond the dune. I would have been tempted to dismiss the invitation, but my curiosity couldn't be denied with the odd sight I could see. On the salt flat that lay behind the sand dune stood a single dwelling, which was typical of what one could encounter in the desert at times. The house had only a couple of rooms—the entire structure including the flat roof was built of concrete. At other times, I'd seen these "houses" where no attempts had been made to disguise the concrete with even a coat of paint. Behind this dwelling, an area had been walled-in to form a private backyard. The backyard drew my attention, for over the concrete wall I could clearly see the black woven top of a Bedouin tent.

I walked over to an iron gate in the wall where I could see the boy proudly holding open a flap in the side of the tent. He ushered me inside. I must admit I became more concerned about the social etiquette of being invited into a Bedouin tent as a guest than I felt about my personal safety. We lived in the golden days of innocence and ignorance before 9/11. As I approached, the boy spoke excitedly to someone in the tent. I ducked my head to enter the tent. I had never been invited into a Bedouin's tent before, I was full of intrigue about what I would find. My first surprise was to discover the interior was relatively well lit, despite the tent having no windows or large open entrances. The light flooded in through the couple of vent flaps in the roof where the smoke from the fire escaped. I felt a little uncomfortable when I realized I stood alone in the tent with only the boy and his mother. Without any hesitation, she bid me to join her in the kitchen area of the tent.

She squatted beside the fire making flatbreads on an iron dome that sat a few inches above the fire. Stoked with dry small branches and twigs, it easily produced a bright fierce inferno. She worked quickly and deftly, without any obvious concern for the intense heat.

Suddenly, the boy found an ability to actually speak a little English, an ability he had kept to himself until then. When I asked him about it, he said all children in Jordan learned English in school. I talked with them briefly while the boy translated for his mother. After a few minutes, I began to suspect, from comments the mother made and how she acted, that the boy had brought other foreign travelers home for an impromptu visit. Such visits didn't appear to concern her as they allowed him to practice his English for a short period of time.

As she talked, she repeated a series of rhythmic movements that looked automatic and, every minute or so, her stack of fresh flatbread grew with the addition of a new piping hot piece. To make each one, she took a large spoonful of batter from a bowl and poured it in a circle at the top of the iron dome. It cascaded down the dome, instantly forming a crust as it came into contact with the extremely hot metal. As soon as the batter started to bubble, she used a stick to lift one side, before she grabbed the entire piece of bread with both hands to flip it over. The entire cooking process for one piece took less than a minute on the really hot metal dome. When she judged each piece to be done she used the stick to lift an edge before she tossed the freshly made piece onto a stack close by. Making flatbread for the family had become a part of her daily routine years ago. She said she followed the same technique many generations of her family had used before her.

I asked them about living in the tent. She said they had descended from a line of true Bedouin stock, and in spite of their strong migrating traditions, the central government had attempted to settle them down. The family had been given the concrete house in the hope that it would persuade them to give up their nomadic lifestyle. All of the family who wanted to be employed worked at the gas station, so they had income. Apparently, the family didn't feel comfortable sleeping in a concrete building. They had turned one room into a large storage shed and the other into a pen for their goats and chickens. They felt quite content to live in their traditional Bedouin tent in the walled garden as it reduced the sand and dust that blew into the tent. During the weekdays, the boy walked with friends across a couple of miles of desert to school. Government regulations made it compulsory for all children between the ages of five to fifteen to attend school. On the weekends, the boy would play around the gas station where he could be close to his father and older brothers. Back in the 1970s, weekends in Arabic nations occurred on Thursday and Friday. I understand a number of Muslim nations have aligned themselves with the Western weekly calendar since that period.

As time had passed, I indicated I should return to my friends. Immediately, his mother took the top two pieces of flatbread, which were the hottest, from the stack and thrust them in my direction. I had no gift to offer in return which would have conformed to Arabic customs. She wouldn't let me leave without the bread and pushed the steaming hot floppy pieces of bread into my arms. I tried to not appear impolite and ungrateful for this kind offering with the heat from the bread searing the flesh from my bare arms. I must have been quite a sight, as I tried to bow a gracious goodbye while juggling the steaming bread as we backed through the tent flap. By the time we reached the top of the dune, the bread had cooled enough for me to stuff a piece into my mouth. It tasted delicious and thoughts of burned flesh receded from my mind.

Penny and Ron spotted us as we descended the dune. They appeared especially happy to see the flatbread as their search of the store had only turned up some Twinkies that looked rather ancient. However, considering their chemical composition, they probably were as fresh as the day they were concocted. My absence hadn't surprised them as we all wandered off at times to commune with nature, away from the crowds. I hadn't been communing with nature this time; I had been connecting with local residents and their day-to-day cuisine. As soon as I'd handed the bread over to them, I dove into the car to search for an already opened bag of English boiled candies. I gave them to the boy who, happily, dashed across to the store to show his father what I'd given him.

Our path south took us around the Jordanian capital, Amman, and, then headed toward the Red Sea for a much anticipated relaxing evening when we planned to stay in a hotel for one night.

Soon, we had returned to the main, two-lane road that wove through golden dunes. Little traffic impeded our progress and I began to relax, hoping it would be a quieter day than we had in Syria. After a while, between the dunes, we started to see rocky ridges that stood out with their pink and gray hues.

Penny commented, "Hey, I hadn't expected there to be as many rocky outcrops in these parts. I have to admit they are a bit of a nice change from the lines of dunes."

Ron took a few seconds to survey the changing scenery. "You're right. The rocks add a great color contrast to the sand. It's just like driving through a kaleidoscope. Forever changing."

Penny looked at me in the rearview mirror. "Speaking of colorful and changes, can we return to the subject of how both of you became thespians in camp."

Ron followed her train of thought and turned to me. "After the art show, you performed in a kid's show, didn't you, Barry?"

"Yes, Patsy had written a play for children that she wanted to produce at the theater in camp. However, after the art show, she changed the play script to incorporate a policeman's role. She then literally told me to come to rehearsals, and I had a minor role in the play."

Penny was curious. "I never saw the first play. We all know, in her next production, you two had the main lead roles. How did that come about?"

I chuckled, "Oh, yes, we never realized what we were in for when we accepted those roles. Patsy told me she'd found a great role for me and asked if I knew someone who wanted the other lead. I talked to Ron and he agreed." Ron looked round at Penny with a resigned look on his face while I continued. "For that second show, we undertook a professionally written two-act children's play, and I fear the playwright would have been appalled by our efforts. As you know, Ron played 'Captain' who commanded our spacecraft and I played his sidekick 'Dunderspeil—the Intergalactic Dragon.'"

Ron and I described the months of rehearsals and the 10 performances that we had inflicted on the unsuspecting camp family members. Several notable memories came to mind and they occupied our conversation for some time.

Ron's role in the play, unfortunately, had about half of all the lines in the entire two act play. He eventually managed to learn all of the lines, but he had a real problem with their order in the flow of the play. So all of the rest of the cast constantly waited for him to accidentally launch into a speech from a totally different part of the play. We would then need to ab-lib lines to coax him back to where he should have been. Meanwhile an English woman, Carol, who performed the unenviable task of being the script prompt, would desperately thumb through her copy of the script in the stage wings as she tried to steer Ron back to the correct part of the play.

My favorite memory of the show followed the first performance.

Our director announced that any children who wanted to see the dragon could come on stage to visit me. Smaller children apparently thought I was a real dragon because, in certain ways, I looked the part. My costume had been handmade of a dark green velveteen material. The main section comprised a full body suit that included a hoodie and an attached six-foot long tail stuffed with newspaper to give it body. A strange sculpture made out of tin foil and wire had been attached to the crown of my hoodie. Patsy had intended it to look like an antenna connected to my brain. On my face and hands, I started with dark green make-up with red spots, but by the end of Act I, it had all melted into ugly green streaks that flowed off any exposed skin.

After our first performance, I cheerfully stood in the middle of the stage with Ron and a few others from the cast. We congratulated ourselves on having steered ourselves through the play to the end via an unrepeatable path through the script. I went to turn when someone in the group grabbed me, urgently, and pointed down. A sea of little, fascinated faces stared up in awe at me. I found such a wide range of reactions among all of those children: some looked scared, some appeared curious, some tried to be brave, and some giggled uncontrollably. As I had been in the costume for a number of hours, I hardly thought about my tail. If I had suddenly turned, my tail could have knocked many of these little ones over and their sense of awe would have been changed quickly. In that moment, my 27 year old male bravado melted under the little ones' stares, which shone with intrigue, wonder, joy and innocence. I saw an unbelievable beauty in those small children's faces and their reactions. My heart skipped a beat as I stared back at them all; I was the one who was truly in awe. Even now, my heart still skips a beat when I think back to that moment. I do wonder how I'd have felt to be a 4 year old on a stage staring up, wide-eyed, at an actual Intergalactic Dragon. Wouldn't it be wonderful for us to lose our grown-up perceptions, our fears, our cynicism, and our jadedness to be a 4 year old, for a minute? Please, give me just 60 seconds, please.

Even though the play felt like a wild rollercoaster ride for us the actors, the adult audience appeared to be quite forgiving as their younger children's imagination took flight, they were fascinated and enthralled by the story. I think the adults felt neutral about the experience as it must have been painful for them to watch; however, to see their children delightedly transported to a totally different imaginary world offset their own personal pain. Despite people's feelings about the actual play, the name Dunderspeil became a household name with many families.

Penny, Ron, and I continued to trade stories about the play as we drove through the open desert that surrounded Amman. A few miles after we left the last signs of Amman, I changed subjects. "We have two choices. Do we want to go and paddle in the Dead Sea, or not?"

"We're close-ish. So why not?" replied Ron.

"I'm not sure how much extra distance it will be. It'll take us on a diversion that could add quite a few miles to today's drive and I'm not certain how long it'll take to navigate down to the water's edge from this side."

Penny tossed in her thoughts on the matter, "You know, I'm all for a nice leisurely relax at a hotel in Aqaba, tonight. Are we sure about this side trip to the Dead Sea?"

Ron looked back at Penny, "I think it's probably just over the other side of those hills," he said, pointing out of his side window.

I corrected him, "We aren't certain it's just over there. Plus, I'm not sure I want to be all salty for the rest of the day's drive to Aqaba. My skin already feels irritated and raw." The heat and the dust had irritated areas of my skin. I happily anticipated the prospect of standing in the shower at the hotel that evening.

Ron sat back in his seat "I suppose we're not sure how far it would be. Penny's right, Aqaba does sound nice. Let's give the Dead Sea a miss. We can always come back here on another vacation, when we don't have to worry about possible Israeli stamps in our passports along with Saudi visas." We had all heard stories about other fellow travelers who had issues obtaining visas to Arabic countries if their passports indicated they had previously been to Israel.

Even though I had not said anything to the others in our conversation, I was happy to not take the venture over to the Dead Sea. All of the driving and constant sense of uncertainty had begun to take its toll on me. If I had not felt so worn down, I probably would have been aligned with Ron and ready to add a few miles onto the trip to visit such a well-known area. But I just didn't have it in me at that time.

Our surroundings had changed from sandy dunes to a more rugged, scrubby desert landscape once we passed the capital of Amman. As we continued south, the heat of the desert intensified. Thankfully, the Blazer's air-conditioning handled it with ease. The black ribbon of the road wound its way across the plains of rock and sand that looked barren and bleak. The ever-present wind scoured the sand from the underlying rock layers which had been tipped up at an angle by tectonic movements and exposed over time. This caused a series of rocky ridges to protrude above the surface of the open wastes. Multiple bands of colors, browns, peaches, grays and pinks wove irregularly along each ridge. The area felt surreal and harsh, and the combination of the colored striations and waving lines of rock strata created a captivating beauty that the harshness of the environment intensified.

The road that headed south across the central Jordanian desert had recently been resurfaced, allowing us to make steady, speedy progress. Along many stretches, we saw no people, villages, or side roads for long periods of time. So we found it a little strange that out in the middle of nowhere, we should find a young man hitchhiking. Hitchhiking was still an accepted mode of transport for many in Britain in the 1970s, so someone trying to hitch a ride in itself didn't surprise us—but this location was in the midst of the Jordanian desert. We screamed past him at 70 mph while we gave him a quick look over and discussed whether we should give him a ride. He was dressed in western clothes and didn't look like most other young guys we'd seen as we passed Amman and other Jordanian towns. When we decided we would give him a lift, I had to backup for quite a distance to meet him as he jogged along the road to join us. He spoke surprisingly good English which made life so much easier for us language-lazy Brits.

He climbed into the back seat with Ron and introduced himself as Abdul. He said he studied engineering at the university in Amman.

After he had finished classes for the week, he decided to head home for the weekend. His meager budget wouldn't stretch to cover the cost of the bus ride, leaving him with no alternative but to hitchhike. His attire and look didn't align with how I expected a young Arab man to dress for hitchhiking. He wore bell bottom trousers, a dark green dress shirt made of a shiny material, and western casual shoes. He wore his dark brown hair longer than many of his more traditional peers.

As we sped south, his line of questioning intrigued us. He wanted to know about life and opportunities in England and Europe. His questions focused on one main topic, how to understand the larger world beyond Jordan. His higher education had opened his eyes to a wider horizon, beyond his own country. He wanted to know what the outside world might have to offer him. Answering his questions made the next section of the drive interesting for us, as we needed to think about our own lives and opportunities more reflectively and objectively. To explain how we saw our possible careers unfolding to a Jordanian young man presented us with unexpected challenges. He only had an impression of life in the west based on a combination of movies and what he had heard at college in Amman. It sounded idealistic; I wondered if he believed all westerners had a genie in a bottle. We all struggled to explain our situations as they were so different to how Hollywood movies portrayed people like us. Eventually, we felt we had given Abdul a more accurate set of ideas about life and opportunities in Europe or America. He tried hard to bridge a huge cultural void that lay between the lives of three western professionals and himself, an aspiring student at a college in Amman. He had dreams and I felt he demonstrated a decent level of intelligence. I could only hope he would find the right opportunity which allowed him to gain a fulfilling career, security, peace, and the comforts of a loving family.

After a little time, Abdul asked us if we planned to stop at the ruins of a Crusader castle that was supposedly a few miles off the side of the road. We hadn't planned on making any side trips, but we knew we had time. Our destination, Aqaba, was only a few hours ahead. He described the ruins as one of the few such castles in the region and, after a few minutes, persuaded us to take the detour.

Shobak Castle had been built by King Baldwin I, of the House of Flanders in northern France, in 1115 when he came to Jordan with the Crusades. King Baldwin had conquered Jerusalem, becoming its first Crusader king. Construction of the castle at Shobak took a number of years. Its being located on a dominant peak gave it control over the territory and routes to the south. The castle had eventually been overrun by King Saladin in 1189 after an 18 month siege. After laying unused for about 200 years, the Mamluks occupied the castle, rebuilt sections of the fortifications, and transformed other parts to different functions, including a school. The Mamluk armies, who originated in Egypt and comprised mainly slaves, held dominance in the Muslim world for a number of centuries before the Ottoman Empire conquered the entire region and far beyond.

Shobak Castle's remaining structures now stood on the windswept, rocky point at the end of a small range of hills. It had become a sun blasted, desolate ruin with walls rising several feet high, archways that had be constructed with both rock and timber, and stone steps that led to where corridors and halls had once existed. In parts, it was easy to imagine servants carrying flagons of wine and platters of meat to feed the crusaders, while in other sections, walls and paths simply faded into dusty drifts. Abdul walked around the site with his long dark hair dancing in the wind; he explained what he knew about the ruins. He looked like he would have been more comfortable at a Los Angeles pool party after a day on a movie set than being a guide out in the wilds of the Jordanian desert.

After another hour of driving and discussion, we arrived at his family's home that lay a few yards off to the side of the main Amman to Aqaba highway. When we pulled up outside, he invited us in for refreshments, which sounded great as we hadn't eaten since the morning's bread feast. I checked my watch, which confirmed my stomach's grumblings about it already being past noon. Abdul invited us into the lounge, it was the front room of the house that was reserved for special guests only. The decor surprised me and challenged my sense of taste. On the floor, a variety of unmatched carpets and rugs of different designs and colors lay scattered, randomly. Along each of the three main walls sat three sofas—their simple box design on short wooden legs and being covered in vinyl gave them a rather unwelcoming appeal. The vinyl covering in the heat made us wish it would be a short visit. Also, the sofas' colors gave us no relief. One sofa looked dull orange, one a muted lime green and one a musky rose red. I felt like I had stepped into a living room from the 1960s, except the shag carpet had been replaced by the random rugs.

Our host walked into the kitchen to talk with his family. On his return, he said tea and food would be forthcoming. His father worked at the nearby factory and his younger brothers hadn't returned from school, leaving his mother and sisters to tend to domestic duties. We had entered a traditional patriarchal household. During the entire time that we relaxed in the lounge, we frequently heard and occasionally saw the mother and sisters in the kitchen. They busied themselves preparing food; they never entered the room to formally meet us. Abdul said social custom dictated this patriarchal hierarchy be upheld in all Jordanian households. I felt uncomfortable in the circumstances, but recognized I may not have many similar opportunities to witness such a household's functioning from the inside. In talking with Abdul about gender roles, he acknowledged the Jordanian society needed to modernize if they wanted to be seen as a viable 20th century country. I hoped he could make such a change when he created his own household.

After a while, despite his talk of change, he fetched the tea as tradition required and announced his mother and sisters would prepare a cooked lunch which would be served as soon as possible. We wondered how long this might take. We also worried about the chicken clucking and scratching that had erupted shortly before in the kitchen. It had stopped rather abruptly.

We sat, drank tea, and talked about his life as a student and our lives growing up in England.

Abdul asked, "So you are all engineers if you work for an oil company?"

I tried to correct him. "Actually, Ron and I work with computers;

we are not engineers. Penny works as an administrative assistant for my department's boss."

"Did you have to go to Saudi Arabia to get these jobs?" he enquired.

Ron responded. "No, we were all employed in London, where Aramco has an office."

Abdul tried to make sense of how everything worked, "So, I would have to go to London to get a job in Saudi Arabia?"

Ron tried again, "I doubt it. If you see a job in a Jordanian newspaper, then the advertisement should give you an address where you need to send your application letter. Then in later letters, a company would tell you where you have to go to interview for the job. You will be told, so you shouldn't have to worry."

Abdul looked over at Penny, "Do many women work in England and America?"

She answered, "I'm not certain about in America. In Europe, more women have jobs, these days."

Abdul scowled a little, "I can't believe it. That means less jobs for men. That isn't right. They need to feed their families."

Ron tried to be diplomatic. "Ah, this is one of the changes we mentioned earlier to you. If Jordan is to be considered a 20th century society, then men will need to understand their traditional roles as the family bread winners will be evolving. Women are now a part of the workforce; they aren't seen as those who only run the household."

Abdul tried to make sense of Ron's words. He tried to hold to what he had always understood. "This can't be true in America? Surely, I mean, I've seen American movies and that's not how it looked to me."

I said, "Abdul, that may be a problem. Remember American movies you see in college, here in Amman, are probably ten or more years old and they portray a different version of American life when women hardly had a voice. That isn't the case, anymore."

He sipped his tea and tried a different line of inquiry, "So, you have friends in London who may want to employ me when I graduate? I am an engineer and I can work really hard."

"I don't know anyone who works in an employment capacity. How about either of you two?"

They both shook their heads. Our conversation covered many topics while we waited. One hour passed and a second hour had almost ticked completely by when a call came from the kitchen. Abdul brought us small bowls of water in which we could rinse our hands. After that, our host brought out an inlaid copper platter which measured about two and a half feet in diameter. He placed it in the middle of the floor. On the platter, a beautiful concentric flower pattern had been created with outer leaves of overlapping rounds of flatbread partly covered by a central round bed of saffron rice. Piled on that lay a beautiful array of cooked vegetables and the remains of what had been clucking in the kitchen, encrusted in herbs and braised in a delicious spicy smelling sauce. Abdul invited us to sit on the floor around the platter, cross-legged. We joined him on the floor as the aromas entranced us.

We waited patiently for cutlery and crockery, but none followed. Abdul invited us to be the first to start. We gingerly put out our hands toward the food, causing our host to let out an utterance that stopped us, instantly. It sounded partly like a little shocked cry and partly a half annunciated apology. He suddenly realized we didn't know the correct etiquette for eating from a formal platter of food without cutlery. Abdul demonstrated and talked us through the gentle art of eating with only our right hand. In their tradition, the left hand was delegated the gentle option of attending to ablution duties and should never be used for eating. He showed us how to rip off a piece of bread, and then take it to scoop up some rice and meat or vegetables. Finally, he rolled up the bread with its contents into a ball that looked perfectly sized to pop into his mouth. The chicken still being on the bone and rather hot made this process more remarkable. He managed to achieve this dexterous maneuver using one hand and his piece of bread without a moment's hesitation.

We spent more time in hilarious gales of laughter than serious eating. We failed to roll any food balls which in any way resembled Abdul's, despite his coaching and encouragement. The contents of the platter balanced wonderful spices, had contrasting textures, and tasted delicious, or at least the small morsels that we managed to maneuver into our mouths tantalized our taste buds with incredible layers of complementing flavors. The majority of what we ate came from the outer ring of bread, with the occasional vegetable or infrequent morsel of chicken that hung precariously from it, when we managed to crush it into a ball-like shape. Despite the amusement of realizing what unadaptable klutzes we appeared to be, we didn't want to be disrespectful and tried to contain our laughter as we knew his mother could hear us. We would see her face look around the kitchen entrance for a quick look, followed by hurried whispers in the kitchen, and then their own gales of laughter. It felt entertaining but frustrating, as we purposefully held our left hands behind our backs all the time so that we weren't tempted to use it. We would have paid highly for forks or our left hands. While we struggled to eat a little of the amazing food, Penny, Ron, and I also had to constantly shift positions as our legs and hips complained loudly about having to sit cross-legged on the floor.

Eventually, we had enjoyed our fill. As to whether we had our fill of food or frustration or both felt debatable. We thanked our host heartily and left him to enjoy his break with his family. We continued south toward Aqaba. On this one night, we planned to stay in a hotel—so civilized a notion.

After a short easy drive, we dropped over the last set of hills and found the city of Aqaba wedged along the northern-most shoreline of the Red Sea. The water stretched away into the distance, a narrow finger of water nestled between two parallel sets of rocky escarpments and sand dunes. We drove through the main part of the town to the beach so we could check out the couple of hotels that had been built along the shoreline. One looked to be more modern than the others and, hopefully, it would be cleaner, as a result. I love the irony of that last sentence—we had been sleeping in fields, ditches, and the desert for the past week or more, and we stopped to consider the cleanliness of our hotel.

Only a few other guests had registered at our selected hotel, which meant we managed to talk our way into two rooms with private terraces overlooking the beach and sea. I sat out on the terrace after taking an incredibly long shower.

Across the water, the dunes settled, their imperceptible movement ceased for a few hours. Tomorrow morning, the wind would rise with the sun and send them slowly drifting forward once again. But for the night, the dunes could rest, the sounds of waves on the beach lulled them, they lay at rest.

I felt clean, and not just physically. I was cleansed inside, too. To be able to relax and not have to worry about where we could eat and sleep felt so wonderful. I felt lighter, thoughts danced, aromas seemed fresher, my senses were no longer dulled. I had shrugged off the fog that had become my world. My eyes saw what was around me, rather than that strip of black asphalt with white lines. I noted we each had managed to pull together mismatched collections of lighter and cleaner wear after our showers.

Penny came into Ron's and my room so we could spend the evening out on our room's section of terrace. It felt so tranquil to not move and simply watch the beautiful red sun sink beyond the distant sand dunes. As we sat relaxing, in my mind, I wondered if I may be reliving one of the infrequent restful evenings that Lawrence of Arabia relished. We watched the Red Sea as it gently lapped up the sands while we enjoyed our gin and tonic drinks. I imagined Lawrence may have done similarly. At times, I became lost in my thoughts. I romantically daydreamed about how many of Lawrence's days may have ended this way. Today as I reflect, I'm intrigued I found comfort in a comparison between our evening in Aqaba and a relaxed evening in the life of Lawrence. For me, Lawrence of Arabia occupied a dare-devil, adventurous, romantic, idealistic, and determined space in my imagination. To relax on the terrace with Penny and Ron offered me a glimpse of that as a reality. It struck a perfectly pitched chord deep in my soul.

In life, the unknown, the uncertainty, the adventure, and the challenge of overcoming the unexpected has appealed to me. I must admit such appeals have changed as the years have passed. In driving to Arabia, the unknown challenges comprised both the physical journey itself and the lack of knowledge about the circumstances we might encounter. It isn't an endeavor I would contemplate nowadays, even if it appeared to be politically or practically possible. Writing about the journey is now my challenge, filled with its own uncertainties. The challenges of writing about it are academic, psychological, and emotional. To be honest, a more daunting sense hung over me when I started to write this tale than the actual drive did, all those years ago.

Penny, Ron, and I agreed we deserved this one night of pampering before we returned to sleeping in the dirt for another couple of nights. We ordered dinner and the staff delivered it to our rooms so we didn't have to move from the terrace. I sat and finished another gin and tonic, before enjoying the multiple flavors of shawarma over a bed of couscous blended with spiced vegetables. I happily knew comfortable beds lay only feet away from where we lounged and ate. In the morning, I noted with amusement that we had finished our meals, but the basket of bread hadn't been touched. No surprise. We probably had eaten our fill of bread on the previous day.

CHAPTER 12

INDIANA JONES—
YOU AND ME, BOTH

الله شاء إن   الله شاء إن   الله شاء إن   الله شاء إن   الله شاء إن   الله شاء إن   الله شاء إن

After checking out of the hotel that overlooked the peaceful waters of the Red Sea, an ambivalent feeling hung over our intrepid trio as we reloaded our bags into the back of the Blazer. We felt intrigued to see what the new day would bring us in the way of adventures, but the relative comfort of the hotel felt so alluring. However, two more nights of sleeping in the dusty desert would carry us back to the Aramco camp and some well-deserved rest in the comfort of our own quarters. I started the Blazer and gave the hotel's seductive luxury no more thought.

Our planned route would take us back northeast toward Amman, the capital. Thankfully, this new direction took us along well-maintained roads that allowed me to cover the first 75 miles of the day's driving in an hour or so.

As we drove, we returned to the subject of Dunderspeil, my role as an intergalactic dragon in the children's play with Ron, but from a different perspective. Penny caught my attention in the rear view mirror. A mischievous twinkle in her eye told me she had been considering how to tease me. "Barry, I understand being Dunderspeil can be counter-productive when it comes to dating."

Ron twisted toward me, taking his eyes off the shimmering horizon. "Oh, this has to be good."

I was cornered and I laughed. "I admit I had a crush on a young lady, Cindy P." I took a second to glance at Ron, "Sorry, you

167

probably don't know her or her family. She was the daughter of the Aramco president. She spent her college vacations back in camp with her family and worked in the same office building as me. I chatted her up while you and I were involved with the play."

He looked intrigued and shook his head, "This isn't going to end well."

Penny settled into the back seat and added, "That's what I gathered but I never heard all the details. Go on, Barry, spill the beans. We have time."

I continued, "After the opening weekend of our Dunderspeil farce, I decided I couldn't embarrass myself any further and plucked up courage to ask Cindy out. I didn't consider how we might spend our date, especially as I had no vehicle and walked everywhere in camp. Surprisingly, she said yes, and we set a date and time when I would pick her up from their family home—one of the larger, executive houses in camp."

My thoughts were distracted by a grove of olive trees that grew down in a gully beside the road. We immediately were drawn by their greenness, despite their dustiness, and thoughts of my date faded. The olive trees' color provided a relief from the scorched sandy tones of the rocky, barren, desert scenery. I commented, "Isn't it interesting how a few green trees stand out so prominently and grab our attention?"

Ron agreed. "Yes. Even a couple of scrubby olive trees look beautiful in this environment. But, enough about that. I want to know what happened next on the date?"

"I'll admit I didn't feel overly self-confident and dating for me was nerve-wracking. To add to my anguish, the night of the date turned out to be incredibly hot and humid. By the time I walked the six blocks to Cindy's home, I looked as if I'd just walked out of my shower, fully clothed. I must have looked like a total disaster, walking up the path to her front door. Plus, having no real plan for the evening made me even sweatier."

Ron turned to me. "Do you have any concept of what embarrassment really means, Barry? Couldn't you have gone home and claimed to have been sick?"

I took my focus off the road for a second to check their facial expressions. Had I revealed too much of my stubborn stupidity? Their expressions revealed curiosity, disbelief, and mainly amusement. I decided the best defense in such a situation would be to join them and admit my unabashed foolishness. I ventured, "Ah, in matters of the heart, there's no space for rational thought. Apparently, bailing out didn't enter my head because I indeed rang the doorbell. I stood in the steamy heat awaiting a response for what felt like an eternity. I tried to calm myself by wondering how long the gardeners spent watering the lawn that stretched, pristine, on either side of the concrete path. Suddenly, the front door swung wide open and I was confronted by Cindy's mother. That possibility hadn't been something I'd imagined in my speculations of how the date would start. With a stern look on her face, she stated, 'No daughter of mine is ever going to be seen out in public with an Intergalactic Dragon' and she slammed the door shut. I instantaneously melted into a puddle of sweat and anguish."

Ron and Penny laughed heartily. After a short break, Penny prompted, "OK, you gigolo, what followed?"

I cringed, "Well, the front door was immediately re-opened by Cindy's mother, but this time with a big laughing grin on her face. She invited me in with 'I'm so sorry, I couldn't stop myself. I loved you as Dunderspeil. We enjoyed the play tremendously.' As I stepped into the hallway, she held out her hand for a handshake—it was a clammy and unpleasant affair. Cindy appeared from the back of the house and tried to rescue me. She was too late—my mind was fried by then. It didn't matter."

Penny followed up with the obvious question, "So, what did you do for the evening?"

"We went back to my place for a drink and talked. I honestly don't remember much about the visit. We had a one-time date and Cindy moved on to other guys. I hope she enjoyed better company with them."

Ron laughed for a while, but managed to say, "The evening may have not turned out so well for you two, but she sure has a weird story to share with her college friends."

I jested back, "Thanks. I had a feeling my tale-of-woe would result in a little more genuine sympathy from you both. Ah, the joys of being with friends."

We pulled off the main road and into the parking lot at Petra which had been a planned stop. The lot had no well-defined borders—an area of packed sand and dirt formed the lot, its boundary simply being where the sand became too soft to negotiate with street tires. Many people have never heard of Petra, also called the Rose City, but they may remember a scene toward the end of *Indiana Jones and the Last Crusade,* which was filmed at a date after my travels. The filming of the scene, in which Indiana finally catches up with the Holy Grail, took place in front of a spectacular rose-pink temple which actually exists—no need for a stage set. The temple which was known as The Treasury had existed for thousands of years, it was one of the most famous temples in the ancient city of Petra.

We joined the small line of tourists who soon would embark on a rather unusual short journey. To reach the ancient city of Petra from the road, we had to enter via the original route on a narrow trail, which ran through a slot canyon in a rocky ridge. The ridge stood hundreds of feet high and the fissure, through which the canyon ran, looked intimidatingly narrow. The trail, known as Al Siq, which literally means the Shaft, became the primary of the two entrances into the city. The trail wound its way down the slot canyon that ran through the cliff and ridge for over a mile.

The historical site of Petra was managed by the Jordanian government. They had learned over many years, people will stand to stare at the formations and colors in the rock walls of the Siq and potentially block the passage way. Also, incredibly hot temperatures could cause tourists to feel exhausted or unwell. Therefore, they tried to discourage people from walking down the passage. The man who sold us our entrance tickets told us we needed to ride donkeys through the Siq, which would hopefully ensure no hold-ups or medical emergencies occurred.

We joined the short line of tourists to wait for our beasts of burden. For the donkeys, their prospects looked like just another day of boringly trudging up and down the Siq; but for us, it held the prospects of a rather strange escapade. Each four donkeys had one handler. He cajoled them, prodded them, cussed at them and occasionally gave them a treat. Our line of about 40 donkeys headed out of the parking lot toward the cliff.

Penny giggled as we headed across the open sand. "You know this is the first time I've been on a donkey since I was a kid. In the summer time, Mum and Dad would take me down to the beach and occasionally they would pay for me to take a ride on the donkeys that were available. Oh, those were the days. I really loved taking a ride, even more than having an ice cream."

"I'll take the ice cream." I countered.

Ron added, "Me too. You know, I was thinking about riding a polo pony as we plodded our way from the parking lot. I never played myself. I always thought it would be bloody good fun. I doubt my parents could've afforded it."

I smiled, "I really can't compare this ride to Lawrence of Arabia charging Turkish gunners on his camel, but it may have been about as close as I'll ever likely get."

"What an interesting bunch of silly notions were floating through our minds, just because of this donkey ride," Ron observed.

I found it interesting to realize how closely I associated Jordanian desert and coastal scenery with Lawrence, no matter if it was him fighting and surviving in the harsh desert or relaxing on a terrace in Aqaba. I felt a kinship I can't explain because I never read any books about him. I presume I heard stories on the radio or TV. I don't recall hearing my parents talk about him, but something about him or his reputation had hooked me sometime in my growing up. For me, he represented a confident, dashing English man who travelled to far distant lands and had great adventures. Knowing I would never be one myself, I suppose he set the example that, in my mind, I aspired to being. I could never explain this type of daydream to my mother. She was too entrenched in following well-trodden paths because they were known and she felt they were guaranteed to be reasonably safe.

In places, the Siq shrank to less than ten feet across and the surrounding walls, carved into incredible rock formations, towered over 300 feet above us. The Siq had originally been cut by flood waters from a large local wadi—a valley, ravine, or channel that is dry except in the rainy season. The rock walls displayed a beautiful array of pastel pinks, oranges, reds, and yellows. At times, rays of sunlight penetrated down to the trail and highlighted the everchanging series of rocky features. Sections of the rock walls were brightly lit for only a few minutes as the sun continued its scorching path across the wide open blue sky. For the majority of the ride through the Siq, we plodded through deep shadows, but thankfully, enough light found its way down to the trail for us to take in much of the beauty of the surrounding sandstone rock strata. Bands of colors wove along the walls, some with distinct boundaries where one color ended and a totally different one began, others bleeding into each other through multiple gradient shades. The depth of the color bands varied constantly as they wove along the walls causing the waves to flatten out in sections or to oscillate in a more frenetic fashion. The patterns, the colors, and even the rock's surface created an ever-changing, consuming, beautiful kaleidoscope. I fell in love with Petra and we hadn't even reached the city and its glories.

The donkey ride progressed slowly and steadily, primarily due to the constant work of the handlers. It took about 10 to 15 minutes to complete the one mile ride. I was sad when we reached the far end of the passageway. I had been consumed by my fascination with the rock strata. The Siq finally opened up into a large rift valley. As soon as we exited the last section of the Siq, we found ourselves opposite the amazing Great Temple, a mere 100 feet from where we dismounted. Indiana Jones had, after many exciting encounters, found the Holy Grail at this temple. Local people and Bedouin referred to the temple as Al Khazneh, or the Treasury, based on local Bedouin folklore, whereas the Nabataeans had originally carved it as a place of worship. We left our donkeys, ready to explore the Rose City on foot.

Originally, the city was built about 2,200 years ago when several important trading routes crossed the region. Traders exchanged goods in a nearby town's market. Soon the original town turned into a vibrant commercial center as the market traded goods and skills from all points of the compass. The town's people, the Nabataeans, charged the transiting caravans toll duty, which created a consistent source of revenue. In time, they became wealthy and felt the need for protection. The nearby rift valley, that had just the two entrances, provided the obvious location for a better protected city. Also, the wealth of the Nabataeans allowed them to bring in artists and craftsmen to carve and build a city of beautiful buildings, both free-standing as well as others which craftsmen carved into the rock walls of the rift valley.

We explored what appeared to be the best preserved buildings that were built on the valley floor. They had been arranged along avenues lined with colonnades. As we walked around the dwellings that were hewn out of the valley's rock walls I was surprised how spacious most of them appeared to be. In many of these cavernous dwellings, particularly in the areas where families cooked, we could see shelves cut into the walls for storage. I was struck by a sense of wonder as I struggled to take in how incredibly large many of these structures had been. The rock appeared to be a softer sandstone, that may have been easier to work, but when I considered the crude tools and the volume of rock that apparently had been removed, I was staggered. I recognized a great deal of planning had gone into the construction of Petra. The buildings that lined the streets on the open flatter ground had probably been built with the rock, which had been excavated from the valley walls. In removing this needed material, the Nabataeans had carved the basic voluminous openings along the valley walls that became other temples, dwellings or storage. They didn't just knock down entire areas of rock face; they burrowed into the valley walls creating useful space.

The Petra city planners were apparently aware the Siq had originally been cut by flood waters and they built a dam at the start of the Siq to divert future flood waters away from the city. They also recognized the importance of water and built a series of canals and channels to bring fresh water into the city, for both drinking and basic machinery such as grain grinding. We found a few places where these old water channels had been carved into the walls of passageways or passed over specially constructed archways and viaducts.

Ron walked up a few steps to join Penny and me. "Hey, I heard our donkey guy talking about an obelisk that was built on one of the nearby peaks. He made it sound quite accessible. Do you want to see if we can find it?"

Penny waved an arm at a fly that was annoying her, "If it'll mean leaving these pesky bugs behind, I'm all for it."

As we walked back toward the Treasury, I concurred, "It'll be fun to gain a little height and be able to see over the surrounding peaks. I'm still amazed this valley has only two entrances."

We returned to the top of the rift valley where we found a trail and an information board that described the obelisk. The narrow trail followed a combination of dirt paths and steps carved into the rock. We quickly rose above the hidden valley. From the higher vantage point, we could see the impressive size of the ancient city. After 20 minutes or so, we found the trail had wound its way up the walls of the canyon and turned toward one single rocky peak. The trail snaked its way higher, giving us a spectacular view of the ruins of the ancient city that had spread across the rift valley floor. When, at last, we reached the peak, a remarkable sight awaited us. Thousands of years ago, laborers had carved a perfectly flat plateau from the peak. It measured about 50 feet across and what had been a perfectly carved obelisk stood in the center. The obelisk had stood about five feet tall and about 20 inches across each of the four sides at the base. It rose in perfect symmetry, except for its sharp top point, which had been lost in the last two thousand years. Weathering had gradually eroded its top 15 inches.

Penny looked puzzled and asked, "Why would these ancient people haul an obelisk to the top of a mountain that they had flattened?"

I was similarly puzzled, "I can't imagine how much effort it took to flatten this area, and then to place an obelisk up here. How wild." I kneeled down at the base of the obelisk to brush the loose sand and dirt away. "Wow. Nobody hauled this obelisk up here. It was chiseled from the same rock as the plateau on which it stands. It was created as the mountain top was chipped away to make it flat."

"You're kidding! I'm not sure if carving it up here along with the plateau was easier than carving it lower down the mountain before hauling it up here." Ron knelt down, next to another side to brush away the dirt to check my finding.

We confirmed that the top of the rocky mountain had been meticulously carved away to create the obelisk on its plateau. To make the coordinated effort to carve it amazed us, but we were left wondering what it may have represented. I could only conclude it was something quite profound for the Nabataeans. I have since learned the city of Petra featured many such obelisks. Most of them formed the main focus of the exterior decoration on tombs constructed for deceased city's leaders. Scholars have suggested the small number of obelisks that were carved on the tops of peaks surrounding the city were created for special ceremonies allowing large gatherings to worship together in a higher place, closer to the gods.

We stayed a while, soaking in the views of the surrounding rocky peaks while we quietly contemplated the original thoughts behind the obelisk and whether its orientation had any special significance. Unfortunately, as we were on the highest point around, we could feel the sun's heat building quickly.

Penny wiped perspiration from her brow before it rolled down into her eyes. "Okay. Are you two ready to drop back down? This sun's getting pretty warm and we have no shade up here. I forgot to bring my water bottle."

Ron agreed, "I must admit I'm in awe. But it's time to go. This place is beyond what I had expected. I'm frustrated that I can't focus on all of these amazing carvings because I'm preoccupied. I'll only be able to relax when I have my passport with the Saudi visa in my hand."

I was still lost in thoughts about the obelisk, its size, its orientation, its use, and what its creators had in mind. "Oh, I suppose we'd better move." Then I realized what Ron had just said. "And I'll also be happier after we have your passport and visa in our hands."

We walked toward the point where the trail started to descend and found another area that had been flattened with an obelisk, but the surrounding area wasn't flat. A shallow step down formed a square, about 20 feet across, around the obelisk. We quickly explored the new find for a few minutes before we descended the trail into the early morning coolness of the valley, still hidden from the sun's intense rays.

We returned to the Great Temple at the bottom of the Siq to await the next donkey train that would return us to the parking lot. While we waited, we listened to a guide who spoke to a tour group. His information answered some of the many questions that we had in mind such as the extent of the city and its population which, at the city's height, was over 20,000 people.

The city fell into decay when the trading caravan trails, particularly those that came from the East and China, had been replaced by longer, but faster, shipping routes. As the city's importance diminished over the next couple of centuries, it was struck by several major earthquakes, which destroyed many of the free-standing structures. The remains lay silent for many of the following centuries. In the late nineteenth century, roaming Bedouin rediscovered the city and started to use it for a temporary shelter when they transited through southern Jordan seeking fertile grazing areas. Within a few years, a small Bedouin community settled in the ruins on a consistent basis. For an unexplained reason, a rumor started among the Bedouin that the Great Temple, at the bottom of the Siq, had been the Nabataeans' Treasury. The rumor also said much of those ancient riches were still stored in the large ornamental urn, which sat high above the main entrance. As a result of this rumor, the temple became known as the Treasury and that particuilar urn has been visibly pock-marked by thousands of bullets that Bedouins fired at it, optimistically trying to release its supposed bountiful contents. Over the years, the solid urn has shown more decay than the rest of the temple's ornamentations while, not too surprisingly, no Bedouins became instantly rich.

The donkeys for our return journey had as much energy and enthusiasm as the ones that carried us down into the city. They quietly traipsed their way up the trail. My last view of the Great Temple, as we made the first turn along the Siq, will stay with me forever. I turned in my saddle to watch the Siq's walls close the gap through which I viewed Al-Khazneh. Its ornately carved frontage, over 12 stories high, was dominated by 6 massive columns that supported the main entrance's portico. Above it, 3 smaller porticos had been carved into the valley wall, adding grandeur to the temple's facade. Above the central smaller decorative portico, sat the pock-marked urn that was rumored to hold the Nabataens' treasury. I had to admit Petra had spoken to me more loudly and deeply than the other ancient sites we had visited earlier at Troy and Ephesus. I have had a long standing love of rocky mountains, the intrigue of natural patterns and colors found in rock strata, and the thrill of stark beauty that can be encountered in harsh, rugged environments. The influence of these three factors had blessed Petra. To me, the city appeared to be a masterful integration of man's creativity and nature's beauty.

Our donkey train took the standard 15 to 20 minutes to plod its way up the Siq. As we emerged into the scrubby desert that led to the parking lot, we crossed paths with a donkey train that headed toward the Siq. I noticed one particular couple in the middle of the pack—their clothes looked American or Western European—they would have fit into Main Street, U.S.A.. The man, mainly, looked out of place in the Jordanian desert.

After we dismounted our donkeys and eased back into walking, we returned to the car but decided to stop for a quick lunch before heading to Amman. Soon enough, we resumed the drive north after we found some fruit and crackers to eat in a nearby market.

After I'd settled behind the wheel, I enquired, "Did you two see the American or European couple on that last donkey train departing for the Siq?"

"No," they replied.

I described the couple. "She wore a light colored summer dress and sandals, which was fine apparel for the heat but maybe not the best for a donkey ride. By contrast, her husband wore a dark serge blue three-piece suit, a white shirt, a striped blue tie, and black leather street shoes."

"No. What were they thinking? A three-piece suit in this temperature?" Penny sounded appalled.

Ron was similarly shocked. "He must have been so uncomfortable. I can't begin to imagine."

I continued, "It looked like his wife probably had to abduct him from his office desk and only took the handcuffs off him when they landed in Jordan. I can't think of another likely scenario."

Ron suggested, "Perhaps she booked the vacation without telling him."

Penny laughed, "I've heard stories like that before. Did you get a sense he was enjoying himself on his wife's vacation?"

I answered, "I'm not going to be that positive. However, his slightly loosened tie gave the one indication of his possible submission to the notion of his being on vacation. I'll admit I felt amazed and rather saddened because he probably was so blind to all of the rich cultural and geological scenery around him. My impression wasn't simply based on his dress; he displayed a bored, disdainful look on his face."

"What a waste. I'm sure she could have found a friend who would've been thrilled to take a trip like this with her." Penny said, still unable to comprehend the situation.

"A good thought," Ron replied.

Looking back now, I remember I met a similarly attired character in a serge blue three-piece suit on my later travels to Tibet. However, he ended up being enthusiastically engaged with the group and a source of expert knowledge regarding Tibetan culture and history. So I hope I misread the guy on his Jordanian donkey.

The road's good condition and a lack of other traffic allowed me to reach the outskirts of Amman by late in the afternoon. I headed to the city center to park the Blazer before we took an hour to explore the area and the main souq—the market. After we wandered around the market stalls, we found a small café for dinner. As the light faded in the early evening and having enjoyed a pleasant meal, we walked out of the café into the warm evening air. We stopped on the pavement where Ron had the totally irrational idea of finding the British Embassy at that time of the evening, with the hope that he could obtain his passport and Saudi Arabian entry visa.

CHAPTER 13
A COUPLE OF MINOR INCIDENTS

الله شاء إن   الله شاء إن   الله شاء إن   الله شاء إن   الله شاء إن   الله شاء إن

Ron was certain it would be easy to find the British Embassy despite the fact the sun would soon have sunk below the horizon and street lighting had been absent on most streets as we drove through Amman. Penny and I had no immediate plans for sleep, so we went along with his idea. We decided to return to the restaurant where we had just eaten as our waiter spoke reasonably good English. He didn't know the location of the British Embassy and turned to ask several of his regular customers. They managed to give us rough directions to the area of the city where they thought embassies had been built. Hopeful, we drove to an area of the suburbs that had larger walled properties and compounds. Thankfully, a few street lights had been installed, they illuminated plaques on the compounds' walls indicating various country's embassies. We continued with a sense of optimism, we needed to keep looking for the British Embassy. However, after about half an hour of fruitless hunting, we became frustrated and decided to ask the few people who we saw on the street. My spoken Arabic met the need to ask such simple questions as, "British Embassy?" On my third try, a man knew the answer. With his guidance, we found the compound with the British Embassy plaque; it was next to a huge heavy wooden gate that would have withstood most vehicles smaller than a tank. Even with the light from a nearby street lamp, we could find no bell or means of gaining the attention of anyone within the walls. Ron couldn't believe it and resorted to pounding several times on the wooden gate with his knuckles. To our surprise, we heard footsteps coming across the paved courtyard toward the gate. A small grill popped open in the gate to reveal the head of a young man.

With an absolutely perfect Bolton accent—Bolton is a city in northern England where people speak with a distinctly identifiable accent—he said, "What do you lot want at this time of night? It's 10:30 and past my bed time."

Ron gave his name and explained that his passport should have been sent in the diplomatic bag from London. The Bolton lad immediately remembered Ron's passport and cheerfully said he would be back in a minute before slamming the grill shut. We stood and wondered, could we really obtain a passport from a diplomatic bag shipment at that late hour—it felt all too easy. The grill re-opened and the lad asked to see Ron's driver's license. After a cursory check, in spite of the dark shadows, he shoved both the license and Ron's original passport through the grill into Ron's hands. With a definitive, "Good Night," the grill snapped closed and his footsteps were heard returning to the main building.

We felt we had just experienced a rather surreal event and that something was wrong. We walked back to the Blazer, only then did Ron realize he hadn't handed his temporary passport over to the embassy, in exchange for his real one. We returned to the gate and, this time his pounding knuckles raised absolutely no response.

I navigated my way back to the city center. By then, my watch indicated the time to be about 11:00 at night and I felt more than a little exhausted. We wanted to find a quiet place alongside a road to take a well-deserved sleep. Instead, we ended up having an even more frustrating time navigating our way out of Amman than what we had experienced in Damascus. There, we needed to head for the main highway to Amman. But in Amman, we wanted to head to the Saudi border—not a definitive destination—rather a vague sense of a road that went in a south easterly direction which, I had heard, turned into a hard packed sand trail. We may have been on the right road, at times, but I lost confidence as it veered away from the direction I felt we needed to be heading. By 11:20, we were an unhappy trio. We passed several late night cafés and tried to ask for directions, only to receive the universal shrug that implied either *"I don't know," "I don't understand," "I don't care,"* or *"I'm too stoned."*

Outside one café, I spotted two 1100 cc Kawasaki motorbikes with police insignias and an array of lights. I apparently hadn't learned my lesson about seeking help from police in Damascus. Undeterred, I turned around and parked outside the café. As I walked in, all eyes fell on me. They followed me as I approached the two motorbike policemen who stood at the counter. I managed to explain my predicament in my Pidgin-Arabic and they appeared happy to help. They downed the dregs of their espresso's before telling me to follow them. I started up the Blazer, thankful that in following them, I would be in good hands. My state of calm dissolved in an instant when my guides jumped on their huge steeds, turned on their headlights and strobe lights before cranking up all of their sirens. If anybody had been sleeping within ten city blocks, they couldn't be for long, with all of the flashing lights and piercing noise. Their motorcycle engines roared into life, their clutches engaged and they hurtled off down the road. And they expected me to follow? To begin with, I unfortunately faced the opposite direction to which they had departed. I jammed into the fastest U turn known to man and sped off in hot pursuit. At times, I flew through small back streets and neighborhoods at 70 mph while I tried to guess where they might head next. Thankfully, the sound of their sirens and the red flashing coloring on building walls led me along an insane 5-mile game of cat and mouse. At points, I may have been a half a mile behind them, but I kept going in their general direction. In the end, their sirens went quiet and buildings lost their red strobe lighting effect. As we drove along a main road in an outer suburb I caught up with the policemen who had stopped on one side. They sat on their bikes having a quiet cigarette as if such episodes occurred every night. I waved a thank you and they indicated to keep going. By then, the time headed toward midnight, and a major adrenalin surge coursed through my veins—sleep? Impossible. We headed for the border.

The road finally wound its way out of the city and changed from concrete to packed dirt and, in places, it turned into no more than a well-traveled trail across open desert. After we left the lights of the city, our eyes became accustomed to the gentle moonlight that lit the desert. A feeling of calm soothed my frayed nerves after the police chase. We simply needed to cross the border, which shouldn't be a problem at midnight. Soon we could sleep.

As we headed out into vast open desert, Ron asked both Penny and I, "Hey, back before we found the two cops, we tried to ask for directions from a few guys who were a little stoned or out of it, in some way. I've heard a few people on the Aramco camp smoke marijuana, but that habit isn't too prevalent, whereas alcohol is almost everywhere. I know you have to be careful in camp, have either of you brewed any liquor yourselves?"

Penny replied, "Living in a house with three others doesn't make that sort of thing possible. It can be challenging getting us all through our dinner and breakfast routines without the chaos which would be caused by that type of activity."

I looked over and agreed, "I understand Penny's concern about living with others and the upheaval making any alcohol can create. After I moved into the efficiency, I could tolerate my own mess and decided to make a batch of ale. I gathered a few recipes that friends offered and determined who would lend me more specialized equipment like a crown capper. I planned to bottle the resulting ale in Pepsi bottles."

Penny asked, "Is it as time consuming as making Sid?"

"No. Beer is quicker. I took a couple of hours to set a batch brewing in a garbage can. Then I needed to be patient while it brewed for a couple of weeks before spending several hours bottling it. I let it ferment in the bottles for a while before sampling my concoction. I described it as not bad and drinkable, definitely alcoholic, but a little yeasty."

Ron teasingly chastised me. "You call yourself a friend? You never invited me over to help sample."

I countered, "I'd finished my beer brewing efforts by the time we became friends. My brew would've been rather evil if I still had any when you first came over for a drink. Unfortunately, my failure to sterilize the equipment after each brew allowed a bunch of bacteria to take up residence in the gear which resulted in some unpleasant tasting beer. So I quit after my third batch."

"What did you do with the garbage can, tubing, and other gear?" Ron enquired.

"Oh, I trashed the smaller gear. I had no easy way to dispose of the garbage can so I kept it with my regular trash can. It actually came in handy later, but that's another story." I laughed to myself.

Ron had apparently talked with others who had brewed beer. He asked, "You had trouble with bacteria in the equipment? Did you buy it from someone in camp or buy it new?"

We talked further about buying brewing gear in the local markets. Most people in camp went to the local city, Al Khobar, to buy non-food items. So I had decided to buy the gear in Dammam where fewer ex-pats shopped. Even though buying a garbage can, tubing, and other equipment didn't, in itself, break any laws, I did feel a certain level of guilt in making these purchases. The act of brewing alcohol in Saudi Arabia constituted an illegal act, so I felt a little uncomfortable purchasing the needed equipment.

One evening, I took the bus from camp to Dammam. Fortunately, I lived in the city for a couple of months when I first arrived in Saudi Arabia and had learned where the stores that sold household items were located in the market. I scouted out a couple of stores that appeared to have the major items on my shopping list. I approached one store owner but he couldn't speak English, so I crossed the alleyway to another store where, to my relief, the owner spoke good English. I found a perfect trash can and a funnel before I headed toward the assortment of clear plastic tubing. I realized I had started to sweat and shuffle nervously as my intent became more apparent with each additional item. The store owner walked over to me and named the next six items I had on my list. I looked at him quizzically. He smiled knowingly and told me he could recognize any Westerner who planned on brewing beer. I couldn't hold onto the pretense anymore and we had a good discussion regarding the relative merits of certain choices. I returned to the bus, relieved I had completed this part of the venture.

Our discussion about making alcohol lapsed briefly while we

enjoyed the beauty of our surroundings. Moonlight gently painted the low sand dunes in black and gray patterns, creating a soft, beautiful landscape that captured our tired minds. After about 45 minutes of what felt like such genteel driving, in comparison to the earlier wild dash out of Amman city center, we encountered a line of trucks stopped alongside the packed sand trail. In unison, we all took a deep breath in anticipation of our last border crossing.

I drove past the trucks as had become the custom. Right in front of the first truck I noticed an un-manned, raised barrier—both felt like unusual circumstances. A short distance from the barrier stood a tent that looked a little more formal than a Bedouin tent. I saw nothing particularly noticeable about it. The fact we saw nobody, unfortunately, didn't strike us as strange, our tired rational minds said most sensible people should be asleep. I had expected to see both the Jordanian exit point and then immediately the Saudi Arabian entry post—not just a single barrier. So I proceeded on, expecting to find the main border point soon thereafter. We drove on into the desert, but soon we began to feel a little uneasy because nobody constructed a barrier across a trail without a level of intent. Beyond the barrier I could see nothing but a sandy trail. Ron said he had heard a rumor that a six mile strip of no-man's land lay between the Jordanian and the Saudi Arabian borders.

That comment made the decision of what to do next quite simple. I turned around to return to the barrier so we could find anybody who could clarify where we should go. When we again could see the line of trucks, we noticed the barrier had been lowered and two armed patrol guards stood at one end. I stopped in front of the closed barrier as I wound down my window. To my slight dismay, one guard greeted me with a broken English phrase, "Welcome, Jordan!"

To which I replied, "Actually, we are trying to leave Jordan."

The guard didn't believe my account of nobody being around the open barrier, a short time before. He countered that he had been at the barrier for several hours without a break. I realized it would be pointless to argue with him. Thankfully, or so I thought, he finally told me to park over by the tent and talk to his commanding officer.

We walked into the tent to find it had been transformed into a spacious office with good quality older furnishings and several hand-woven rugs scattered around to disguise the floor being compressed desert sand. The officer paid no interest in my discussion with his barrier guard, he simply requested our passports so he could inspect them. He checked Penny's, stamped it and returned it to her. Next, he repeated the process with mine and then opened Ron's.

He flicked through the passport several times, and with a look of frustration, pointed the passport at Ron and said, "Where is your entry visa?"

Without a moment's hesitation, Ron pulled his temporary passport out of his back pocket and tried to replace the one in the officer's out stretched hand, saying, "Oh sorry, it's in this one!"

Oh shit! I felt like the world suddenly stopped spinning. The officer's face became an amazing cross between outrage, fear, shock, and delight, all at the same time. The officer may have been in charge of a border post, out in the middle of nowhere, but he knew nobody should have two passports with the same name from the same country. If Ron had a designation like '007' associated with his name, then a more positive outcome may have resulted. Ron didn't have the '007' designation or 'Bond' as his surname—we were in trouble. I assumed only people who were members of international drug or arms smuggling rings would possibly have two passports. Ron didn't fit into one of these categories and his hurried verbal explanation caused the officer even more confusion and consternation. Penny shuffled nervously while I started to mentally imagine the inside of a Jordanian jail and wondered how long we may be incarcerated. Suddenly things didn't look good—the evening had turned into a never-ending nightmare. Why had I agreed to obtain Ron's passport that night? Perhaps in the light of day, Ron would have acted differently or we may have passed this checkpoint without a thought.

Penny and I added our voices in Ron's defense, which did nothing to help. We had to admit the situation looked rather strange and the more we tried to justify it probably made it worse. Minutes ticked by and I sensed time had shifted into slow motion. The officer tried to telephone someone, but nobody answered his call. The whole concept of diplomatic bags made no sense to him, so our explanation fell apart before it started. After multiple attempts to talk our way out of the situation, I quietly suggested to Ron we change tactics. I whispered to Penny and Ron perhaps we had reached an appropriate time for a bribe. We all agreed it probably wouldn't make anything worse. While the officer looked at both passports intently, I fished my wallet out of my pocket and extracted $100. Back in 1977, that amount of money would have paid to go shopping for the week's groceries for an American family of four at Safeway.

Ron placed the money on the desk, next to the passports, saying, "I hope this helps you understand." Without looking up, the officer opened Ron's original passport, stamped it with an exit visa and handed them both back to him.

The officer pocketed the money, said, "Good Night," and returned to the papers he had been reading as we entered. We bolted out of the tent and back into the Blazer. I may have driven around the barrier, rather than under it, in my hurry to depart Jordan. I wanted to waste no time before I returned to the uncertainty of no-man's land.

In the relief that flooded over the three of us, Penny and I insisted Ron pack his temporary passport deep in his bag, so he would never again be tempted to use it, under any circumstance. I don't recall if Ron ever offered to pay me back the $100, but it was a cheap price to avoid possibly being jailed. Now that I think about this incident, I recall the officer's attitude changed immediately Ron placed the money on his desk. Had he simply played with us while he waited for the bribe?

After our second adrenaline rush in a matter of hours, I felt rather unsettled to be in an international stretch of no-man's land. If for any reason the Saudi Arabian border post refused to allow us entry, we would have to return to the Jordanian tent to try to gain re-entry there. After our recent encounter, re-entry into Jordan couldn't be guaranteed or it could cost us more money than we had in handy cash for a second bribe. At most borders, the exit process from one country slowed our progress with only a brief formality, before immediately being forced into the entry process to the new country that sometimes presented us with more of a challenge. All prior borders had all felt like one continuous process with just a switch of uniforms.

The Jordanian/Saudi Arabian border's six mile strip of no-man's land, without sovereignty, felt unique and uncomfortable; however, it felt a little better than the situation from which we had just extricated ourselves. In the moonlight, those six miles of no-man's land seemed to go on forever. Eventually a structure arose out of the gray desert. Its steel frame and harsh halogen lighting looked modern and efficient in contrast to the tent, from which we had just escaped.

*A Bedouin mother prepares her family's daily
flatbread supply in northern Jordan.*

*Ron, Penny, and Abdul gathered with his family,
before our departure for a night in Aqaba, Jordan.*

The upper porticos of the Treasury (Al Khazneh) in Petra, southern Jordan.

*Ron, donkey and handler prepare to return through
Al Siq after we toured Petra, southern Jordan.*

*I met many new friends while meandering the
Art Show dressed as an English policeman in camp.*

*Our two vehicles ready for us to descend into the chasm
created by the collapse of a cave's roof.*

Walt, Sandra and Brendan relaxed under a tree
for our last lunch in the Empty Quarter.

The Blazer on top of a rocky ridge in the vastness of the Empty Quarter.

The photographs that have been included in the book, as well as additional ones, are available in color on my website at: www.bdhwrites.com.

CHAPTER 14
THE HOME STRETCH

الله شاء إن الله شاء إن الله شاء إن الله شاء إن الله شاء إن الله شاء إن الله شاء إن

We pulled up to the inspection area under the steel canopy at the Saudi Arabian border. A young Immigration/Customs officer checked our passports for our entry visas and did so without any problems, thankfully. We breathed a communal sigh of relief, thinking we had crossed the last hurdle. The officer then indicated he wanted to check the contents of the back of the Blazer—not just take a quick look. I tried to explain that the lock on the tailgate didn't work in a combination of pidgin Arabic and sign language. I thought he understood my predicament, but he still insisted. This meant we had the unenviable task of unpacking everything through the front passenger door.

After the large pile of boxes, bike, and assorted items laid out on the sandy concrete, he took a long look through all of our belongings and boxes, but he appeared to be unsatisfied. It was after one o'clock in the morning and we sensed this one suspicious customs officer had us directly in his focus. He apparently had no plans for sleep and no other travelers to check. We repacked the car, after which he returned to question us further. When the officer, with his gun slung conveniently over his shoulder, started to interrogate me in Arabic, I felt this night would never end. I suspected we might need a second bribe in the space of a single hour. After a short time and, to my relief, I thought I understood what he expected to find.

He had seen the boat on the roof rack and I suspected he may have drawn an incorrect conclusion. He knew one word in English, "*engine*", and he repeated it multiple times. I wondered if he could be of Bedouin stock and hadn't seen many boats in his past. Possibly every previous boat he had ever seen had been crossing the border and almost all of them had been speedboats. When I thought back to what Hughie had told me, I realized the regulations probably said all boats had engines and import duty needed to paid on the engines. Thus he required an engine so he could ascertain the size, which would determine the duty I would have to pay. I tried to tell him I didn't have a speedboat—this was a sail boat. Sadly, this meant absolutely nothing to him. So at 1:30 in the morning, I started to draw pictures of sail boats in the dusty dirt on the back of the Blazer. I drew an Arabic dhow and made comparisons to my boat. He appeared to have about the same level of understanding of a dhow as an iceberg, so that approach failed.

Despite my exhausted state and frustration, I came up with new ways to explain I had no motor, but he continued to counter by saying "*engine.*" The harshness of the overhead lights began to blur my vision and a headache started to pound in my forehead. Penny and Ron walked away when they reached their limit of frustration and they saw a look of blind determination cross my face. I'm not sure what I said or did, but eventually I managed to persuade him I had no engine, without need for bribery. He stamped our passports and we drove into Saudi Arabia at long last. After a few miles, we pulled off the road. Ron and I fell asleep in a ditch while Penny enjoyed sleeping in luxury in the back seat of the Blazer.

The next morning, we all decided to take a hike up a nearby sand dune to take a little time to relax before the arduous section of the drive that lay ahead of us. We felt better after stretching our legs and a little exercise. The desert looked peaceful and beautiful in the early morning sunlight. Soft sand dunes surrounded us. Golden orange color warmly glowed on their eastern flanks while their shadowed sides felt warm and comforting despite being dull gray tones. We sat and simply reveled in the joy of not moving or arguing with border guards. As we relaxed, my mind was captured by the beauty of the expanse of dunes. I was surprised how quickly I felt rejuvenated when I simply allowed myself to be present to the colors and patterns that surrounded us.

I had one concern that lingered in the forefront of my mind. I had noticed one of my front tires had slowly lost a noticeable amount of air. I had been unable to find a working airline in the gas stations where we had stopped recently. I hoped we could fix the problem when we stopped for gas at Al Qurrayat, the first Saudi town we would encounter.

Our peaceful composure on the dune ended abruptly. We heard the annoying buzz of a small engine—it reminded me of a mosquito—it was coming from the open expanse of desert to our south.

I heard it and I groaned, "Oh no. That is precisely what I don't need right now. I wanted a few moments of quiet and no more hassle." A lightness that had filled my mind as I relaxed turned dark and dread hung over me. I was surprised how quickly my mood changed. *Mother, I don't need your doubting thoughts, right now.* The long drive was wearing me down.

Penny, understanding my concern, brushed some sand off her dress as she said, "Do you think it's a Bedouin out scavenging? We could hope he doesn't spot us and keeps heading in another direction."

Ron, at that time, hadn't spent much time in outlying areas where such encounters tended to happen. He optimistically added, "I think we should wait to see what happens."

I felt too tired to move and decided to do as Ron had suggested, wait. "Ah, we'll see soon enough."

Many Saudi Bedouin had been given Toyota pick-up trucks by the government. They drove around the desert where they could be quite aggressive scavengers and petty thieves. My suspicions proved to be correct when we saw a small pickup cutting over the dunes. He apparently had quickly spotted my Blazer as it stood stationary near the road a ways from us, its black body highlighted against the pastel shades of the sandy desert. He made a direct line for it.

The Toyota circled around the Blazer and came to a stop alongside the front tire that had been causing me concern. The driver apparently saw the one tire that looked a little deflated in comparison to the others. I decided I had better go down to check what this guy intended doing. Before I had moved too far down the dune I stopped in my tracks. The driver had got out of the truck and walked to the back of the open flatbed. He pulled on a rope and a few seconds later a small two stroke motor spluttered into life. He pulled an airline over the side of the truck and squatted down next to my tire. I tried to hurry straight down the dune, but I found myself wading through soft sand which slowed me down. By the time I reached the bottom, he had filled the tire, turned off the motor and recoiled the air line. He drove off, without paying any attention to me or the other two who had followed me. When we arrived at the Blazer, the front tire looked like all of the other three—perfect and ready for the road.

I found it interesting to note my immediate trepidation when I had first heard his truck. But, in the middle of a dusty strip of desert, he had inflated my tire because he had the means. He did it without need for any acknowledgement or thanks. He didn't turn out to be one of the scoundrels I had feared him to be. Instead he adhered to the ancient traditional desert ethic of, *If you can help a fellow traveler, do so. Your reward will be when you are in need of assistance yourself.* We wondered if we had just witnessed a miracle. I couldn't begin to guess the chances of encountering someone with an air pump and airline out in a desolate patch of desert.

We stopped in Al Qurrayat for gas, breakfast, and other supplies. Soon afterwards, we left the soft sand dunes and started across the plains of open sabkha—barren salt flats. The prospect of the section of the drive that lay ahead of us challenged my confidence and gnawed at my resolve. This road had been built years before so that maintenance crews could gain easy access to a major pipeline that went from the eastern province of Saudi Arabia up to Lebanon. The pipeline, for the main part, drew a straight line across open desert for well over 800 miles. The road ran parallel to it for the entire way. That defined our immediate futures driving along a straight two-lane road for many mind-numbing miles with a pipeline about 100 feet off to the left and the never-ending shimmering flat desert disappearing in all directions without any noticeable features.

Very few other vehicles used the road making it easy to cruise along at about 75 mph. Along the length of the road, we saw no towns or villages. Thankfully, Aramco had several maintenance yards along the road where small groups of workers lived so they could perform necessary maintenance tasks. As I worked for the oil company, I could stop at these yards for gas and food.

Out in the midst of the open desert, temperatures rose brutally by the middle of the morning and they didn't drop until well after dark. We sheltered from it in the Blazer's air-conditioning. After some time, I realized just having to look out at it constantly kept us all feeling uncomfortably warm. I had also never before realized my sight could physically sense heat. It caused me to break out in sweat if I didn't look at something cooler for a period. We couldn't imagine being outside the Blazer in those conditions. If we had broken down, we would have stayed in the car until someone came by—we may have had to wait for a couple of hours or longer. The possibility of being stuck in the car didn't feel pleasant, but we would have survived.

The road went on, mesmerizingly straight and unchanging. At times, if I focused on the horizon, I felt we stood totally still. Only the road and the pipeline gave us any real sense of movement. Hours ticked by and the miles did pass. While I had felt really happy to have company for the entire journey, I especially felt thankful through that section of the drive. I remembered my friend, Hughie, had driven back on his own, and this particular road must have been unbelievably tough for him. We occasionally saw signs for the next camp. If it said only 30 miles to go, we felt the camp must be in spitting distance. To reach one of the camps was wonderful as we could take a little walk to buy food in the small store, and thankfully fill the gas tank or clean the windscreen. We saw such small tasks as pleasures because such breaks from the mind-numbing sameness of the passing miles in the scorching heat helped to revive us.

I have seen movies in which people were tortured by desert mirages and incredible hardships in the ravaging heat. We certainly didn't suffer in any such way. Along certain sections of the road, however, we began to experience a few of the mind-altering phenomena that vast open expanses of heat shimmering desert can cause. The smallest object that broke the unending specter pulled at our minds' attention like a magnet attracted a nail. Ghostly beings emanated from the shimmering heat. Time stood still and in many ways lost meaning. It felt good to be cocooned in the coolness of the car and grounded by our conversation.

Over the miles, we entertained each other with topics like the latest political shenanigans in England, our experiences of school, why a single shriveled tree could stand alone out in the middle of this blasted desert, and what we would consider to be a relaxing holiday for our next vacation. At one point, I had a follow-up to our conversation about alcohol from the previous night.

I started, "Hey, you recall my failed beer brewing endeavor? Well, my search for a satisfactory alcoholic beverage wouldn't be deterred by that failure. So one evening, I headed to the library to find if any cookbooks may have an alternative brew that would please my taste buds."

Penny rolled the sleeves of her shirt higher and looked at me in the rear view mirror, "Barry, I have to give you credit for persistence, but for many reasons I'm not expecting a successful end to this episode either."

Ron shifted to look more directly at me, chuckling, "I agree with Penny. You don't have a good track record. What happened this time?"

I gathered my thoughts and launched into another tale. "I actually found a recipe for alcoholic ginger beer which looked like a winner as it had alcohol and, secondly, I really like ginger. So I gathered all of the necessary ingredients and, thankfully, the recipe required minimal equipment that I knew I had or could obtain."

Turning to look at Penny, Ron said with a grin, "Now, that seems like a successful venture, so far. Do you agree, Penny?"

With a sarcastic tone, she agreed, "Oh, right."

I continued, "I made a small batch to test it out. After I had completed the process, I had nine bottles of ginger beer crown capped in Pepsi bottles. The recipe indicated it would be best to let them ferment by laying them on their sides in a dark and cool place. I didn't have much space, which meant the floor of the little pantry in the kitchen appeared to be the most appropriate spot available to me.

I laid one row of five on the floor with the other four on a second row. They needed to be left quiet for about four weeks. The one detail that caused me concern was the temperature wasn't really cool."

While I took a drink of water, Ron commented, "I sense this isn't going to be good."

I looked over at him with a contrite smile. "Several weeks later, I awoke at about 1:30 in the morning to the sound of breaking glass. My immediate reaction concerned the saber rattling that had been going on between Iran and Iraq, and Iran's threats toward Saudi Arabia, as they appeared to side with Iraq. I assumed, in my sleepy state, Iran had pre-emptively bombed our camp's radio tower to deter the Saudis. I dove under my bed—not that its 2-inch foam mattress provided any protection. Rational thought filtered back into my brain and I realized the sound had been much closer."

Back in 1980, hostilities in the Iran/Iraq war began, but for a number of years before, an escalating war of words had worried all in the region. Aramco employees were given a daily newssheet that was supposed to give the international news that may be of interest to us. It was fascinating to compare the news given on these sheets against what we could read in English and American newspapers after they were censored in stores in Al Khobar. The Aramco sheets always followed the Saudi Arabian government's distorted version of reality. Now that I think about our current situation here in the U.S., there are parallels to the reporting by supposed news outlets that support the administration's misleading explanation of current events.

Ron and Penny listened to my story about being awakened at 1:30 and shook with fits of laughter. Ron managed to wave, to indicate I should carry on.

"I took a quick circuit through the unit and found nothing out of place. As I found no broken windows, I prepared to go back to bed when a small amount of clear liquid oozing from under the pantry door caught my eye. When I opened the door, I found where nine bottles of ginger beer had lain, the space then only held seven. Glass shards from the other two bottles had been randomly buried in the underside of shelves, walls, and the back of the door. I realized I no longer had bottles of ginger beer, I actually had seven volatile hand grenades."

Penny stifled her laughter to ask, "What on earth did you do next?"

Any embarrassment about this ridiculous story had passed and I told them, "I considered opening the last seven to defuse them to be the best solution. I delicately wrapped one bottle in two beach towels, held it over the sink, and waved a bottle opener at it."

Ron suggested, "Gingerly, I assume?"

I laughed and agreed, "Absolutely. After a few tries, I connected, and the precise flight path of that cap will never be known. It bounced off several walls and objects before it came to rest behind the fridge. I looked in the sink to find not a drop of fluid and the bottle's inside looked barely damp. When I had released the pressure, the entire contents of the bottle had vaporized in an instant. After that, my shredded nerves could take no more. I grabbed my old beer brewing garbage can and my regular one, forced one inside the other, and loaded the six remaining bottles inside them. I prayed they would then be contained until morning. I tried to sleep, but I had more adrenaline than blood flowing through my veins."

Ron had been staring out at the open expanse of desert while I talked. He repositioned himself and inquired, "If you wanted to contain them, why didn't you put them in the fridge? They would have become colder and less volatile."

His suggestion made sense. "That would have been sensible, however, at 2:30 a.m. and somewhat freaked out, I couldn't think clearly. Anyway, in the morning, I talked with Hassan, my Lebanese team lead, about my predicament. He was a volunteer fireman and had led teams who fought big refinery fires. Unfortunately, he could only advise me to protect myself as he knew nothing about grenades. He lent me his helmet and visor along with his industrial strength gloves. But I still had no plan."

"You couldn't just leave them, could you?" Penny said.

I acknowledged her thought after I took another sip of water and munched a couple of crackers. "I called a friend who had a company truck. He drove over and we loaded the garbage cans, with the grenades, in the flatbed. We knew of a garbage disposal area to the south of camp. We simply hurled the last bottles out into the rocky terrain on the edge of the garbage piles. They all exploded, as hoped, except for the last one that bounced without incident on some soft sand. I didn't feel right to leave it as other people used the dump. We threw rocks at it until one snagged the cap. It took off like a balloon that had been released before it could be tied. Thus ended my fateful career as an alcohol manufacturer."

With such banter, the miles of driving passed. We stopped at one camp for dinner as no other options existed, and then drove a few more miles before we called an end to the day. In the morning, as soon as the sun had risen over the horizon, we arose too and returned to the road. Out in the vast open sabkha, it didn't take long for the sun to send the temperature into the 100's. We retreated to the air-conditioning of the car. More miles ticked by and a few more hours passed.

When I saw the first road signs, I knew we were finally approaching civilization. We first passed the road that headed to Ras Tanura where Aramco had their export terminal. A short time after, we started to see the outskirts of Dammam, a relatively large city for Saudi Arabia and the location of the local government.

At first, I felt a little uncomfortable with other vehicles around me. But the traffic moved easily; it flowed along. The last few miles sent me on an internal emotional roller-coaster. I desperately wanted to be able to relax, but I also wanted the adventure to continue. I probably simply shut down and focused on driving. When I saw the top of the main Aramco office building, a mixture of bitter-sweet emotions hit me. We had made it back—the journey would barely last two more miles.

I certainly had felt a level of strain and internal tension for the entire journey. Plenty of opportunities for incidents to not go smoothly had arisen. A few turned into challenges while others became delightful memories. Continual anxiety and uncertainty over the two weeks had accumulated and taken a toll on me. Over those last few miles, the build-up of tension was difficult to contain. I don't know how Ron and Penny saw me in those last few miles, but inside

I was shattered, I was thankful, I was happy, I was sad, I was confused, I was one hell of a fortunate human being for experiencing an incredible journey, and I had been with two amazing souls. We had been through so much without an argument or heated words. I was done.

I believe, at a deeper level, I realized what I then faced didn't present me with an ending of a journey, but rather a time of transition. All people go through life and experience pivotal events that shape who they become and how they see the world. I now know the experiences of that journey have been a major influence on who I have become. The essence of lessons learned continue to influence my decisions on a regular basis. As I drove those last few miles to Dhahran, I sensed the boy who left London, just two weeks earlier, no longer existed.

I pulled up to the main gate to sign in. I had no more energy to give, physically or emotionally. I felt I had come home. Everything looked so familiar, safe, and comfortable. I could even see my efficiency perched up on a rise beyond the parking lots. I made the few turns to pull into the parking lot next to the radio tower and my efficiency. I unlocked my front door and we all collapsed onto my sofa and chairs, with a sense of camaraderie that only an experience like we had been through could ever forge.

Ron beamed at me, "Congratulations! You succeeded in driving your Blazer from London to Dhahran. What took you so long?"

Penny gave Ron a puzzled look. "How can you be so perky? Aren't you tired?"

He slumped further into his chair, "OK. I'm exhausted too. How are you doing, Barry?"

I paused before saying, "You know, I don't honestly know. Are we really here? I feel tired, but I'm so wired I don't know how to feel. Do I want to laugh, talk, cry, or what?"

"Man, sit down, relax. You deserve a damn good rest," said Ron.

More small talk filled the void while the three of us tried to take in the experiences we had just survived. Despite my own swirling emotions, I felt for Ron in that moment because he had missed the first half of the journey. I sensed he was disappointed he had missed several events by not being with Penny and me as we drove to Turkey.

After we had spent an hour or so relaxing, I dropped Ron at the bus stop so he could take the shuttle over to his hotel, and I then took Penny and her bike over to her efficiency. Finally, I unpacked all of the gear from the back of the Blazer. The Laser sailboat would stay on the roof rack until the next weekend when I could transport it down to the beach. I finally sat down in my lounge alone and no longer moved. The Blazer and I could settle at my Saudi Arabian home. I was about to start a new chapter of life and what an adventure that would turn out to be.

"Did I ever contemplate doing it again?" is a question I have been asked several times over the years. I honestly don't recall if I said a definitive "*yes*" or "*no.*" To have done it once brought me so much satisfaction and happiness; I had achieved my goal of having a reliable vehicle to venture out into the Saudi Arabian desert, to take longer road trips, or simply arrive for a squash game in plenty of time. I had no reason to prove I could endure another 5,500 mile drive. And, what could I possibly have used as an excuse when my mother asked me why I wanted to do it for a second time?

CHAPTER 15

POST JOURNEY

O n the weekend after our arrival back at the Aramco camp, I took the Laser that I'd left strapped to the roof rack of the Blazer down to its new home. Aramco had a facility on a sheltered piece of coast line that lay about 15 miles south of the main camp. The Aramco beaches sat on the side of a secluded bay that enclosed about 20 square miles of sea water, which was almost as saline as the Dead Sea. The bay was attached to the main Persian Gulf by a narrow neck of water which allowed porpoises and, occasionally, large pods of jellyfish to enter the bay. The water was always crystal clear and wonderfully warm. Some days, when the wind wasn't blowing, water skiing on the perfectly flat water was a surreal experience. As I skied, I felt I looked down on the coral which covered much of the sea bed through a sheet of glass.

The swimming beach, which nestled below a sand dune, allowed people to relax in the warm water, or shelter from the sun's intensity under permanent canopies. I could only assume the canopies had been constructed by a pipeline construction crew with scraps of their left-over steel. The canopies looked functional, strong, but not at all attractive.

About half a mile away from the swimming beach, on the other side of a sandy point, the boat beach had been constructed. Employees' boats could be stored securely in that facility and launched safely. Steel canopies again protected the pale skinned ex-pats.

As soon as I arrived at the boat beach, friends recognizing my new black Blazer came over to help off-load the sailboat's hull and sections of mast. I looked forward to joining the fleet of Lasers which were designed to be sailed by one person. My friend Anna had given me one brief lesson in the English Channel when I picked up the Laser. She had sailed her Laser alongside me, calling instructions. Now I would have to work it out for myself. It would be a few more weeks before I dared bring the sail and other gear down for my first outing on the bay. It felt good to have it stored securely on the racks with other people's Lasers. I felt happy to have all my unpacking finished and I began to take in the delights of having my own vehicle. I could easily reach the beach when I judged conditions might be good for either sailing or water skiing. Soon, the Blazer became essential when I moved to a new bachelor house that had been part of a major expansion. My commute to the office changed from 200 yards to about three miles which I could walk unless the weather became extremely hot or humid.

After the journey from London, it took me quite a number of days to resettle into the repetitive side of life on the Aramco camp. During the drive, my routine had become based on movement, progress, and a lack of time-based schedules. To be driven by a watch felt so artificial. Life on the road had at times been challenging, but overall it had been a richly rewarding, ever-changing, and an incredible adventure. To do the same job each day didn't feel satisfying. An uncomfortable funk clouded my state of mind for a few weeks.

Following a few weeks of re-acclimatization in camp and time to look back on the journey, I could see how the stress had accumulated as we made progress. I was glad we had taken the one night in Aqaba to relax and given us a chance to rejuvenate ourselves. Happily, I couldn't recall one time on the journey when we had any angry interactions or any one of us being really upset about anything. When I considered our fatigue and the list of stressful episodes, that was quite remarkable.

The bond that had been struck between the three of us kept us in an ongoing friendship during the rest of our time in Saudi Arabia. After we each left, the bonds did dissolve and I know nothing of Penny's or Ron's lives in later years. I would be intrigued to hear their memories of this two week journey. They may disagree with some of my recollections. To know how they remember various incidents would be fascinating. I would want to know which events they recalled as significant, but I've since forgotten.

The gas pumps incident in northern Syria, in which we were almost shot by two soldiers, stayed front and center in my mind for a long time. The understanding that life is precious was profound; I had understood this message for several years before the journey. However, to feel its true meaning, physically, shifted my comprehension and it motivated a much more engaged approach to how I lived my life. I found new ways to interact with the world and, in doing so, I became more confident, more assertive, and a damn sight happier.

Several incidents when we had been on the road stood out as great examples of what I started to learn about life. The time I bought rope in Izmir taught me two lessons—don't expect others to do tasks in the same way I would and don't be over assertive, such as speaking angrily or louder, in order to solicit help. In Greece when I needed the tire fixed, I found listening to my gut, rather than my head, was a better course forward. Those mechanics may have worked in a back-country workshop, but they were highly skilled—they fixed the puncture and returned us to the road. That tire never gave me any problems after that. I also learned I couldn't push myself without a break. I needed the night in Aqaba to revitalize myself. I couldn't drive myself on continuously and probably the funk after our return to camp was a necessary way for my body and mind to impose their own need to take time to recover.

Over the course of the 15 day drive, I had come to see I couldn't expect much out of life if I didn't become my own mover and shaker. Nobody else was going to make my life happen—it was up to me. If I wanted to do something, then I would be the one to plan and make it happen. While I had worked in London and lived in Brighton, I hadn't been particularly interested to learn about other people's lives or their cultures, but I certainly had been aware of the diversity of people that could be found. However, to actually witness people of other cultures as they lived their daily lives had stirred an interest in me that made me consider my own heritage and my place in it. What did it mean to be British? How did people of the former Great British Empire see me as I traveled around the world? What did I assume about myself or others? I may have not realized it at the time, but a seed had been planted that later blossomed when I took periods of time to travel in other parts of the Middle East as well as the Indian subcontinent. Through those travels, I realized there were answers to my many questions. My eyes were poised ready to see when I opened them and my mind and heart were ready to understand my surroundings more deeply. I received an education about life, the likes of which could never be found in textbooks. To witness people adapting to the circumstances of their natural surroundings was an education in ecology. Communities coming together to overcome times of hardship was an education in social structures and economics. Understanding the significance of a consistent and clean source of water to remote villages expanded my thoughts about health and the need for basic hygiene. These were lessons I would never have learned if I stayed safe, at home.

On the section of the drive that ran alongside the 800-mile pipeline, we had fallen quiet for periods of time. I easily and quickly became absorbed by my fascination with openness, my surroundings, that had no boundaries other than the sky. I felt connected to the joy I had experienced as a teenager when I had conquered my first mountain peaks and sensed the immensity that could be seen from such places. That section of the drive wasn't a spiritual awakening, but more like a door to spirituality being opened just a crack.

In the period while I re-established my routine around camp, I took several trips to the beach each weekend. I crossed open plains of sabkha and became familiar with the dunes that lined the side of the bay; they started thoughts about adventures in Saudi Arabia. I had a reliable vehicle that I could take on the road or out into the wilds. The possibility of new explorations helped to settle me down; I knew the future wasn't only about work. A whole load of play and fun awaited me. I was ready.

CHAPTER 16
AL HOFUF

I soon settled into driving around camp and, on weekends, down to the beach. I decided I needed to venture off camp and join roads driven primarily by locals. The most obvious destination was the nearby city of Al Khobar, about six miles away. However, the route to Al Khobar crossed the junction with the road to the International Airport which had a bad reputation for dangerous and reckless driving. Ron crossed it every day on his commutes to and from the office. He had told me a number of stories of grave stupidity and how many drivers behaved irresponsibly. I chose a quieter period of the day and managed to navigate to and from Al Khobar without any problems. After several such outings, my confidence with driving on the busier local roads grew quickly.

After I unloaded the Laser from the roof rack, I noticed a problem with the Blazer's roof. Back in England, Mike and I had positioned a tire on the roof of the Blazer to support the Laser's hull so that we could securely tie it down. Over the course of the journey, the tire had ground a patch of paint off the roof and in the acrid desert air, rust soon appeared. I took the Blazer down to a paint shop in Al Khobar to see how easy it would be to fix. While they fixed the rust, they suggested repainting the entire roof white, instead of its original black. I accepted their proposal as a white roof would be much cooler than a black one.

After we had been back in Dhahran for about six weeks, Penny, Ron and I decided a little off-camp outing would be good for us. As I hadn't yet felt like driving out into the wild desert in my new vehicle,

I hadn't taken time to buy off-road tires. I still had the truck-grade tires that had brought us from England. They worked perfectly well on the local roads, as well as the main roads that crossed the open expanses of desert which could, without warning, turn into packed sand trails. The one slight concern I had about the Blazer's tires was the fact the spare was still the repaired tire from the puncture in northern Greece. But, I knew the repair still held pressure, so a local expedition on the roads seemed like a great idea.

On a free weekend day, we went to the ancient city of Al Hofuf. My route took us to the south of Dhahran for a couple of hours, toward the Empty Quarter. Al Hofuf had been established in an area of open desert that had several well-known oases. These precious sources of water had drawn camel trains to converge around them in centuries gone by. The caravans traded goods, causing a market and ultimately a permanent settlement to be established. In the modern day, the oases allowed for the development of large areas of date groves. Local farmers tended the groves that produced extremely good quality dates. The three of us had all been to Al Hofuf previously, but none of us had taken the time to explore it and familiarize ourselves with its layout.

We left camp early and had to drive north for a few miles to join the road that made a long sweeping left to head south into the wilds of the desert that surrounded our camp. The blacktop road gave us the one point of relative solidity, otherwise sand dunes surrounded us as they slowly moved under the control of the winds that appeared to be as constant as the scorching sun. The gusting winds blew up one side of the dunes, carrying sand upward toward their tops. Ultimately, much of the sand that reached the peak of each dune was picked up by the wind and carried away. A little of it simply fell down onto the sheltered side of the dune, while other grains floated away to land in drifts or on other dunes. With this constant action, the dune neither grew nor shrank in height much, the dunes gradually crept in the direction dictated by the wind. It depended on how strong the wind happened to be. Its strength varied constantly, but the direction of the winds remained reasonably constant for months. Direction changed depending upon the season. The dunes in our region of

Arabia inched primarily toward the southeast without a care for roads or other obstacles. Mankind could bulldoze the sand to make roads and build structures, but the wind re-sculpted the dunes and they kept shifting in the wind's direction without a concern for man's futile efforts to control the sand or impede the dune's progress.

In places, drifts of sand had been deposited on the road. As we drove through the dunes, the wind caused by our passing picked up some of this sand and it danced wildly behind us for a period before it settled once again. The entire road surface appeared to continually move as each passing vehicle etched a new pattern in the drifts that came close to or onto the road. I felt I drove through a live, ever-changing piece of art.

As I drove south in the early morning, the sunlight created beautiful colorful patterns on the dunes and the drifts. I had to focus on the road with its drifting sand so that I wasn't mesmerized by the beauty that surrounded us. I looked over at my companions. The passing splendor had captured their attention, too.

I said, "The light on the dunes is amazingly vibrant. Once in a while, the grains of sand sparkle when the light hits them just right."

Penny responded enthusiastically, "Absolutely. It's unbelievable how many shades of color are yellow or gold. With all of the wind-driven sand flying in places, it's forever changing."

Ron took a drink of water before adding, "I have to admit when I decided to take the job here, I never had any idea about the desert or what I'd see out here in the wilds."

Penny looked intrigued. "So, what did you expect to see out here in the desert?"

"Well, I did expect to see sand dunes and camels, but the subtlety is what has caught my attention," he answered as he twisted around to look at her directly. "The sand isn't only yellow. One single dune can display all of the variations of colors that can be found in the color spectrum. I'll admit, at first, I saw all sand as yellow and couldn't understand people's love of the desert. Then, one afternoon, a co-worker gave me a lift back to my hotel after work. He cut across a section of desert on a trail after we got clogged in a traffic jam.

To my surprise, he stopped in the middle of nowhere and just looked at a nearby dune. I did the same. As I sat there, I realized I was actually looking at a natural kaleidoscope, it blew me away. I hadn't ever taken the time to simply stay still, for even a moment, and really see what I'd looked at so many times before."

Penny thought about his reply and with a twinkle in her eye asked, "So when we came down the Pipeline road and you appeared to zone out for periods, you were really taking in the desert and not taking a snooze?"

He jibed back, "Gee. Thanks. Yes, I was looking at the desert and I admit I also took a few moments to rest my eyes. However, I remember one of our party who happily took frequent little naps in the back seat." His attempt to look hurt switched to a beaming laugh. We all sniggered as we each took a few seconds to think back on the drive back to Dhahran.

I looked over at the two of them. "Now, children, I don't want you two squabbling!" I couldn't keep a stern fatherly expression which caused us all more amusement. It felt good to know we still had the ability to joke with each other.

We cruised easily down to Al Hofuf where I found a good place to park next to the old fort which lay near downtown. It didn't take us too long to find the market. I had heard it could be a reliable source for Arabic crafts such as basketry, copper work, some painting, and crude jewelry. We enjoyed a walk around the stalls, looked at crafts but made no purchases. Each of us kept mental notes of possible future ideas. When we had our fill of crafts and market stalls, we took a quick tour of the fort that had fallen into serious decay.

In the days before the tribes of Arabia had been united by the House of Saud, the fort at Al Hofuf had seen a few small battles as its location had been considered to be strategically important. I had learned that the equivalent fort in Riyadh had been the sight of the final and crucial battle which allowed Saud to conquer and unite the twelve Arabian tribes. In stories that I had heard about Riyadh Fort, Saud had attacked the Riyadh Fort's main gates with a small party of warriors. They had forced the gates open and in the ensuing fighting,

Saud had driven his sword into one of the gates so deeply the gates couldn't be re-closed after the defenders successfully repelled Saud's group. The sword continued to obstruct the closing of the gates as the defenders couldn't extract it. Saud returned soon afterwards with a larger force, fought his way into the fort and won the day. His sword remained impaled in the gate and had to be broken off. Whether or not this tale held any truths didn't matter to me; it represented a beautiful example of the endless stream of folklore stories that can be found in Arabic culture. For thousands of years, similar stories have been told by the Bedouin who crossed the deserts in great caravans, such stories spreading from tribe to tribe and from generation to generation. A few storytellers wanted to enhance their storytelling reputations and added new words into the Arabic language to highlight a nuance or to shift a story's meaning subtly. I heard, as a result of this flourishing tradition of storytelling, the Arabic language became the most verbose language in the world. The English language has a plethora of words, but not as many as Arabic.

We later returned to the Blazer as we had one other place to visit in Al Hofuf. We didn't know precisely where to go, but I had been told what to look for. As hoped, we saw a low rocky ridge beyond one section of the date groves that circled the main center of the city. We wove through smaller side-streets along which houses and small stores had been built. As to whether they had been built 100 days or 100 years ago looked difficult to determine. Aging, dustiness, and decay had been the fate of such houses or stores before their first coats of paint had even dried. The desert's climate could be harsh, relentless, and unyielding. It could destroy mankind's structures relatively quickly, but some of the results of the climate's sculpting could only be described as exquisite.

After a few blocks, the road turned into a packed sandy trail as we entered the shade of the date groves. Alongside the trail ran an irrigation channel with crude wooden and metal gates that allowed farmers to regulate the water flow. The trail started to rise up toward the rocky ridge as the date palm groves became thinner. A short distance ahead, we could see several vehicles stopped near a sandy rock face that had several caves at the base. Deep fissures broke the rock face into sections.

We parked on a convenient patch of dirt and felt we had found the correct area when we saw westerners hiking the short distance to and from the caves. In the first cave, we found one of the local artisans who spent every day at his potter's wheel. He had a crude wheel made of wood that required him to perpetually control the speed of the wheel with one foot. He had to take his sandal off as the sandal's leather sole would have given him little control. The potter had a limited variety of small finished products: Arabic water pipes, vases, jars, and bowls. When he had completed one item he would transfer it from the wheel to a small flat piece of wood that he placed outside for the item to bake in the 100+ degree sun. Despite the end products not receiving a final coat of glaze, they could still be functional. Many were used by the local people on a daily basis to hold dry items for long periods and liquids for shorter times.

We wandered between the caves and their potters. The differences in their styles fascinated me. Some used primarily their fingers to fashion the spinning clay while others used a variety of sticks as tools. A few spun the wheel at a reasonably consistent speed but most changed the speed depending on how they needed to shape each piece. Several had family members who worked the crowd outside and hawked their products after they had dried, while other potters talked in both Arabic and English as they spun to engage with their potential customers. No matter which style a potter choose, their end products and their prices were all similar. So we each selected a different potter, from whom we each made our purchases. Most westerners who bought these pottery items simply used them for decoration around their homes and didn't actually use them.

We stowed our goods in the back of the Blazer. I still relished the wondrous delight of being able to actually use the tailgate. An aircraft mechanic friend, Jason, whom I had shared a house with in my early days in Dhahran, had amazed me with how easily he had been able to fix the tailgate lock. It had taken jamming a piece of wooden coffee stirrer into a spring in the middle of the lock to stop it from turning.

After we stowed our fragile purchases, we noticed a local guy who sold sodas and ice cream. "Now there's an opportunist," Ron laughed.

Penny smiled at the prospect of an ice cream. "He probably realized these potters attract more ex-pats than local people and ex-pats do like their sodas and ice cream. I say we check out what he has. The ice cream I've had here in Saudi Arabia tastes just like it does back home. I wonder where they get the milk to make it."

I suggested, "Probably import it, like so many things. I can drive with an ice cream cone in one hand. Let's go."

"I think we should make sure they are frozen solid. His two coolers are pretty beaten up. I wonder how well they're insulated," she warned.

Ron headed toward the vendor, "It had better be in frozen condition because I need some relief from this triple digit temperature. Can't it cool just a little? It's late afternoon."

I turned to him saying, "I'm betting on the ice cream being solid, not on the weather—it won't cool down." The vendor opened the coolers and I could see the ice cream was hard. I asked for three cones.

We stood quietly taking bites of soothingly cold ice cream while we watched the sun begin its descent toward the horizon, not a guarantee of a drop in the temperature. We returned to the Blazer, turned on the A/C, and dropped back down through the groves into town while we demolished the last of our ice cream cones.

It didn't take too much effort to navigate through the small city center and return to the open main road that cut a path northward across the open desert. With the sun in the west, the shadows on the dunes formed more intricate patterns as their windward sides faced the sun. Sand, carried up the dune by the wind, scoured small channels in the surface of the dunes, carving a network of shadows. They created fine designs that could have competed with the finest gold filigree. They competed for our attention, but I needed to focus on the road.

We relaxed as the miles ticked by. We all felt the day had been a good first expedition for the Blazer. Without the car, we could have visited Al Hofuf, however the experience may not have been conducive to absorb the beauty and reality that had been all around us. I had found my awareness and engagement with the dunes had been heightened by my need to focus while driving through this ever-changing landscape. I realized I wasn't simply driving down a road. I, along with the road, the drifts, the dunes, and the act of driving were all one. It was as if the subject, the object, and the activity all blended into one. No separation existed. I, the dunes, and all points of connection lost our individual identities—we all were one. I was consumed.

After this first trip outside of the camp, I felt more confident and ready to take trips out into the desert on trails and across the desolate stretches of sabkha—salt flats. Before such trips, I needed to head to Al Khobar or Dammam to purchase balloon tires. These types of tires had no distinct sidewall nor tread. Their cross-section looked more bulbous, which meant they hopefully would have less of a tendency to dig themselves down into loose sand.

CHAPTER 17
DIVING IN THE RED SEA

الله شاء ان   الله شاء إن   الله شاء إن   الله شاء إن   الله شاء إن   الله شاء ان

Amonth or so after I had resettled into camp, I joined a group of friends whose company I enjoyed, even though I didn't see them often. We chatted about various subjects, one of which recurred frequently for most people in camp. Many talked about plans for vacations as such trips certainly lifted people's spirits—not that we felt depressed—far from it. Occasionally, I perceived a slight claustrophobic quality to life around camp because some people stayed in camp for long periods. I recognized that most of the people who I thought of as my friends were the adventurous and engaged ones, while others hid from the opportunities the region offered.

One couple in the group, Jay and Marsha, said they planned to head to the Red Sea for a diving trip in mid-November. That caught my attention as I had brought a small amount of dive equipment in the Blazer. They asked if anyone else would like to join them. A couple of other people and I said we were interested.

Jay gave the basic details, "I've been trying to find contacts in Jeddah who could help us connect with a dive store. I've heard about a dive store which rents tanks and they can refill tanks as needed. It will mean driving into the city at least once a day."

Marsha added, "After looking at different places, we've decided that an area north of the city, called Twenty-Nine Palms, would be the best. It's as close as we can get to Jeddah and be on a good area of the coast for diving."

I felt really excited at this unexpected opportunity and asked, "How long a drive from Jeddah to the camp site?"

Jay squinted at Marsha before replying, "Roughly 30 minutes, if we're lucky." He turned to face me with an inquiring expression. "Time out. Barry, you've just driven your new car back from England. Are you really interested in another long drive so soon?"

"I'm game. When are you planning on going and how long will you be diving?" I enthusiastically replied.

Marsha, more assured of the dates, jumped in and explained, "Before Jay gets it wrong, I'll tell you. We plan on leaving on Thursday, November 17th. That should mean we will be one day ahead of the main Hajj rush to Mecca on the Friday. It will be bad on that Thursday, but far better than a day later. Then we will take a few days off work so we can return on the following Monday. That will give us three days for diving."

I really loved the idea of another road trip, especially to a new area. Additionally, I needed to work on my diving skills; I knew the basics and had just a little practical experience. I felt hesitant to make a decision as I had a few concerns about driving across Arabia two days before the start of the Hajj.

The Hajj, the annual pilgrimage to Mecca and Medina reputedly brought together one of the largest gatherings of human beings— official counts put the number of pilgrims attending each annual Hajj in the millions. My mind toyed with the possibilities; I had recovered from the drive to Dhahran, I felt confident driving on Saudi roads, this would be a new experience and a chance to get to know this group better—I was going. I quieted my remaining fears and inquired if I could ask other friends to join me in the Blazer. Jay and Marsha had no objections and said they would be happy to have a good-sized group.

Over the next few days, I asked a couple of friends whom I thought might be interested. Soon enough, Jim and Tom indicated a desire to join the group. Neither of them had ever been diving before but wanted to give it a try.

For myself, I had taken a scuba diving class when I still lived in England. I understood how to dive and the equipment, but I didn't yet feel proficient or confident. The prospect of submerging myself in the beautiful, warm Red Sea after learning to dive in the murky, cold waters of Swanage Harbor on the South coast of England felt unbelievably alluring.

Closer to the date of our departure, Marsha distributed rough maps of how to find the Twenty-Nine Palms section of the coast north of Jeddah. It couldn't be defined as a campsite or resort. Literally, 29 palm trees grew along a strip of sandy beach. The group of trees had wedged themselves between the open desert and the gentle waves of the Red Sea.

The date for the start of the Hajj could be determined using the Arabic calendar, which based its months on the lunar cycles. Marsha determined we would be fine driving on Thursday after she looked at the Arabic calendar. Many of the pilgrims made the same determination and planned their journeys so they arrived at Mecca on Friday evening in time for the start of activities on Saturday morning. Pilgrims found it easier to camp alongside the road, while en route, rather than have to deal with the overcrowded camps around Mecca itself. So it would be optimal for the pilgrims to arrive on Friday evening. We decided this timing would be best for everyone, the pilgrims and our dive party.

However, life didn't turn out to be that simple because the determination of the Hajj start date wasn't contingent on only the published Arabic calendar. The date actually depended upon an ancient custom. A chief Muathin, a religious leader, in Riyadh declared the start of the Hajj based on when he, with his naked eye, could distinguish between a black thread and a white thread by the light of a new moon. As he aged and his eyesight became compromised, his ability to declare the start of the Hajj correctly became problematic. Indeed, on the year of our planned trip, he apparently again failed to declare the correct date, calling the start of the Hajj one day earlier than the calendar. The main rush of Hajji's would occur on the same day as our day of travel—not on the following day, as had been expected. This became apparent to our group just a few days before we departed. After some discussions, we all decided to continue with our planned trip.

Our dive group travelled in four vehicles. The journey ahead would cover about 450 miles in one day. Despite my recent two-day 800 mile drive down the Pipeline Road, it still felt a little daunting. We left camp early on Thursday morning and drove north toward the junction where we could branch off to Riyadh. Initially, the traffic didn't appear to be too heavy and everyone drove in a restrained manner. The first few hours saw us cover a good distance toward Riyadh. Even with a gradual increase in the volume of traffic, our four cars saw each other on a fairly regular basis. As soon as we reached Riyadh, we merged with a large number of Hajji's—pilgrims—and many drove anxiously, as they probably worried about being late.

Jim sat calmly in the passenger seat to my right, but suddenly he jumped and tried not to scream, "Shit!! That idiot just came out of nowhere. How did you avoid hitting him?"

I quickly looked over at Jim, acknowledging his concern, "Luckily, I had seen him in the rear view mirror, he had been pushing his way through traffic for a while. I saw him edging up on me and could see he would try to get around me."

Tom added from the backseat, "I saw the driver, when he came up alongside us. He had a glazed, maniacal look in his eyes. He's headed to Mecca today or else he's going to heaven, having just taken out a few infidels—us—along the way."

Jim said, "It certainly is an advantage driving a higher vehicle. You can see the traffic flow and anticipate potential problems and idiots."

I agreed. "You've got that right. I'd feel really unsafe if I drove one of these old, beaten up, smaller saloon cars," I said pointing at the mass of cars which surrounded us.

Jim took a long look all around before he explained, "I wondered if I could still see any of the others from our group. I think we've been totally separated and I imagine the volume of traffic isn't going to lighten until we've passed Mecca, which is a good couple of hours ahead."

As we left Riyadh and returned to driving the main highway to the west coast, the volume of traffic lessened a little; however, a sense of urgency dictated how many drivers behaved. Despite the well-designed seats in the Blazer, I sensed my shoulders becoming tighter as the drive continued. I constantly needed to monitor drivers ahead of me as well as those behind me. I also kept a watchful eye for traffic coming from the other direction as a disturbing number of their attempts to pass lacked due consideration. I could only imagine several such attempts depended on the drivers' cries of "*Inshallah!*— God Willing?*" and also on my taking drastic avoiding action. Another consideration that seriously concerned me were the occasional cars headed west, like myself, that had either broken down or stopped for a nature break. Most of these cars had parked on the hard packed sand alongside the road's asphalt surface, but a few simply stopped on the road without any apparent attempt to clear the roadway. This became especially dicey where the road narrowed to a single lane each way. Even where the road had two lanes each way, the volume of traffic made these types of circumstances difficult and potentially dangerous to negotiate.

After several more hours, we reached the point where the Hajji's headed off toward Mecca. Apparently, security tightened on all roads that led into the holy city to prevent infidels, like ourselves, from entering. I was really surprised when I found that we were still surrounded by congested traffic even after the Mecca turn off. We continued west in a solid line of fast moving traffic, despite many cars having turned in the direction of Mecca. The much anticipated quieter drive into Jeddah had apparently been canceled by whoever oversaw such matters.

As we dropped down the escarpment side of the Asir Mountains that run along the Western side of Saudi Arabia, the road became a series of wide sweeping bends that snaked their way down onto the coastal plains. The road had two lanes in each direction with only the solid white line to separate the two halves of the road. As slower traffic clogged the right lane, I pulled into the left-hand lane. A minute later as we rounded a curve to the left, I took a quick look around us and let out a shriek, "Oh crap! Jim how many cars can you see over to our right?"

"Fuck! Three. Is that one over to our left?"

I double-checked, "Nope. Two fucking idiots are overtaking me on the wrong side of the road and I'm in the left lane!"

I hit the brakes hard, but it actually didn't help as the entire group hit the brakes at the same time. We had realized the same horrifying reality, we six cars abreast flew downhill and faced a comparable line of five cars abreast that screamed up the hill toward us. I had no space to stop or get out of the way. The cars on the outside of the bend headed onto the hard pack sands, while their drivers tried to control the abrupt transition. Cars on the wrong side of the road careened further out and the rest of us barely had time to head to what looked like a space in the ranks of the oncoming vehicles. We all screamed *Inshallah* while I tried to not close my eyes. Two cars went past on my left and I saw one upcoming car zoom past my right wing and it was gone in a flash. We couldn't believe what had just happened; eleven vehicles went into a potential disaster and all of them continued on their ways, without a scratch on any of the vehicles. But, we drivers and passengers couldn't hide our frayed nerves.

Tom put it quite simply, "Christ!! I've never thought of myself as a Christian, but I just witnessed one bloody good advertisement for becoming a sodding Muslim!" We all laughed a little nervously at the truth in his words.

I ran my shaking hand through my hair and said, "I thought after we lost all the Hajji traffic we would have saner drivers. I was wrong. These drivers appear to feel like Allah is right with them. I'm not saying they're right or wrong. I'm just really pleased to know Allah's on their side and apparently on ours, too."

Jim looked over at the driver to his right and whispered *Inshallah* at him.

The rest of the drive into Jeddah passed quietly. The maps that Marsha had prepared proved to be useful as we managed to miss the city center and made our way to the northern edge of the city. We then drove along several miles of trails that wove through small dunes lining the upper side of the beaches. Eventually, we saw several palm trees ahead and as we approached them, we could see two familiar vehicles and a group of people about to set up camp. After we parked next to them, we crawled out of the Blazer to stretch and greet Jay, Marsha, and the rest of the group. Half an hour later, our last vehicle arrived and we started to organize our trips to the dive shop to rent dive tanks and other gear.

The next morning, Jay and a couple of others drove into Jeddah to find the dive store. Jay had arranged to rent gear from the store before we came across to the west coast. While the rest of us relaxed on the beach, we paired up with a buddy so we could keep an eye out for each other during our times underwater. As Jim and I had built a level of rapport on the drive across the country, we decided to be a pair. Jay had been designated the lead diver of the group as he was most experienced. We all knew to follow his instructions at all times.

Jay returned several hours later with the gear that had been requested. We distributed it and then ensured each of us had everything necessary. While waiting for Jay, several of us checked out the water; its beautiful warm temperature felt inviting. I knew as soon as we started to descend into the depths, the temperature would drop noticeably, but I felt certain wetsuits wouldn't be needed.

We helped each other put on the heavy diving gear and staggered through the soft sand into the shallows. We had heard that stonefish which had poisonous spines along their backs lived along this stretch of the coastline. These flat fish settled into the sandy bottom and, apparently, were well camouflaged. Before we sat in the water, we kicked around in the sand to encourage any stonefish to depart the area. Having sat on the seabed without incident, we struggled into our flippers and put on our goggles and snorkel. Our group swam easily out into deeper water. We bobbed on the surface for a few minutes to perform several last minute checks. Jay warned us the water was about 10 feet deep at that point, and it would soon drop away down a near vertical cliff. We switched from our snorkels to the regulators which were attached to our tanks.

We swam down into the sparkling waters and were immediately tantalized by an array of multi-colored corals that competed for our attention. The corals stretched in bands across the sandy bottom far into the distance. Throughout the heads of corals, a myriad of beautiful fish swam, their array of colors appearing like shards of rainbows that darted or wafted through the water. I knew which were angelfish, clownfish and pufferfish, but hundreds of other types swam by me. I felt they displayed an apparent scorn for me as I didn't know what types they were. Many displayed single bold colors while others dazzled in festive combinations of vivid colors woven into complex patterns. Their ever-changing spectacle of colors and motion reminded me of a fireworks display in which new colors and patterns thrilled my senses briefly as one burst of beauty was quickly replaced by another. The corals' muted earthy tones became a dull backdrop to the intensity of the fishes' iridescent kaleidoscope of colors. The fishes' only consistent detail was the vibrancy of their colors, whereas the corals were muted and rarely vibrant.

Scattered in the sand, as well as in certain areas of the coral, mollusks moved at barely perceptible speeds. Each mollusk carried a shell for protection; they covered a range of shapes from simple domes to tightly spiraling cones. In occasional rocky crevices, the heads of eels darted out to look for a quick mid-day snack before returning to wait for the night-time hunt for larger prey.

As we moved further out and into deeper water, we could see an apparent end to the sandy and coral sea bed. Beyond there, we knew a near vertical cliff dropped down into the blackness of the depths, far deeper than it was safe for us to ever contemplate. A darker shade of blue stretched out beyond the dividing line.

When we swam out over the top of the underwater cliff, I was awestruck with a sense of both joy and curiosity. To be weightless, floating in a warm bottomless body of water while surrounded by the beauty of the reef life was astonishing and profoundly moving. We headed over the edge and down we swam. Ledges crisscrossed the cliff face and formed perfect environments for other varieties of corals and fish. Mesmerized, we gradually descended deeper and deeper. A tug on my arm caused me to turn quickly and I found Jay trying to grab Jim's attention, too. Jay indicated we needed to surface immediately. To return to the surface was an exercise that had to be performed carefully; if it was done too quickly it could cause 'the bends.' This condition was produced by air bubbles being released into the body during decompression. It could result in paralysis, joint pain, or possibly a rather painful death. Ascending from the depths needed to be slower if the dive was deeper or for a longer duration. I had to keep an eye on the tank's pressure gauge and the time to ensure I had enough air to allow for a necessary slow ascent.

When the entire group had gathered back on the surface, several minutes later, Jay took his regulator out of his mouth and in a concerned tone asked, "Do any of you know how deep we were when I told all of you to surface?"

As soon as he asked the question, I realized I hadn't taken any notice of my depth gauge as I had been so drawn in by the sights. Several people made various attempts at guessing.

Jay responded, "None of you are close. We were at 75 feet when I stopped us. I sensed nobody else had checked their depth gauges. I would suggest we stay at 60 feet or above so that we conserve air and can remain on the dive for a longer period. There's plenty to see on the top section of the wall."

We all agreed before we returned to the blue world that lay just below the surface. Keeping focus on our depth needed to be a priority. As we descended to deeper depths, pressure increased within our bodies, which resulted in a drop in cognitive functioning. What may have been a simple rational decision on the surface could become a challenging conundrum if we dove to 100 feet and spent more than a few minutes at that depth. I had heard stories of divers in such circumstances who reported having trouble working out which way to swim to reach the surface, even though the sky was the brightest feature in the environment and divers' air bubbles always floated upwards to the surface.

I was fascinated with the incredible variation of colors, shapes, and textures found in the beautiful array of coral heads. Their varieties appeared to be endless: delicate fans, dense clumps, long spikey arms, and groupings that looked like fields of mushrooms. In the clear water, the bright sunlight penetrated deeper, allowing the stunning array of earthy coral tones to vie for our attention. Add in the multitude of fish with their iridescent colorful scales, their incredible variety of shapes, their sizes, and their range of activity levels, and it was an unbelievable vista and experience that words failed to describe fully. Photographs could capture the essence of what we saw in their flat two-dimensions—a picture. However, to actually be in that environment, entirely surrounded by it, I was captivated by the experience. It was so surreal that it felt like an additional dimension had been added. We no longer witnessed the experience, we were the experience. I felt such a deep sense of joyful wonderment that, in my mind, the physical world and my perception of it blended with concepts of Mother Nature's power and forces beyond our knowing. I recognized I might never walk in space and feel a real connection to the universe, but to float at ease in that underwater world gave me a glimpse of an endless universe and the powers which created it all.

We were absorbed by everything that could be observed on the cliff face or that swam in the crystal clear waters. After Jay's warning about our depth, we constantly monitored our gauges. The one gauge that dropped too quickly was the one which indicated the amount of air remaining in our tanks. We had been on the dive for only about half an hour when our gauges pointed to the red caution level. It was time to return to the surface. We slowly ascended and joined several other buddy pairs who relaxed in the warmer surface waters using their snorkels.

Gradually, our entire group gathered on the beach in states of wonder. None of us could imagine a better venue for diving. After we cleaned our gear, we relaxed on the beach before arranging who would take the tanks into the city for refilling. While we had been diving, a few other dive groups had arrived and set up camp. We would need to share the pristine waters with more divers. Several of us felt a little disappointed by this change; to swim with so few buddy pairs in such a treasure-trove of underwater beauty allowed an intimacy with our surroundings that heightened the experience. Encountering more divers in the depths could dilute the sensation.

Over the next few days of diving, we gained confidence and, with each dive, our breathing became more relaxed and allowed us to extend the duration of our dives. We explored many areas of both the shallows as well as other sections of the cliff. Nowhere lacked for a point of beauty, interest, or intrigue.

On one dive, Jim and I had moved further along the cliff. We went around a rocky point, about 50 feet down. I looked back into a sheltered quiet alcove in the cliff. Below me, a diver sat on a ledge, while he quietly read a book. I did a double take to make sure I wasn't losing my mind. Indeed, a guy read a book, while he sat on a ledge about 60 feet below the sea's surface. I went over to check it out; it was a book of fish with descriptions of each species. The book was apparently well waterproofed as the pages wafted in the currents. I will admit I could have learned much by reading it; I may have been able to identify a few more of the fish that swam around us.

On another occasion, we had explored a sandy and rocky ledge where anemones were concentrated. We were about to swim further along the ledge when I saw what I had hoped to see. A lion fish swam along the sandy section of the ledge. I pointed it out to Jim so he knew it was close by as they can deliver paralyzing, painful stings. I had seen pictures of these fish previously and had been fascinated by their beautiful appearance and mysterious motion. The fish, which probably measured 12 inches in length, was a golden orange color with light brown vertical stripes. Along its body were about two dozen spiny fans that wafted in the water as the fish swam slowly along. The spines were about six inches long, they pointed straight out from the body, and it was their wafting motion that "hypnotized" other fish, and sometimes humans. At the end of each spine was a tiny barb that caused the stings. Their stings killed fish almost instantly and could cause death for divers in minutes. Aware of their danger, we kept our distance while admiring the beauty of this one's coloring and flowing motion.

On our last dive, Jim and I had decided that once the first of us was out of air, he would return to the surface and keep an eye on the other one, still using the remaining air in his tank. After about 40 minutes, Jim indicated he was out of air and headed up to the surface. When I saw he had switched to his snorkel, I continued along a section of the cliff and headed toward a bluff that jutted out from the main wall. After I'd swum around the bluff, about 40 feet in front of me was the largest fish I had ever seen. I have since learned it probably was a humphead wrasse. It slowly swam straight at me. To encounter such a large fish, about 45 feet under the surface, frightened the heck out of me. Later, while we sat around a driftwood fire on the beach, Jim told everyone about my encounter. Apparently, when I saw the fish, which was possibly twice my weight, I simultaneously appeared to let out a scream that expelled most of the remaining air in my tank and I attempted the impossible task of swimming backwards. I hadn't wanted to turn and swim away from the giant as I sensed a need to keep an eye on it. It ignored me and continued along the cliff, leaving me to quietly ascend to the surface and join my friends as I was almost out of air, after my scream.

I felt a deep sadness as I surfaced on that last dive because I had a suspicion I might never again have the opportunity to experience diving in the warm beautiful waters of the Red Sea. That suspicion has become my reality with the passing of many years. It was an incredible opportunity that left me clear and joyful memories. I was overwhelmed with gratitude for the opportunity to share that amazing world which lay a few feet below the gentle waves that rolled up those sun-drenched beaches.

To witness an ecosystem, which humans can only experience with artificial aids, connected me to an understanding that I, like most people, have a limited knowledge of much of the world in which I live. As a human, I live in an ecosystem that is so close to the oceanic ecosystem, yet they are both so distant from each other. I realized that only by taking the time to observe and comprehend the relationships between such environments can I begin to live in true harmony with the earth. My trying to control environments isn't the answer; I need to learn how humans can make changes without any negative impact any of the earth's ecosystems. I will be appalled in years to come if environments like the oceans are polluted by man's activities, acts of stupidity, and greed, denying my child and her children the wonderous opportunity to enter a world that is so alien to our human existence and yet so close.

After all of the dive gear had been returned to the dive store, we relaxed around the fire and shared stories. We expected the return journey would be a more relaxed drive as, hopefully, we wouldn't meet up with too many Hajjis on the road.

Indeed, the return drive turned out to be relatively sane and carefree. The one episode that caused us concern occurred as we approached Riyadh. The road took a right-hand bend, but it turned out to be much sharper than most drivers anticipated. About ten minutes ahead of me, the driver of a fully loaded gasoline tanker had misread the bend, lost control, and rolled onto his side out in the desert on the far side of the road. Other drivers stopped, more interested in the spectacle than actually helping. They milled around, making a social event of the accident. As I approached, I could see the truck driver stood with a couple of uniformed men who I assumed to be motorcycle police. When I surveyed the scene, I actually accelerated to leave as quickly as I could. The overturned tanker truck lay on its side with rips in the tank that allowed its load to slowly drain out. One group of bystanders were engaged in a serious conversation near the truck and they caught my attention. Several of them had lit cigarettes, despite the growing lake of gasoline. I kept going and didn't wait to find out what happened. I kept a careful eye on the rear view mirror for quite a while and felt relief to see no plumes of black smoke rising from the area.

The return trip took about seven or eight hours to complete with one or two stops. I didn't feel too tired after I had resettled in my efficiency in camp, which was good as I had to return to the office the following day.

It had been a really incredible experience that I may never have entertained on my own, but Jay and Marsha made it happen. Since then, I have dived in other spectacular locations, but the Red Sea still stands out as the most wonderful. Could it have been the thrill of my first time diving in such beauty? Had it been the potential dangers such as lionfish, stonefish, conger eels, rays, or sharks that lurked in those waters? Had I sensed diving in that location to be a unique opportunity because, at the time, the area could only be accessed by westerners who worked in the country? Had our awareness and enjoyment been heightened by the release of anxiety that had been generated by the drive to Mecca with all of the pilgrims? Probably it was a combination of all of those factors that led me to have such powerful feelings. I am grateful to have survived and to carry those memories for the rest of my days.

When I look back on my life, I have found the voice that told me to stop and not do activities came from two places. First, I needed to listen and not ignore my natural inherent sense of self-preservation. A second factor concerned my comfort, in several different regards. Was I worried that I was capable, did I worry I could embarrass myself, was I lost in thoughts about my possible personal discomfort, would I push my personal boundaries and move out of my comfort zone? All of these doubts could be raised whenever I considered taking part in a new or even known, but scary, activity. At a younger age, I sometimes allowed these considerations to negatively influence my decision-making. However, I learned by facing these confining possibilities, I realized I still stood upright, I still breathed, and I may have "egg on my face," but who actually cared? When I took more such risks, I found I could quite easily accept my failures and foibles because I found I could also be successful. I learned to love myself. I'm not perfect, I'm just living life and like everybody else, I will fall down occasionally. I learned the message—get over it. I needed to be authentic and live—not hide. Life could be an amazing and joyous experience, if I allowed it to unfold fully.

When I sat in my efficiency, after the drive back, I considered. *Now, it's time for a new type of adventure. What shall I try?*

CHAPTER 18

UPLIFTING WINDS

الله ه شاء إن   الله ه شاء إن   الله ه شاء ان   الله ه شاء إن   الله ه شاء ان   الله ه شاء إن

After the dive trip to the Red Sea, I decided to buy balloon tires so I could explore more wild desert areas. For this purchase, I headed to Dammam, where I knew the locations of most of the larger tire stores. I checked out several that had good selections and tried to haggle their prices down. I don't remember if these efforts really saved me any money, but I recognized haggling met with the traditional Saudi approach to making any purchase larger than a bag of groceries. Eventually, I found a good set of balloon tires and rims. The price still felt high to me, but I didn't want to have to return on another evening and reluctantly agreed to the salesman's price. The store's mechanics mounted the tires on the rims and we loaded my new balloon tires and rims into the back of the Blazer.

The following day, I took everything to the small garage we had in camp to have one of their mechanics check that the tires were correctly mounted on the new rims. They then exchanged them for the truck-grade wheels and tires that had been on the Blazer since it left New York. I had a little more confidence in these mechanics' technical abilities than the store's mechanics. Thankfully, I never had reason to doubt the camp mechanics.

With the new tires, the Blazer stood a few inches higher than it had previously, and it took a few days before I became accustomed to it. The Blazer looked ready and I felt set to start exploring the wilds of the desert. I wanted to find an easy outing to test my state of readiness. I knew on the opposite side of the bay from where

Aramco had their beaches, expanses of sabkha—salt flats—as well as smaller sand dunes extended far to the south. It would be a great place to experiment with driving off-road and off the packed trails. I invited Ron and a colleague of his, Steph, to join me for this outing.

The next weekend, I took time to look through the packing boxes I hadn't emptied since I moved into my house. As hoped, I found two kites in the boxes and decided to take them with us.

After lunch, I picked up Ron and Steph from the bus terminal near the offices. I headed down the road toward the beaches. On that 15 mile stretch of open sabkha, only two features broke the monotony. A single track railway line crossed the road. It ran alongside a thin snaking line of palm trees that wound their way to an old, dry oasis. As soon as I crossed the railway line, I turned right onto a packed-sand trail. Perspiration broke out on the palms of both hands as the reality of heading off road for the first time hit me. We continued around the end of the bay before I left the trail to head in a southerly direction.

I turned to Ron and Steph with a beaming smile, "Oh wow! I'm actually driving out in the desert! This is such a blast. The entire area is so flat and open. Where shall I go next? I could get high doing this. Who needs to drink Sid?"

Ron glanced over at me and said. "Barry. Stay sitting in your seat. You're driving. I don't want to have to walk all the way back to camp."

Trying to contain my enthusiasm, I looked around and thought I saw what appeared to be concrete beams out in the middle of open sabkha. "Hey, what d'you think that could be?"

Steph looked up from his camera, in which he had loaded a new roll of film, "What? Where?"

Ron pointed to the beams. "Over there. D'you think anyone lived out here at some time?"

I made a bee-line to the structure, "Beats me. Let's take a shufte." Shufte was a London slang word for 'look' that coincidentally derived from the Arabic word for 'to look.' This slang word derived from when New Zealand and British troops occupied Egypt in World War I.

As I wanted to check out the remains of the building, I stopped nearby, so we could wander around the concrete columns which jutted out of the sand that drifted up against what was left of the walls. To determine what the structure had been originally looked impossible. After just a brief stop, we continued on our way, and I drove east toward the coast. I wondered out loud to the others if we might be able to see Bahrain.

I leaned back into my seat as I felt more confident of both myself and the Blazer with its new tires. After I had crossed several miles of open packed sand, I found my way to the coast and quickly realized I'd steered too far to the south to see Bahrain. However, I realized I had ended up a mile or two away from a Saudi Coast Guard Station. I believe back then, only a couple of them had been built around the entire country.

Ron, Steph, and I surveyed the sand and rivers of running water that lay between us and the station to see if we could determine an easy path across the area.

I frowned as I searched for a path. "I don't see an easy way across to it. I suspect that is an estuary flowing between the station and us. It may be shallow but it looks pretty wide. I can't tell if the water in the estuary is due to the tides in the Gulf or if it came from water originating in a local spring."

Ron grunted agreement and with shoulders slumped, he said, "Damn, it would have been interesting to forge a route across."

Steph looked more resigned and added, "I think you should avoid it. Any water out here, in the desert, would be highly saline and tough on your Blazer's new bodywork."

I drove back inland to a point where my route meandered between two low rocky ridges. I saw loose sand being blown off the ridge tops and suggested we try flying the kites. Both Ron and Steph agreed enthusiastically as we could feel the wind being funneled through the gap where I'd stopped. We pulled the kites out of their packaging and soon assembled their aluminum frames before we attached the nylon sails. Each kite had two lines, which would give us more control over their five-foot wingspans. The kites flapped, almost anxiously, in the wind that whipped around the Blazer. We released them and immediately realized we needed to be standing solidly on a good footing because the strong wind grabbed their pliable wings and drove them powerfully skyward. I wouldn't say we learned the art of kite flying in the hour that followed. Those kites couldn't have been better or more forgiving teachers. They forced us to understand the potential exhilaration of handling their double lines to control them, and they repeatedly bounced back when we mistimed maneuvers that sent them plunging into the sand. All three of us enjoyed the thrills of working with the surprising forces that the kites withstood and we needed to control as we flew them in twists and turns. They soared and dove. Ron passed one of the kites over to me and as soon as I had it under control, one of the two lines broke, which caused the kite to take a rather ugly spiraling dive. It hit the ground at a fast speed, breaking and bending several of the frame's spars. Ron and I gathered up the lines and pieces and tossed them back into the Blazer. For a while, we watched Steph as he experimented with a few new kite handling techniques. His delight disappeared in an instant when he accidentally lost his grip on the two spools of line. We made a dash to grab the spools, but they hurtled away from us, dragged by the free-flying kite. We could only stand and watch the kite disappear over a nearby ridge.

We stood like three kids who had unfortunately kicked their ball over a hedge and had nothing else to play with.

Steph twisted his feet deeper into the sand, "Well, crap, that's the end of some really fine fun. Barry, I probably owe you a kite."

Smiling, I looked up at the ridge top and said, "Well, no, but I think you'll have paid your penalty by the time you've walked back to camp. Come on, Ron, we should be leaving."

Ron's face lit up, "Actually, I think he deserves worse. No Sid for him for the next month, after he walks back to camp."

"Agreed," I replied as I meandered back to the Blazer.

We continued to hound Steph as we slowly made our way back to the side of the bay and the rail line, where we relaxed for a short period. My first venture out into the real desert had been a success. We may have experienced two casualties, the kites, but we had fun. To fly them in such wild conditions had brought me back to a lesson I learned in Syria. Life made no guarantees; I could only live in the here and now. That meant I needed to always live my life fully because I never knew what tomorrow, or even the next minute, might bring.

Potentially losing two kites was a small price to pay for an entertaining afternoon with friends, but if a choice of action could possibly have cost me my life, then I would have been highly unlikely to make that choice. The vast majority of decisions I made in life lay between those two extremes. Many factors influenced how I viewed decisions—none were definitely right and none definitely wrong. Circumstances, timing, and other factors swayed each of my decisions, even ones that were repeated.

I rounded the end of the bay before I rejoined the trail that ran parallel to the rail tracks. A short while later, the three of us relaxed with a drink back in my efficiency.

Ron asked, "So how's driving on balloon tires? You knew the original truck tires pretty well."

I took a sip of my drink while I thought, and then replied, "There're a few subtle differences. On the road, the tire noise was less than before, and when I made turns, I didn't sense the same immediate responsiveness. However, out on the dirt, I felt like my tires almost floated at times. I didn't sense the tires digging into the sand at any time which felt really good."

Steph beamed broadly, "Well, that sounds like we may have to go out and do it all again. Do you both agree? Do either of you know anybody willing to donate a kite or two for our entertainment?"

We all smiled and decided another expedition should be penciled on the calendar. I wasn't surprised that both Ron and Steph expressed interest in reaching the Coast Guard Station, which we had seen, if we ventured in that direction on a later trip. At the time, the station was the only one on the entire eastern coast line.

This Saudi Coast Guard Station featured prominently in an incident that occurred about a year after our afternoon's expedition. When I heard the story of that incident, it provided a perfect example of the unbelievable happenings that often transpired in Saudi Arabia. Let me digress and relate the story.

Our Laser fleet had arranged a large regatta with sailors from other local companies, over one weekend. When we had gathered at the beach, everyone agreed to race, despite the fact that winds blew above the normal top limit of 15 knots. On the second leg of the first race, I foolishly tried a jibe—a maneuver only competent sailors should attempt in high winds. I wouldn't say my capsizing craft tossed me gently into the sea. Rather it slammed me down into the water hard which proved my decision to always wear my life jacket was an excellent one. As I floated in the water and recuperated next to my Laser, I realized several lines had become untied in the upheaval and my center board had come loose. I couldn't fix these problems while I bounced around on the churning waves. So I clambered up onto my upturned hull to wait to be rescued. Sadly, quite a number of other boats ended up in similar states, challenging the rescue boat to keep up with the need. As I drifted further toward the narrow bay entrance that led to the open sea, I caught up with my buddy, Hughie, who also sat on his hull and needed help. Without any concern about the temperature dropping, we happily basked on our sailboats' upturned hulls. Later, our complacency disappeared when we realized our masts, which pointed straight down into the depths, began to bounce along a shallower coral reef that lay across the entrance to the bay.

"Shit," Hughie uttered.

Surprised, I called over to him, "What's up?"

His voice had a concerned edge, as he explained, "My mast just bounced on the reef, which means we're getting into shallower water. I hope the top of the mast doesn't get stuck in a crack because that would make it difficult to stay secure on the overturned hull."

I didn't like that prospect either. "That doesn't sound good. I reckon we may be some of the last boats to be rescued as we're so far down the bay."

A short time later, we were heartened to see the rescue boat head in our direction. They helped to right both of our boats and then towed us back to the boat beach and safety.

When all of the racing fleet had been successfully returned to shore, the rescue boat crew breathed a sigh of relief and retired for the day. Unfortunately, in their work to rescue the regatta fleet, they forgot the non-racing sailors who had gone out for the sheer hell of it. One of them had also been capsized, disabling his boat and he floated further down the bay. He was washed out of our protected bay and into the open expanse of the Persian Gulf. Hours later, the tides carried him ashore a number of miles to the south. Fortunately, he struggled onto dry land within a short distance of the Coast Guard Station. He didn't realize the building's function, but relieved and happy to see the only building on the barren coastline, he walked into the station to ask for help.

By that time, the sun headed toward the horizon; he had been lost at sea for over 6 hours. Meanwhile, a number of his friends, wondering where he was, had raised the alarm in camp.

The Coast Guard told the sailor the station had been open for just over a year and in all of that time, they had never rescued a single soul. He would be chalked up as their first. Despite his protests that he had walked into the station, they joyfully wrote his name on the first line of their log book. When he realized the time, he was concerned that he had been lost for all those hours. He asked them to arrange transportation back to camp or at least try to get word to camp that he had reached their station. Sadly, both requests failed because the radio operator had been sent home sick. They ignored the sailor's concerns about the time and the station commander sent three of his crew to an out building to slaughter a fat goat. He wanted a celebration feast, that evening, after their first-ever rescue. They treated him as an honored guest. Only after a sumptuous feast did they agree to drive him and his boat back to Dhahran. He returned to camp a short time before midnight. The Aramco head of Security gratefully filed away his plans for a search mission at first light.

I have always wondered if that guy ever went sailing again. But, I'm more intrigued to know if he ever told his grandchildren that his name became the first entry in the Coast Guard station's rescue log book.

In most activities, I felt like I had at least one toe still firmly planted in what I called my *comfort zone*. However, one activity pushed both of my feet outside the circle that enclosed my safe zone. It again concerned my Laser sailing boat I had brought back from England.

Primarily during the spring, the eastern side of Arabia was subjected to strong winds and sand storms. They occurred several times each year and could last a day or two. Winds could blow at over 40 miles an hour, stirring up a great deal of dust and sand. Occasional stronger gusts carried sand particles that flew horizontally for long distances and sandblasted everything that was exposed. Most people considered those days to be ideal to hide indoors, but when the sand wasn't flying too badly, a gang of us would head to the beach and rig our Lasers for an outing. To sail a single-handed sail boat solo in 40 mph winds was almost impossible; however, with the weight of two of us, we could sail one of these boats with one person to fight the rudder while the other struggled with the lines and sail. We had to be coordinated if we needed to change positions with space in the craft being really tight.

In those high-wind conditions, the general direction of the wind was from over a nearby sand dune, which gave us a chance to leave the beach and be settled before the full force of the wind bore down on us. Soon we screamed through seas with waves that ran from 4 to 6 feet high. It was like being on a good rollercoaster, except water isn't as consistent as the steel rails of a rollercoaster. We would scream up a wave until we flew over the crest and plunge down the far side. At the bottom of each wave, either the bow bounced up to carry on up the following one, or it buried itself deep underwater in the base of the wave. If the bow went under, then the boat's speed was killed instantly, and the two of us were sent sliding forward down the deck as we clung to the rudder or lines for stability. We didn't have to worry about being thrown forward for more than a moment because the buoyant bow would emerge from underwater, sending a tidal wave of water down the length of the craft. This wall of water was far more likely to wash us off the stern of the boat. To say sailing in such conditions was an adrenaline rush would be an understatement. For much of our time on the raging waters, we had no choice but to let out the most primordial of screams—they were the only emotional response that suited the wild exhilaration. Each time we went out, we rode the waves in the bay for about five minutes, then turned around and flew back. After every brief but adrenaline-charged outing, we needed a few minutes to recover our strength and our courage.

After each of these sessions, I would drive back to camp, encrusted in dried salt, and think about the outings, *Wow, what an experience! I cannot count how many times I was petrified. That was wild!* Part of me wondered if we would soon have similar weather conditions in which we could have another outing like the one I had just survived. And I'll admit another part of me hoped we had seen the last of those windstorms for the season.

CHAPTER 19
SPELUNKING IN THE DESERT

الله شاء ان   الله شاء ان   الله شاء ان   الله شاء ان   الله شاء ان   الله شاء ان   الله شاء ان

After a few more ventures in the desert, I felt ready for a more challenging outing. I mentioned this to my friends, Walt and Sandra, who I knew had taken many overnight trips out in the wilds. I asked them, "Hey. I've been taking a few drives out in the desert and want to go further out. I should probably team up with somebody who has experience. Would you two be available for a weekend outing sometime?"

Walt immediately replied, "Oh, yes. We know a great place for an amazing quick trip. Sandra, do you think we should take him up to the collapsed cavern that's out northwest of Jubail?"

Sandra thought for a moment. "What a great idea. We haven't been up to that region for ages. We should warn you, Barry, this trip does require rappelling and climbing, if you are up for it. We should think about who we could invite along as a fourth."

I hadn't been rappelling or climbing for a number of years, since my serious climbing accident. In the excitement of this new adventure, I completely discarded any thoughts about the agonizing years of recovery. I knew neither Sandra nor Walt had been hard-core climbers, so I didn't expect anything too difficult.

After a short discussion, we invited a mutual friend, Brendan, to be our fourth member. Between all of us, we found we had all the camping equipment we needed and Walt had the climbing rope and gear that we would need for the rappelling. We set a date, a few weeks ahead.

Early on a Thursday morning, we gathered at their house and double-checked we had packed all necessities. I followed Walt out of the camp gates and we turned left onto the road that led toward Dammam. Our route carried us further north, parallel to the coast that lay several miles to our right.

After about an hour and a half, Walt pulled into a gas station and as I pulled up next to a second pump, I said to Brendan, "Well, I assume life will soon start to be interesting. If we are filling up with gas here, then I expect we will head off-road soon."

Brendan looked across the road. "We are out in the middle of nowhere, surrounded by plains of sabkha. This certainly looks like the area that Walt had described."

"True. We've been driving through this type of terrain for the last hour." I wound the window down as a garage worker headed over to fill my tank. I called out, "Salaam," to him as he headed directly to the fill cap; he knew the routine. I turned back to Brendan and said, "I'll ask Walt how far we have before we leave the road."

I crossed the dirt to Walt's Toyota. "So, how much further before we hit the sabkha?"

Walt and Sandra looked up from a map that they studied. Sandra looked across at me and teased, "You ready to get those new tires dirty, are you?"

I smiled, "They're dusty and I'm ready to get them dirty now. So how much further on this dusty road?"

Walt looked up from a compass he held. "About another five miles and then we take off to the left. We need to follow a compass bearing when we leave the road."

"I will follow your lead." I said before I returned to the Blazer to pay for the gas and ensure the cap was on tight.

After a short time, Walt turned on his left signal and crossed over onto the packed sand. We continued in as straight a line as we could; in places, drifting sand, rocks, occasional shrubs and stunted trees caused us to take little deviations from our course. For much of this driving out in the wild, we could drive at about 40 to 50 mph, provided we kept a keen eye out for larger obstacles. However, I quickly realized I couldn't follow Walt as the dust kicked up by his tires blinded me. I pulled abreast of them, with a 30-yard gap between us.

We progressed out into a gray sea of rocks and hard-packed salt flats. Once in a while, the dusty green of hardy shrubs and trees broke the vista. I had settled into driving out in the environment and felt quite at ease, even though we were headed into a huge expanse of nothingness. I noticed Sandra wave at me, indicating I should stop. I pulled up alongside them and wound down my window. Thankfully, we had been blessed with a cloudy morning that felt cool and delightful. I made the quick decision to leave my window down to enjoy the pleasant temperature, which would soon be lost when the cloud burned off.

Walt peered around Sandra with a detail that surprised me, "Barry, I suggest we drive much slower until we reach our destination. You will find a drop-off and you don't want to accidentally go over it!"

"A drop-off? How much of a drop-off? Like a cliff—drop-off?" I responded.

We continued in the same direction, at about half the speed. As the minutes ticked by, Brendan and I felt the level of tension rising as we didn't know what we expected to find, except a drop. The landscape appeared to remain the same patchwork of sand, salt flats, and rocks. I scanned the area ahead of us and could see no breaks in the desert's surface. As we headed up a slight incline, Walt honked and slowed down to a crawl. I followed suit as we slowly inched forward. We both stopped when Walt saw indications of the drop-off. I couldn't see a dip or a slope. It looked like the desert suddenly stopped—it no longer existed.

Rather taken aback by what I could see or rather by what I couldn't see, I said to Brendan, "Well, I guess this must be our destination."

A look of concern crossed his face as he replied, "That looks a bit scary. Let's take a closer look. Suddenly, I'm not so sure about this outing."

We both got out of the Blazer and walked to where Walt and Sandra stood. When I stopped still, a quaking sensation rippled through my core. I viewed the incredible sight with awe while noticing a clammy sweat had broken out in the palms of my hands. My legs shook slightly as I stood overlooking what appeared to be a hole in the surface of the desert. It measured roughly 100 yards across and about 70 to 80 feet deep. The sides of the hole rose almost vertically, and they comprised loose, crumbling layers of sandstone, shale, sand, and strata of a darker rock. The bottom of the hole had the same appearance as the desert we had just crossed, with piles of rock debris in areas.

Brendan and I still stared in disbelief at the vista, when Walt offered an explanation, "According to geologists who I have questioned about this hole, they said most likely a huge cavern system had been cut by flood waters over the centuries. When more floods undermined the rock columns that held up the roof of the cavern, it was only a matter of time before the entire roof collapsed. It must've been extremely spectacular the day it went down."

I heard Brendan swallow hard and I could only manage a grunt of acknowledgement. My mind questioned the sensibility of rappelling into a pit, down a fragile vertical wall of loose rock, which looked rather unstable and uninviting. I could see one undeniable simple fact and I couldn't begin to fathom it out—the hole's perimeter looked round. If this natural hole had been created by a cavern's roof collapsing, why had the resulting chasm been reasonably round? I always thought Mother Nature preferred more randomness—and I didn't think round shapes qualified as being random.

Needless to say, it took me about two seconds to overlook my doubts and we set about parking the two vehicles parallel to the edge of the hole in preparation to drop over it. Walt told me to never park facing the hole, in case the park brake failed. We anchored the climbing ropes to the front axle of Walt's Toyota and threw the remaining lengths over the cliff. Brendan and I walked around the edge until we could see that the ends of the ropes had reached the bottom.

Walt attached himself to the end of the safety line, which I held so I could feed line to him as he descended. I had anchored myself to the Toyota so I couldn't be pulled over the edge. Walt dropped over the edge while I let out controlled amounts of the safety line. He descended smoothly down into the chasm and soon called up that he had reached the bottom. We switched the ropes around so that Walt could control the safety rope. Sandra descended next, followed by Brendan, and I took last place. Once I maneuvered over the edge and started to descend the loose face, I felt happy and quite enjoyed the rappel by the time I joined the others at the bottom of the pit.

We tied the ropes to a large boulder so scavengers would not be able to steal them. As we did this, I noticed a cave entrance in the base of the perimeter wall on the opposite side. I confirmed we would head to the cave with Sandra who indicated it would be amazing, but without any details.

We worked our way to the cave that stood almost as high as I was, which made my skull quite prone to frequent encounters with the roof. Thankfully, the cave's width exceeded its height, significantly, which allowed plenty of light to penetrate into the depths. Flashlights only became necessary, when the cave narrowed to about ten feet and we had turned a couple of corners.

Walt suddenly stopped. "I knew something didn't feel right about this place. Sandra, do you know what's missing?"

She gave a couple of seconds thought and cried out, "Bat Guana! There's hardly any bat shit smell. For goodness sake, where are the god-damned bats?"

"Absolutely! The other times we've been in here, millions of bats have hung from the cave roof. And, today, I don't see a single one. How totally weird!" he exclaimed.

We stood for a few minutes while we proposed multiple theories as to why the bat population would depart their cave. We didn't have a plausible answer that we could all agree on.

Walt looked at Brendan and me, "Are you two ready for the fright of your lives?" He turned and winked at Sandra.

Brendan hesitated a little before saying, "OK. Give us your worst shot."

We walked deeper into the cave until we stood in a small chamber with a domed roof. I could see no continuing passageway—we had reached the back of the cavern. Walt purposefully looked down at the mud floor, causing us all to do likewise. He brought his flashlight up towards both Brendan's and my head before he stamped hard on the mud floor.

We stood silently for about ten seconds, still staring at the floor, and then we heard a distant thud. After a few more seconds a fainter thud followed. Both had reverberated from far below us.

Quickly, Brendan and I realized we stood on a layer of mud, and probably rock, that jammed a hole in the roof of another huge chasm. I uttered, "Oh, geez," as my head shot up to take in the looks on the others' faces.

Brendan's eyes were open wide. They scared me almost as much as the chilling realization of where we stood. "Wooo," was all Brendan managed to say. We all exchanged fast nervous looks as our minds wrestled with this rather frightening reality. The mud layer was apparently thick enough to hold the weight of four people, but thin enough for Walt's foot stamp to send sound waves reverberating down into a huge chasm underneath and bounce back to us, seconds later. We stood there taking this all in. Instead of retreating to a more solid area of the cave, we stayed there, trying additional foot stamps. They also became faint echoing thuds after the same delays. We realized we probably stood at the top of a vertical passageway, blocked by rocks and a layer of silt. The bottom of the passageway probably opened up into a huge cavern, far below us. The hair on my neck stood stiff and a cold shiver crawled across the skin on my arms.

I will admit I felt a whole lot happier and safer once we had retreated from the open mud layer. We slowly made our way to the entrance and daylight which brought with it the sun's heat. We didn't delay; we made a direct path to the ropes.

Walt untangled a couple of the ropes as he organized our ascent. "I will go up first so I can take the safety line from the top. Barry, can you secure yourself and take the safety line for me?"

"Sure. I will come up last after Sandra and Brendan. Okay?"

We all nodded our approval as we prepared for Walt to climb the rope. He would use jumar clips which allowed us to climb a fixed rope in a similar style to climbing a ladder. He demonstrated how to use them to Brendan who hadn't used them for a number of years.

As Walt had a strong and wiry frame, he ascended the 80 feet to the Toyota in a matter of a couple of minutes. He lowered the jumars and the safety line down for Sandra who ascended without any problems. Brendan took a little time and coaching before he understood how to use the jumars to climb the rope. His jubilant cries indicated his sense of relief as he finally crawled back over the edge. It took me a couple of mistaken movements before I recalled the best technique and then I ascended the fixed rope without any problems.

We stopped for a while to enjoy a little water and food. It had been a tiring but exhilarating couple of hours. We drove a short distance so we could relax in the lee of a small band of rock. It didn't take too long to set up the essentials for our overnight camp. We sat around and talked about caving in Arabia, as it had been Brendan's and my first taste. I doubt I would have really grasped how it had felt, if I had only been told about the experience. When we stood on the open mud layer at the back of the cave and the "*oh shit*" feeling of fear clamped a grip on my stomach, I knew then this experience could never simply become a standard memory. This one had been seared into my memory under the category of "frightening", never to be forgotten.

Sleep came easily that night after the physical and psychological exertions. We all awoke bright and ready for a new adventure as the sun began to climb into the clear blue sky. Cooler weather didn't look to be in our prospects for that morning. After a quick breakfast and hot coffee which we had brought in thermoses, we again drove further away from the road. The open sabkha started to bake, even though it was still well before noon. A few shriveled trees and boulders caused us to change course slightly while we tried to keep on a straight path. Walt drove across the open desert based on a compass bearing as features were few and far between. He and Sandra searched for a couple of rock slabs that barely protruded above the surface layer of sand.

After an hour or so, Walt and Sandra said we had reached the right region, but our target wouldn't be as large as the previous day's. We took an hour or more to explore the area before they happily leapt from their vehicle to announce that we had arrived. Indeed, we saw no hole. It was nothing more than a fissure in a slab of rock that formed part of the desert floor. Without much delay, we had all of the rappelling and climbing gear set up. We anchored the ropes to the Toyota and dropped the rest of the rappelling rope into the fissure.

Walt attached himself to the rappel and safety lines before he slid into the fissure. He inched his way down an angled section of rock and disappeared. A few moments later, he let out an excited, "Alright!!"

After a couple of minutes, the lines became slack and we heard Walt call up to indicate Sandra could come down to join him. She attached herself to the rappel rope and slid into the crack. She soon let out a squeal of delight as she dropped slowly down to meet Walt. Brendan found the descent unbelievable and we had to encourage him to continue as he wanted to stop frequently to inspect all of the fascinating features he passed. I hadn't prepared myself for what I saw once I disappeared down the angled rock. The rappel line fell free from the apex of the cone-shaped cave. As I descended, I simply spun around as I looked at different aspects of the cave's walls. I hadn't expected the water and the dampness on all the rock, which caused large areas to be covered in green moss, algae, and lichen. The variety of greens looked beautiful and rich, but they also felt cold and eerie in the light of our flashlights.

We found no side passageways or other caverns to explore, so we clambered over the rocks and boulders that covered the floor of the chamber to look for the source of water, some of it pooled in the lower areas. It didn't take long to complete our tour, but we couldn't find where the water came from. The variations of greens that were highlighted by our light beams intrigued us, beautiful and compelling. But after a short time, the dampness felt heavy and depressing. We decided it had been a good contrast to the previous day's outing, and we needed to head home.

Walt ascended the rope with the jumars. As it hung free, it made the effort to ascend much greater than when we had a cliff wall alongside of us. The height of this climb looked to be probably one and a half times the previous day's climb, and it took Walt over twice as long. Both Sandra and Brendan took some words of encouragement and coaching to make it to the top. As for myself, I had to take quite a number of rest breaks over the course of the climb, which concerned Walt for a while. Eventually I poked my head out of the fissure and felt more than delighted to sense the sun's intensity burning me once again.

We relaxed for about half an hour before we packed up the two cars. I told Walt and Sandra I would always be grateful to them for taking Brendan and I out on this amazing adventure. Spelunking in the desert could never be considered the safest of activities, but the simple act of driving to Al Khobar would never make a list of safe activities either. If I hadn't been caving a number of times in Britain, before I moved to Saudi, I may have had second thoughts about this outing. I understood the basics and I recognized a few of the risks. Absolutely nothing in life is free from risk, even hiding your head under the warm blankets of your bed isn't guaranteed to be safe. I saw caving in the desert simply as an activity I considered to be risky, it was on the border of my comfort zone or, possibly, a little outside it.

To be honest, it is having survived various times when I thought, *Oh Crap! I maybe shouldn't have done that*, that have given me the resiliency, the faith in myself, and the guts to face the demanding challenges of my later years. To run from life would have never prepared me for the future or for getting older.

CHAPTER 20
WHAT NEXT?

الله شاء إن   الله شاء إن   الله شاء إن   الله شاء إن   الله شاء إن   الله شاء إن   الله شاء إن

ollowing the spelunking trip, Walt, Sandra, Brendan and I socialized frequently, playing bridge and discussing other potential wilderness adventures. We worked well together and enjoyed each other's company. So we started to think about a more significant outing. After considering and rejecting various ideas, we decided to tackle the most obvious challenge—the Empty Quarter—the Rub' al Khali. It covered the majority of the southern half of the Arabian Peninsula—nothing but baking sand dunes and huge expanses of sabkha extended for thousands of square miles. Bedouin and trading caravans had traversed the region using their 'ships of the desert,' camels, for millennia. Geographers say that the Empty Quarter is the largest contiguous hot sand desert in the world, measuring over 250 thousand square miles.

Why would I choose to take a trip out into one of the hottest and largest desert regions in the world? And, more significantly, why would I travel into that wilderness for multiple days? Such questions are valid and they have caused me to think hard about why I followed that course of action. The most obvious concern would be my basic state of sanity but, despite my occasional rash decisions, my sanity has never been in doubt. Did I have a suicidal tendency? Absolutely not. So what drove this desire to head out into potentially hazardous surroundings for more than a quick cursory visit? To answer this question, I need to look back at my adolescent years.

As a youth and a young adult, I enjoyed both mountainous regions and open expanses of ocean. Those environments gave me the freedom and, in some ways, an invitation to think about the world, why it existed as it did, and why I personally was a part of it. In this quest for understanding, I'd mulled over the concepts of open expanses and infinity. I saw and understood my surroundings as numbers and patterns. I truly was and loved being a numbers guy. Openness was a form of natural environment in which I felt satisfaction, but an intrigue with how and why it existed—a spiritual quest. The Epilogue—Part I has a more in-depth discussion of my decision to venture into the Empty Quarter.

While driving down the Pipeline Road, when Penny, Ron, and I returned to Dhahran, I reconnected with the whole notion of vastness and endlessness. I again sensed an awareness of human frailty and vulnerability. I don't recall being spiritually moved for most of that time. However, while we sat on the dune in the early morning sunshine, before the Bedouin came buzzing like a mosquito and pumped air into my tire, I had sensed brief moments of spiritual peace. We had been sitting quietly and I could simply meditate on the vast expanse of sandy dunes and ridges. After the stress of the drive, spending a few minutes at peace was uplifting and it has stayed in my memories, as clear as when it actually happened.

Thinking about spending several days in the Empty Quarter, I discovered I wanted to reconnect more deeply with a sense of inner peace in that empty environment. While I acknowledged obvious dangers existed in the idea, I felt drawn to the opportunity to experience vastness and repetition in a way few other places on earth could provide. In many ways, the loneliness of our small party, our obvious human frailty, and our removal from day to day comforts would allow me exposure to the spiritual without too many distractions or assumed levels of safety. It would be raw living.

CHAPTER 21
THE EMPTY QUARTER

الله شاء إن   الله شاء إن   الله شاء إن   الله شاء إن   الله شاء إن   الله شاء ان   الله شاء ان

Walt and I discussed how to best prepare our vehicles for the trip. We decided that we would head out for a five day adventure. Walt's Toyota was equipped with jerry can carriers that allowed him to carry additional fuel equal to the amount he could pump into his standard tank. It gave him a range that would suffice for the five days we planned to be off-road. My new Blazer presented us with a significant problem in this regard. My tank gave me a range of about 300 miles at most. I had no means of attaching jerry can carriers. Luckily, Walt was an engineer and said if we removed the rear seat in the Blazer then he could install a second "gas tank" in that space. I agreed to his proposal, but I only found out the real details later when we came to do the work.

I bought a brand new 55-gallon drum and one weekend we replaced my back seat with the drum. It lay on its side on a makeshift cradle, and we locked it down with steel cables and tensioners. It certainly didn't move, but I wondered how it would fare when it had a large volume of gasoline washing around in it with the accompanying shifting of weight.

We bought enough canned and packet food to last us for the full five days. Even though much of it didn't need heating, we had a couple of stoves for when we wanted to warm water or food. Walt and Sandra had enough desert camping gear for all of us. The four cots that kept us off the sand while sleeping would soon become our most prized item of equipment. We completed all of our preparation a few days ahead of our anticipated departure date; we had arranged to take a week-long vacation.

Our journey started by heading toward Riyadh, the capital of Saudi Arabia, which lay in the center of the country, but closer to the east coast where we lived. We drove through it without any issues. Our course then turned to the south. We continued until the road had lost its asphalt surface and a number of villages had no gas for their gas stations. Fortunately, Walt had determined the last village where we could make the purchase of large quantities of gasoline. We continued on to that village and pulled into the gas station. Walt filled his tank and jerry cans while I filled the Blazer's tank and then proceeded to fill the majority of the 55-gallon drum. I felt happier when I had the drum's cap firmly screwed back in place. As we paid, the garage owner tried to question us as to where we planned to go with such large amounts of gas. Walt had anticipated such an encounter and answered saying we had Aramco business down at a drill site. We hoped the garage owner wouldn't report our large purchases to local police. Sandra and Walt had previously been followed by the police and interrogated after they bought a large quantity of fuel in this same region. It wasn't that buying large quantities of gas was illegal, but it caused the police to wonder what these ex-pats intended doing—the police didn't trust infidels.

We drove a few more miles down the road as Brendan and I regularly sniffed until we agreed that we couldn't smell gas leaking from the drum. However, a sense of tension hung over our vehicle until Brendan and I became a little more comfortable knowing we had about 80 gallons of gasoline onboard. After a few more miles, Walt saw a strip of open sand that ran through a group of squat shrubs and headed toward a couple of palm trees. He departed the road and drove out into the wild as I followed close behind. We had started our big adventure. I was driving on desert sand and I wouldn't see a black top road for another five days.

We soon lost sight of roads, trails, villages, and other signs of civilization. After only a few miles, the wilds surrounded us. I felt a different sense of awareness that skewed how I saw my circumstances. I came face-to-face with the fact we ventured alone out into an immense expanse of wilderness. I wouldn't describe the feeling as being uncomfortable, but suddenly, the normal priorities that drove my daily life became irrelevant. I had, for years, sought adventure and many times I had found it. But this felt different. The adventure and I were one—only adventure existed. Where would I dare go, what would I chose to do, when would I pull back into a safe space, who would I be at the end? I knew of only one way to answer all those questions; it lay further out there, possibly beyond the ever-receding horizon.

If we had driven straight out, it would have been several hundred miles before we encountered any humans who lived or worked in a permanent location. I felt humbled and amazed by my reaction to the vastness of our surroundings and the power the desert held over me. A sense of fear, mixed with exhilaration, coursed through my veins. I glanced at Brendan who also appeared to be lost in a rapturous daze.

I broke his trance saying, "Can you believe we are about to drive off into one of the largest expanses of hot desert in the world, without any real plan, other than to return to civilization in five days?"

Brendan took a few seconds to pull himself back from his musings. "I know what you mean. To leave the road and take in all of the wilderness that lies ahead of us is such a profound experience. I'm already having a blast and I cannot thank you enough for including me as your vehicle buddy."

I smiled, "Let's get through the trip before you thank me. We have no idea of what may lie ahead of us."

Brendan wiped sweat off his brow before it ran down into his glasses, "Okay. We may not know much of what lies ahead, and one simple truth is my next shower lies six days ahead. I hope you brought deodorant."

"Sure. Along with my smoking jacket and slippers."

We both smiled and fell silent while we thought of all the items we probably had forgotten to pack.

We navigated through drifting sand and rocky outcrops. The horizon tormented us as the desert continued in an unbroken expanse of sameness that made the horizon feel like an unattainable goal. We drove across the sand-swept salt flats that shimmered in the afternoon heat. If we left the comforts of the Blazer's air-conditioning, the heat didn't feel like a normal daily type of sensation, it manifested like a physical barrier that stopped us immediately.

Walt saw a short line of old telegraph poles out to our left. We skirted around a small rocky ridge to reach the poles. To our surprise, the remains of a structure lay close to a distant pole. We headed to the remains. As we reached them, we found they were tinged with the blackness that cakes concrete after a fire. Within the outer walls, we discovered machinery and valves which had been ripped apart and torn off their foundations.

Walt surveyed the scene before he speculated, "I think this was an old GOSP that must have been destroyed in an explosion. It's difficult to tell how old it may be. Older GOSP's had serious problems and quite a number did blow up." GOSP stood for Gas Oil Separation Plant. Many had been built across areas of the desert where wells were producing oil.

I realized I had never before been around the remains where an explosion had taken place. The mangled pieces of metal and the fractured concrete columns spoke volumes to the force of the explosion. I felt humbled by the story of fiery destruction that the rubble told as I meandered through the wreckage. I found a section of a six-inch cog wheel and thought it would make an interesting memento from the trip. I kicked sand from a couple of nearby areas where it looked like other machinery fragments lay, partially buried. I explored the debris I had turned up and I found two more pieces from the same cog. I put them together to form one completely perfect cog wheel. I stowed the cog fragments in the back of the Blazer before we departed for further wide open spaces.

As the sun dropped toward a blazing red sunset, we found a quiet area that lay in the lee of a ridge. We quickly set up camp alongside the vehicles. Sandra searched around for a flat spot to put her sleeping cot when suddenly she let out a shriek. We all dashed in her direction. She stood still and looked down at a point a few feet in front of her. We all followed suit and saw a small snake that lay coiled in the sand.

Sandra stammered, "Wow. I almost stepped on it and I'm barefoot."

Walt looked down at the snake, "I'm not sure what type of snake it is. By the look of its size, I would guess it's a baby snake and if it's poisonous, it could be really nasty. Little ones haven't learned to moderate how much venom to release, they give a full load with every bite. I'm glad you didn't step on it. We're four or five hours from Riyadh and the nearest hospital. I suggest we move." The snake raised its head slightly letting out a small rasping hiss. We all backed away from it, quietly.

When Walt suggested moving, the other three of us had no arguments. Soon we all wore shoes and warily walked around as we packed up our gear. After a few more miles we found a spot near two gnarled trees that stood utterly alone among the drifting sand. They became the backdrop for our camp that night.

The following morning, we used the sun as our navigational guide and drove south toward the dunes. As we crossed open plains of sand and occasional slabs of rock, Walt slowed to take a look at a couple of the slabs. He pulled up next to one. We all checked out the area, and as he had suspected, Walt found crevices and holes in the rock into which he could crawl. Soon, we all squirmed into openings and down into snug underground passageways. Our flashlights helped us navigate through tighter areas where we needed to plan how to maneuver past problems to avoid becoming stuck. We explored several of the openings and discovered many connected into a complex of channels and tiny caverns. In places, they became too small, which meant we had to back out of those spots that were challenges we couldn't overcome. The labyrinth of passageways ran within a foot or two of the desert surface, which may sound close enough. However, when I became stuck in a tight area and needed assistance to reverse out, I will admit I felt rather scared. Afterwards, it took a few minutes to calm my nerves before I returned to sections where I had been previously and felt confident enough that I could negotiate the passageways.

Before we departed, Brendan asked, "Do you think this passageway network was cut by rain water?"

Walt replied, "Yes. I would imagine that's what happened."

Sandra looked over at us. "You mean that little network could, in a million years, become another collapsed cavern, like the one we explored north of Jubail?"

Walt thought for a few seconds, before replying, "I suppose it could happen. It all depends on the rock strata that lies below this area."

We returned to driving across miles of open sabkha. Our surroundings appeared as an endless sea of grays, creams, and golds. With no solid points of reference, the colors intermingled and merged into a visual representation of eternity that, with each passing mile, became almost real and concrete in our minds.

We simply drove straight out into that flat nothingness, mesmerizing us as we proceeded in a reasonably straight line at 50 or 60 mph. Brendan and I found no reason to talk for quite a while. Our thoughts and feelings were consumed by the sense of vastness. Out in the sea of grays and golds, a tiny speck of black stood out. In that never ending area, which redefined the words uniformity and infinity, that black speck became a magnet to my eyes and attention. My mind attached to it, which caused me to deviate from Walt's path by a few miles. In the openness, the perspective of miles and inches felt relatively the same. I drove directly at the speck, which with the passage of miles became a single rock, daring to stand out defiantly to break the flatness. As I closed in on the rock, I could see I had been drawn by just a small rock; it probably was a little larger than a standard house brick. Despite its small size, in that vast expanse of sameness, I couldn't avoid its alluring pull. It stood alone, one unique feature in the environment. When I reached it, I actually ran over the rock with my right front tire—I couldn't miss it. I was amazed to witness how such a small, but so seemingly out of place, object within the shimmering mirages could grab and hold my unflinching attention.

Brendan chuckled and said, "I knew you were gonna' run over that rock. There wasn't any way you could do anything else. Impossible."

I couldn't deny it. "I knew it too and it simply pulled me in its direction. It had my name on it. This desert plays games with our minds."

Brendan, who worked as an editor for Aramco, replied, "Oh. This trip is going to make a great story for the company magazine."

Gradually, we moved from the open plains of sabkha to sandier terrain that had been blown by the wind into undulating hills. We stayed as much as possible in the valleys between the hills as the sand became packed and easier to cross. After miles, we drove along the edge of the hills where they transitioned to become a huge plain of open golden sand. The firm surface allowed us to drive easily at 40 to 50 mph. Walt had pulled about a quarter of a mile ahead of me when he suddenly stood on his brakes and made a U-turn. Walt and Sandra drove slowly toward me, slowly sweeping closer to the hills as both of them hung out of the windows to check the ground. Walt stopped abruptly and both of them launched themselves out of the car. They started to dance around, screaming excitedly as if they had both walked unexpectedly onto hot coals. I tried to stop next to them but they indicated to park further away. I did so. Then Brendan and I walked back to the dancing pair where we looked down at the ground and also started to hop around. We couldn't stand still on one spot because every inch of the area held remnants of tools and weapons that probably dated back thousands of years.

Over a matter of hours, we crawled around a reasonably large area and discovered stone scrapers, knives, axes, arrow heads, and various broken pieces. If a small section of ground looked barren, we only had to wipe away a layer of sand to reveal hidden treasures. In prehistoric times, a sea that had long since dried up probably existed in part of the area where the Empty Quarter now resided. As we talked and explored, we surmised that we may have come across the site of an ancient fishing village. We each had our own collection of treasure. The range of different rocks found in the tools and weapons surprised me. This added to the supposition that this had been a fishing village and probably a market where traders came from foreign parts to exchange goods such as tools and weapons.

After a long time, we decided we shouldn't delay any longer as someone could have spotted us and reported our activity to the authorities. The local government had been charged with keeping people away from such ancient sites. They didn't want artifacts being removed. I had heard the Saudi Arabian government only considered history to have begun with the start of Islam—nothing before it existed. So Stone Age tools that predated Islam didn't fit with the government's view of history and, therefore, to them such tools couldn't exist. If we had been caught with such objects, they would have been confiscated and we could have been in trouble.

As we prepared to move on, Walt commented, "Hey, we happened to find this site today. Who knows when it last saw the light of day. The sands are shifting perpetually. Who knows, this area may have been buried under six feet of sand a year back."

Sandra followed his train of thought, "You're right. I wonder how many other ancient villages we have driven over, not realizing some artifacts are barely inches under the surface."

Brendan added, "Can you imagine how much history and the many clues about how these ancient societies worked are hidden in this terrain? Nobody needs to dig through hard-packed soil. Here we only need to brush the sand aside and all these fantastic ancient objects are laying there awaiting our discovery. It's extraordinary. I'm appalled the value of this history is ignored and even denied."

Walt smiled and said, "Let's get moving, before we stand here longer, discussing the potential this area holds."

We agreed we needed to leave the open plains, we started our engines and headed toward a line of dunes which we could see miles to our southwest. We kept a closer eye on our surroundings all that afternoon until we hoped we had travelled far enough to have lost anybody who tried to follow us. Obviously our tires left unmistakable trails across the desert, but in surprisingly little time the wind had scoured away all signs of our tracks. If the police or any other officials had pursued us, it would have been difficult to deny we had poached the artifacts even if we had managed to dump them. Out in that wilderness we probably had been the only ex-pats within a couple of hundred miles. And, Stone Age tools would only be of interest to ex-pats. I suspected locals, if they even saw them lying in the sand, would have driven over them without a care. A more difficult situation could have been created if local officials accused us of planting the artifacts in attempts to create revisionist history that could undermine the foundations of their Islamic roots. I had heard enough stories to know such "paranoid" thinking did exist, especially when it came to infidels.

Let me be clear—this type of problem wasn't my every day experience. Such extremist thoughts existed in pockets of the country, but I can't think of any country, including the U.S., where such "paranoid" thoughts don't exist among certain factions.

Eventually, we found a beautiful shallow valley for our camp. While we looked through a box of food, Sandra looked over at Walt. She shared, "Hey, I just had a thought about how we danced around when we found those first few tools. It reminded me of when we had family gatherings and people would dance. Our leaping around felt reminiscent of a dance called the Tarantella Two-Step."

Walt smiled broadly. "Yeah, that's right. I remember you talking about it. We should name this the Tarantella Find."

We all agreed on the name for the site. While not recorded officially, it would be our name for our collections of ancient tools. As to whether the field of tools and treasure lay exposed for decades or minutes had been impossible to tell. We may have been the only people to explore it and it may be centuries before the artifacts surface again. The Tarantella Find was ours.

Later, as we sat around eating, we decided to pull the best six pieces out of our collections from the day to show the group. We all spent a few minutes to sort through our pieces to decide what to show.

Sandra displayed her six selected items. When she held out her third one, she commented, "This blade, I assume, is obsidian as it's so intensely black and polished."

The top half of a finely shaped knife/scraper blade sat perfectly in the palm of her small hand.

Walt gave it a glance and leapt from his stool. "That's unbelievable. Hold that blade—I need to pull another piece from my other bag."

Two minutes later, he returned with an obsidian piece—it had been the bottom of a finely chiseled blade. Not believing the possibilities, Sandra and Walt brought the two together, they fit almost perfectly. By the light of a flash light, we could just find the join line.

When they recalled where they found their piece, Sandra and Walt realized they had been over a hundred yards apart. We sat there, amazed they had uncovered both halves of such a beautiful blade in such a fluid environment. What was the likelihood of finding both of them? We concluded the possibility to be just short of miraculous, especially given the environment of ever-shifting sands.

We found a bunch of broken, dried branches in a gully close to where we set up camp. They allowed us the opportunity to enjoy a warm fire for a short time. The temperature of the open desert plummeted as soon as the sun dropped below the horizon. Often, at night, the temperature dipped down into the 40's. After darkness fell, we welcomed the fire and a warm jacket, especially on that evening, as we needed to unwind after the excitement of the day.

That night we started a nightly routine in preparation for the following day. I needed to transfer gas from the drum in the back of the Blazer to the fuel tank. Unfortunately, I had been unable to find any siphon pumps in any local stores and had to purchase a length of ¼ inch tubing. To manually start the siphon action by sucking was relatively easy with that size tube, but it took hours to transfer a decent amount of gasoline. However, with each nightly process, I felt happier as I knew less fuel wallowed around in the drum, only feet behind Brendan and me.

When convenient, we boiled water to be stored in a couple of thermoses. Having hot water available allowed us to make tea and coffee whenever we felt like it, without the hassle of starting a stove. This became a less essential need in the last few days as we would soon head toward Riyadh where we could buy refreshments.

Even with our coercing, the fire gave out so we decided to crawl into our sleeping bags to keep warmer. We pulled out the cots, some warm clothing, and the bags. Soon we had all snuggled into our cocoons, and warmth tried to lull us to sleep. But our minds continued to churn and the notion of sleep never made it into our heads. We lay on our cots telling ghost stories, which actually didn't help to settle us down. Then we started to hear the scurrying of creatures that had buried themselves in the sand for protection from the sun during the day. The darkness and dropping temperatures told them to come out to hunt and feed. Their perpetual movement added a level of nervous tension to our camp site. We were still trying to slow our thoughts down and sleep when the clocks had ticked into a new day.

At about 1:00, Sandra realized why she couldn't sleep, "Will somebody please turn out the lights? That Milky Way is far too bright."

I chuckled, but couldn't deny the truth of her words. Not a cloud dimmed the stars and, as we were far from cities and civilization, their ambient light didn't distract from the stars' light. The Milky Way sparkled in its finest glory and the moon's icy silver glow gave it a presence and power that I had rarely witnessed.

Sandra shuffled around for a few seconds and then pronounced, "Oh. This is crazy. I can read my book by the light of the moon and stars. Now, that's a first."

We all smiled at the thought of reading by starlight. We slowly relaxed, wishing the new day might hold ventures that would be as unbelievable as those from the previous one, a day which danced in our minds and competed with our desire for sleep.

The following morning's trails soon had us in different terrain and, with it, we encountered new challenges. We had reached an extensive area dominated by large dunes. We soon found their golden sands to be unpredictable. After we had driven up one ridge without issue, we thought a similar looking ridge would also be no problem. However, the sand had other plans for us. When either of us tried to accelerate and any of our wheels was in lightweight sand, which felt similar to dust, then that wheel spun ineffectively except for digging itself deeper into the loose sand. It didn't take more than a few seconds for the wheel to be submerged in sand, up to the axle. The time for us to endure hard labor had arrived—out came the shovels, pieces of grating and anything to gain a little traction. Three of us pushing the stranded vehicle forward provided much of what it took to dig ourselves out of particularly bad sand. We climbed dunes, we followed ridges, we partially slid and drove down steeper faces. Our bodies and minds fought many battles, but eventually they bathed in the exhilaration of having traversed lines of dunes that rose beautifully and bright. Their golden sands rose 100 to 200 feet high. I loved being on the crest of a tall dune where I could view the surrounding lines of dunes with their interweaving ridges and valleys. Earlier in the day, the harsh sun created dark shadows that accentuated the patterns which flowed in all directions. By midday, the overhead sun blasted all shapes and details into a flattened monotone yellow wasteland except for the few dunes that immediately surrounded us; we could still make out their features.

The perpetual uncertainty of what was ahead as we traversed the dunes restrained my intrigue and love of being in the midst of such giants. We could barely cover a mile before we returned to digging one of us out of loose sand. I will admit most of these times when we needed to dig a vehicle out, it was my Blazer. I found driving on dunes was an art that required me to be able to read the sand and I had to gain much more first-hand experience. Even when I followed Walt's tracks, I soon found there was no guarantee I would find a navigable path.

One of the real challenges we faced involved plotting a course through the dunes. We had to avoid the steep faces while anticipating how wide ridges might be and skirting around deep loose sand. It required a continual state of awareness and observing. While we were observant, our senses were tantalized by the sand dancing in the wind; its constant movement caused the sand's colors and their multiple shades to shift subtly. Many people could dismiss sand as simply being orange or yellow, but to be a part of that intricate landscape forced me to see the sand, the dunes, and the entire environment with so much more depth. The beauty of the colors and their shades was magical, the patterns that were carved in the sand by the wind were amazing, and the size and consistently repeating profiles of the dunes were riveting. Such aspects drew my thoughts along joyful avenues of wonder.

The subtle color variations, along with gradients of brightness and the infinite spectrum of grays danced in my eyes, constantly tiring them despite my tinted sunglasses. When I sensed my eyes becoming tired, I became concerned knowing I needed to focus clearly for driving. We all took time to quietly let our eyes rest until we felt normalcy returning to them.

The winds that blew for much of the time were accompanied by rumbling tones as they inched the dunes forward. But the winds' voices took on a shrill quality when they whipped more closely around us, blasting any exposed skin with dusty sand. It didn't sting all the time, but it stuck in the ever drying layer of sweat, leaving a crusty feel to the skin. Blowing sand had no discernible taste or smell, but these two senses possessed a quality that could only be described as "dry." It was the first time I realized dry was a taste and an aroma.

We negotiated our way back north as the sun began to descend on the western horizon. As we drove, we noticed the sky had become heavy and the wind had gained strength.

I said, "Well, it looks like we are in for an entertaining night."

Brendan grimaced as he replied, "I sure hope this doesn't turn into a Shamal tonight." I knew what he meant by Shamal. They were the annual wind and sandstorms that hit eastern Arabia each spring, a time when a few of us went out for wild sails, with two of us to hold down each Laser. Shamals could hit the Empty Quarter at any time of the year. The unrelenting strong winds carried huge quantities of a red sand from northern Iraq, depositing these sands all over Saudi Arabia.

Before nightfall Walt found a secluded canyon in the dunes where we felt sheltered from the main wind gusts. We quickly organized ourselves, as we all intended sleeping in our vehicles that night. After we snatched a little food, the four of us jammed into the back of Walt's Toyota. By the light of our flashlights, we played card games to while away a few hours before sleep. We became aware the wind direction had shifted and we could feel the force of the gusts directly. The sound of sand being hurled at the Toyota became almost deafening. While we sheltered inside, we felt safe.

A particularly strong blast hit us, causing us to immediately stop everything we had been doing. The windward side of the Toyota had suddenly dropped about an inch.

Walt, pulling clothes out of the bag on which he had been sitting, told us tersely, "Wrap spare clothing around your heads to protect your skin and your eyes. We need to barricade the wheels. The wind has begun to scour the sand from around and under the tires. Bury anything that is large or heavy by the wheels to stop the wind scouring. We need to do that on the two windward wheels of both vehicles. When people have failed to act in circumstances like this, a few cars have been rolled over, so we need to protect the tires from the wind."

Brendan and I staggered across the ten-foot gap to the Blazer while we tried to protect our faces from the sandblasting. Having wrapped shirts around our heads, we buried wood and other heavier equipment around the wheels in attempts to stop the wind's action around them. We retired back to the Toyota to play a few more rounds of cards while waiting to see if our protection was effective. When we felt assured the scouring had halted, Brendan and I retired back to the Blazer. As the backseat had been removed to make room for the drum, Brendan snuggled into the front passenger seat while I tried to pretzel my 6' 3" frame around the steering wheel. Not too surprisingly, hours passed without my having more than a few minutes sleep before a cramp or back pain awoke me.

By 1:00, I felt utterly miserable and may have been optimistic thinking the wind had lost some of its power. I decided I would go to sleep under the front bumper where I would be out of the main wind gusts. I laid down on the soft sand in the warm comfort of my sleeping bag. I faced the underside of the Blazer's radiator and pulled the top of the bag around my head. I fell asleep in a matter of minutes.

Cries of, "Barry, Barry," awoke me. I groggily tried to undo the top of my sleeping bag, but my body didn't want to move. *What is wrong with me? Have I had a stroke or something? Why can't I move? This isn't good.* I struggled to move my legs, but they felt weighted down.

I heard a more urgent, "Barry, where the hell are you?"

I called out, "I'm in front of my car." I heard footsteps fighting their way through deep soft sand and then Walt's head appeared behind one of my front wheels.

"Ah, there you are. Do you realize your sleeping bag is completely buried in the drifting sand?"

"Oh good. That probably explains why I can't move too easily."

I heard hands dig away the sand behind my back. Eventually, I rolled over to see Sandra and Brendan standing close by, both looking relieved that I hadn't been suffocated. I realized the wind had dropped, but it had changed direction overnight, causing it to drift up against my back. Fortunately, I had faced under the front bumper and inadvertently become a barrier that stopped the wind scouring under the front of the Blazer.

It didn't take us long to break camp as we hadn't unloaded much gear. However, to move out of the little canyon in the dunes presented us with a problem. Soft sand had been blown into the canyon and much had accumulated around both vehicles. The newly deposited sand had also changed the slope of the dunes, requiring us to change direction to find more solid sand. So, for the first hour or two of this new day, we occupied our time with digging, swearing, more digging, more swearing, finally pushing and still more swearing.

We really only appreciated the glorious sunny morning that came without a whisper of wind when we had managed to navigate a few miles across the dunes. They wore a beautiful cloak of red sand which had been deposited by the windstorm. It wouldn't take a day for the new layer of red sand to be mixed and lost in with the more yellowy golden sand, the dunes' normal tone.

To sit on the crest of a dune and look out over a sea of sand dunes mesmerized my mind. In the early morning sunlight, the dunes and the drifting ridges that joined them threw harsh shadows into the intervening valleys. A rhythm and a sense of order prevailed. Patterns and repetition ruled my surroundings. I wondered if the Dutch graphic artist Escher had ever witnessed such natural beauty that perhaps inspired his work. I had read that he didn't consider himself an artist, that he sought to express infinity in his works. These dunes appeared to go on for ever and ever—perhaps in the far distance lay infinity.

Our path lay to the north as we needed to find our way back to "civilization." Our route cut across lines of dunes and through hills of packed sand and rocky ridges. When we sat on the crest of one dune and saw an open expanse of sabkha that headed north by Walt's compass, we charted a route across the remaining, smaller dunes to access the sabkha. Soon enough, we could drive at a steady 50 mph across the plains of dusty nothingness, leaving the majestic dunes to slowly march along a path chosen by the prevailing winds.

After several hours, the terrain became rockier with low ridges that had escarpments running along their southern flanks. We navigated into dried-up wadis that cut between the ridges. In the sheltered areas of these river beds, we came across thorny shrubs and thin grasses that looked deceptively fragile, but they had to be extremely hardy as they endured the scorching temperatures. We enjoyed their greenness as we hadn't seen much for a few days. Driving along the wadis, we found side trails that ran along the banks of the dried river bed. Walt and I enjoyed deviating from the river bed to these side trails and back again. Our exact location still remained unclear to us.

At one stop, I asked, "Hey Walt, do you have a sense of where we are as yet?"

He looked around Sandra with a broad smile while saying, "What? You want to know where you are? You should be used to this state of being lost."

"Come on, Brit, you lot ruled the world for centuries. You mean you don't have your map, compass, and sextant?" Sandra teased.

I jibed back, "Thanks. No, I don't have my sextant and, yes, I'm happy being lost because that forces me to be with you two happy souls. I know we're in the Arabian desert."

Walt looked around quickly then answered seriously, "Based on the terrain and the position of the sun along with the time, we probably could already be approaching the southernmost outskirts of Riyadh. I hope we'll reach there by early afternoon."

I asked Brendan. "Are you ready for that shower, now?"

Brendan's eyes had lost the sparkle that I had seen in them, while we were exploring. He answered flatly, "No. I'm not."

I tried to add some vitality to my voice and cajoled, "Come on. We need to go back to work if they are to keep paying us. And I don't think the desert's going anywhere soon. We'll be back."

We continued up the dry wadis, weaving between trails until I had the misfortune to meet a junction that turned out to not be a junction at all. A trail I chose on the right bank appeared to make a left around a shrubby bush and rejoin the wadi. In reality, on the other side of the bush, the trail stopped, immediately followed by a two foot drop into the wadi. Most people don't believe Blazers could fly. Mine made a mighty good attempt to prove those people wrong. I came to a halt in the wadi, a little shaken and still on four wheels with a drum of gasoline holding steady on its cradle in the back. Sandra had seen my path headed toward a problem and apparently screamed at Walt to stop. They both watched, wide-eyed, as I descended. We checked the suspension, which appeared to be fine, and then we continued with a little less weaving between trails.

Eventually, we reached the top of the wadis and found a pleasant little sandy open area where a few palms grew in addition to smaller trees and shrubs. We stopped to seek shade under a couple of the trees and sat next to the vehicles for our last lunch in the wilds. As we sat, reminiscing about what a great trip it had been, we heard the sound of a distant truck engine. We suspected it to be a Bedouin and, as expected, he found us minutes later. He parked a short distance away before walking over to where we relaxed.

He greeted us, "Salaam Alaikhum," and we returned the greeting, "Wa Alaikhum is Salaam."

He sat on his haunches, as most Saudi's did. They could stay talking in this position for ages, and it never failed to impress most ex-pats. Through a combination of pidgin Arabic, a few words of English, and plenty of hand gestures, we learned he was going to check on his flock of goats further along the ridge. As we knew a few of the traditions of the desert, we felt obliged to offer him a little refreshment as he had come to our temporary camp. We mentally took an inventory of the few food stocks we had in both vehicles. We had plenty of water, but next to nothing in the way of beverages. Sandra remembered she had a single tea bag in her bag. However, the last time we had refilled the thermoses had been two days before. Walt thought we had enough hot water for one cup of tea. He offered the Bedouin a cup of tea, which he gratefully accepted. Walt and Sandra walked over to their Toyota to do what they could to produce the cup of tea. They returned a few minutes later and handed a cup to our guest.

When he took a sip, he considered it and managed, "Shukran"—Thanks, to which Sandra replied, "Afwan"—You're welcome.

The Bedouin inquired where our travels would take us and where we had been. A surprised look crossed his face when he realized that we, ex-pats, had been out in the Rub' al Khali—The Empty Quarter. He said he rarely saw foreigners out in that region, which didn't surprise us. It didn't take him more than a few minutes to finish the tea. He excused himself and departed for his truck. We did feel a little awkward we had only been able to offer him a really bad cup of tea. Walt indicated the thermos held barely enough water, and the water may have been hotter if we had simply left it out in the sun. Lukewarm water doesn't make even a halfway decent cup of tea. We packed up the few items we had pulled out for lunch and returned to the trails across open expanses of packed sand, so much easier to drive on than the wadis.

Soon enough, we encountered a trail that had been used by traffic on a regular basis. The trail wound through a few low hills and small groves of palms. It carried us to where we had to reluctantly re-enter the domain of settled humans once again.

As we skirted around a hill, both Walt and I stopped suddenly. We had had our windows rolled down and all four of us sat sniffing the breeze that wafted around us until Walt broke the quiet, "What on earth is that smell?"

Sandra gave a thought, "Pomegranates? It's so strong, it almost seems unnatural."

"Strawberries?" I suggested.

Sandra screwed up her face and shook her head, "Nah. I agree its definitely fruit. But what?" A pungent sweetness begged to be recognized.

"And I'm sure it's not citrus," Brendan added.

"I suggest we go find out as we seem totally stumped," I concluded.

We continued along the trail for another quarter of a mile before we found the surprising answer. A huge field of the largest, most sumptuous watermelons lay off to our right. The abundance of ripe fruit as it lay in the field immediately answered the unknown aroma. Hundreds, or possibly thousands, of beautiful, large, ripe watermelons basked in bright sunlight on their dark green foliage. Like the rows of sunbaked dunes, this magnificent field of fruit held us spellbound. I had never before smelled a fruit's aroma with such intensity. The sweetness overpowered the subtleties I normally associated with the aroma of watermelon.

The field gave us the first sign of our return to "civilization." A sad sense that the adventure lay behind us dampened my thoughts and spirit. I drove along the trail, following Walt. What had been excited anticipation of what the next minute or the next turn could present to us quickly dissolved into, not dread, but a let-down that sucked the spirit out of me. I had been hyped up for five days and it was over. Weariness embraced my body and mind in its mantle. But I couldn't surrender to it as we still had several hours before we would be back in camp.

Beyond the field, irrigation channels ran alongside a grove of palm trees. The canopy of the palms' fronds cast shadows over the channels, providing welcome relief to the farm workers. A few dilapidated buildings that the farmer used for equipment and supplies also sheltered under the canopy. We wove through several more fields with a variety of crops and produce before we reached the first small village. It marked the start of the city of Riyadh. The wilds lay miles behind us, leaving incredible imprints on our minds and, most significantly, in our hearts.

When we reached the first store that appeared to have fresh fruit, we immediately pulled in. That field of watermelons had reawakened our desire for any sweet-tasting fruit. We bought a selection of fruit as well as cold drinks and other snacks. Both Walt and I reckoned we didn't have sufficient gas in our tanks for the drive back to Dhahran and planned to buy more at the first gas station. By then, Walt and I agreed that we were tired, but still prepared for a few hours of driving on black top. It felt rather strange, at first, having to think about road signs and other traffic. I was surprised to realize how quickly I had become accustomed to off-road driving. At least, we could stow the shovels as drifting sand wouldn't be a potential hazard for the rest of the trip.

The drive back to the eastern edge of the country took about three or four hours. A bittersweet mood draped itself over us during the last hundred miles.

When we could see the camp, I looked over and said to Brendan, "Can you believe that the adventure is over?"

"No. I really wanted the time to continue, but here we are back at camp and I presume they will require us to work again."

"I know what you mean. How can five days have passed so soon? Well, we left camp as two guys looking for adventure and we certainly did that, didn't we? I don't know how you feel, but I need that shower."

Brendan smiled and agreed, "You got that right. We both need one. And I know I'll enjoy mine."

After I resettled in camp, I sometimes spent long periods considering how I previously had understood concepts like vastness, sameness, flatness, eternity, and infinity; they had been the mere juggling of thoughts. To face their actual realities out in the Empty Quarter was an undeniable experience that gave these terms such life and profundity. This deeper understanding could never be reversed. Until I confronted the realities of these terms, I had absolutely no idea how concepts could be granted the power to amaze. They challenged my normal thoughts, they took my perceived reality and stood it on its head, and they took normal rational thoughts and questioned their bases. Such ideas played games with my mind. It felt uncomfortable, at the time. However, now I'm so glad I experienced them and to have grown through them.

I think many people would look at an area of sandy dunes and be more impressed by the surrounding heat or their size than the fact that dunes are simply piles of sand that are moved by the wind. However, every single dune is a pile of sand of such enormity that one dune is possibly made up of more grains of sand than the total number of breaths ever taken by all humans who have ever lived. Each of those grains of sand conforms to certain crystalline structures. What are the chances all of these uniformly structured grains of sand should accumulate into one sand dune? These are the types of questions that crossed my mind and caused other day-to-day thinking to be reconsidered.

To travel in such a desolate, but beautiful place as the desert for a period of time opened my eyes to thoughts about life, opportunities, consequences, fear, self-responsibility, and mortality that have been influential in how I've chosen to live my life. Throughout these adventures, I faced situations that gave me the option to face my fears or give in to them. This five-day adventure presented me with many opportunities to confront that choice. During my life, I've decided to walk away from a number of different activities, but not many. Who could say if I made a right or wrong decision to do so? To be honest, I don't care. More important to me is the motivation that prompted my response or reaction. Motivation is an interesting phenomenon to me because I believe it comes from both the heart and the mind. I think my long-term engagement with the concept of motivation has been a profound lesson for me that started with these adventures.

CHAPTER 22
LIFE THEREAFTER

الله شاء ان   الله شاء ان   الله شاء ان   الله شاء ان   الله شاء ان   الله شاء ان   الله شاء ان

Now that my tale of the drive from London to Dhahran and later experiences in Arabia has been told, I must confess my surprise at how the act of writing the story touched me. I'm not sure I'm finished; I'll always find more to write. The writing has become a journey in itself, challenging me in ways quite different from the drive. As I said earlier, the period of time that covered London to Dhahran could be seen as a lifetime of experiences packed into two intense weeks. Now some highlights of the journey and other adventures have been packed into the pages of a book.

I have found it difficult to be objective while writing about these experiences. I'm certain a few people who have had their own wild and extreme travel experiences may scoff when they read about these ventures. And, alternatively, I'm sure other readers will find it absolutely unbelievable we made it to Dhahran, or I survived my adventures around Arabia. I believe reading or writing any such account forces people to make comparisons and judgments. That is neither good nor bad; all writers and readers are human with vastly different sets of experiences and comfort levels, which generates a huge spectrum of reactions to what is read or written. In the act of writing this book, I've had to reflect on my experiences, 40 years ago and since. Through this process, I've learned a great deal about myself and my life's journey.

My experiences along those 5,500 miles forced me to face feelings about self-reliance, perseverance, and trust that I may never have needed to confront in other situations. I certainly didn't resolve many of them during the journey. However, as I had opened the box that held those feelings I knew I could never shut it again. Perhaps my stubbornness wouldn't allow me to avoid the discomfort of only holding and not facing these feelings. To find peace with such profound feelings and thoughts has been part of my life's challenges and one of its richest rewards.

During the journey, I soon found many interesting lessons awaited me. I recognized what I put into life was what I would get out of it, and I was able to finally shed the immature attitude that life owed me.

Not only did the overall experience evoke many emotional feelings, but life lessons fell like an abundance of low-hanging fruit. A prime example was the lesson about not expecting people to act as I normally did, like the Turkish hardware store owner who sold rope by weight. I understood other lessons after time, study, and later experiences helped to clarify their meaning. Probably, for me, the most obvious example was the reflection regarding the likely changes along the Yugoslavian coast. In places, now, large commercial resorts and hotels have replaced the naturally beautiful old groves of trees which overlooked the peaceful sandy beaches. After years of experience and observing life, I came to acknowledge more deeply that everything constantly changes—absolutely nothing remains the same. Mountains rise and gradually erode away; cities are built and eventually crumble; we are born, age, and die; cosmic forces created the earth and it constantly changes under human influences as well as cosmic rhythms.

One specific lesson—live life fully—occurred when we were almost shot after I accidentally stopped at a military refueling point. Before the trip, I hadn't really thought about the possibility of making an irrational decision, because of fatigue. Should such concerns have stopped me from making the journey? They were grouped together with other unknowns. By definition, I knew nothing about them until they happened. But I did survive the encounter with two Syrian soldiers who almost shot us, and I learned a huge life lesson. I would never have gained a deeper understanding about life and death if I had hidden under my bed covers. Lessons are only to be found in the unknown and potentially risky.

I'm thankful to have these 40-year-old memories and reflections from the journey and adventures in Arabia and to have woven them together to form my adventure story. Although the world is different now, forty years later, I believe it is still unbelievably beautiful and incredible. For me, world travel was an amazing education, the likes of which I could never have found in classrooms or text books; it could only be gained by experience. I encourage all people to go out and have adventures—take care for your safety, and leave faint footprints along the way.

Over the last 40 years, I've transitioned from a rather immature and internally insecure 28-year-old to a 70-year-old spiritual care volunteer supporting the chronically sick. I've been able to make this transition due to the experiences described in this book, as well as other later influences. The Epilogue—Part II has a more in-depth discussion of this shift.

For the first ten years or so after my 1979 venture into the Empty Quarter, memories of that trip remained in my focus and brought me spiritual peace. I continued to seek a spiritual philosophy that aligned with my nature-based understandings, my acknowledgement that life wasn't always easy, and that life was influenced by the unknowable. In 1989, I had a work assignment for six months in New Zealand, where I eventually turned a significant corner.

One evening, soon after I arrived in the New Zealand capital, Wellington, I was waiting for several work associates in my hotel room. With nothing better to do for ten minutes, I checked out all the drawers and cupboards in the hotel suite. In the bedside drawer, I found a copy of Gideon's Bible and a book on Buddhism. I picked up the book on Buddhism and started to read. In just minutes, I realized I had found my path. So many of the basic premises resonated with me. Karma made sense to me, seeing all "souls" as equals felt so right, reincarnation—continuing life's journey toward enlightenment—filled a void in my thinking, and giving of ourselves spoke to a truth that would manifest in me later. I studied the teachings, in an academic sense, for several years before recognizing I wanted to take "refuge," which is the Buddhist equivalent of Christian Baptism. I admit I haven't become a conventional

Buddhist, I don't belong to a Sangha—a community, I don't attend teachings often, and I don't meditate. However, I try to live my life by Buddhist principles and find great joy and satisfaction manifesting those principles in my chaplaincy work as a spiritual care volunteer. I fondly remember a conversation I had years ago with a woman who had been following Buddhist practices for most of her adult life. I asked her how her daily practice had been recently. She surprised me when she said her daily practice didn't matter, she said what mattered was how she lived every moment and the feelings she held in her heart. That simple statement released me from a need to follow the conventional path. It allowed me to find comfort and have confidence knowing my own foundation was based upon Buddhist principles and teachings. Sensing my own strong spiritual grounding and understanding has allowed me to walk alongside the terminally and chronically sick, and to give them all spiritual support, no matter what faith or beliefs they professed. I find great joy in taking a Buddhist teaching and couching it in terms that a patient of a different faith will understand and seeing how it can help them view their situation differently.

I have found a path that gives me an understanding of my place in life and my journey—to gain enlightenment. However, I admit one significant unresolved issue still hinders my progress to a place where I can say I accept and understand basic Buddhist philosophy. In all of the teachings and readings, I have never found a satisfactory Buddhist explanation for our earthly environment; the dawn of the universe; the Big Bang; and the existence of vastness, openness, and endlessness. Questions about these concepts continue to drive my spiritual quest. Now in my later years, I've reached a point when I am happy to not have these answers. To not understand is a good reminder to me that I'm not omnipotent and that my journey still needs to continue. I would be unsettled if I thought I knew all the answers, spiritually speaking, as I would become complacent. To have what I thought I already knew reaffirmed isn't satisfying, but to seek answers to what is unknown by me continues to be enriching. And, most importantly, seeking the unknown requires me to have what I hold to be faith. And I do have faith that Buddhist principles are correct for me and they guide me along a compassionate path, even though I still have questions. Such principles are valid for me, just as other philosophical/religious tenets guide other people. I am joyful in their choices of which teachings to follow. To my way of thinking, there is one truth, no matter how we label that truth, be it God, the Divine, Buddha Nature, the Sun God, or whatever. More importantly, I believe there are multiple paths to the truth and it is that one truth which all beings seek. We each choose our path and, depending on our circumstances or understandings, we can choose to change to a different path. They all bring us home.

I will admit life has had its struggles and I do at times wish I could relive certain periods of my life. I don't think of myself as exceptional; I have been blessed with exceptional circumstances. I have learned to face challenges where they primarily involved just me, but I'm constantly frustrated with resolving issues that involve others. To recognize and admit such failings dampens my joy of what I've managed to achieve in this life. This understanding simply highlights another truth—each new day gives me the opportunity to learn and grow. Life's trials have been incredibly powerful opportunities for me to become a better person. And I appreciate it is my past experiences, both pleasant and not so, that will guide me to a point of understanding, which will bring forth the fruits of learning.

When I take time to recognize the significance of my stay in Saudi Arabia, my mind often drifts back to those transformative days. They were amazing, an opportunity I was fortunate to have found; it had been by accident—not by design. Once in a while, my musings wander back to an alternative path that I had escaped by moving to Arabia, *Perhaps, instead of going to Arabia, I should have stayed in London, bought a house, and spent my time tending to my garden.* Then my saner side takes over. *Really? No—not a chance!*

EPILOGUE

Part I
My decision to venture out into the Empty Quarter

When I was a young man, I thought about both the immense and repetitive side of nature and the incredible complexities of human and animal physical forms. I couldn't avoid the simple conclusion that a reason for these realities existed. As I had rejected standard religious doctrines as a teenager, I found comfort in a nature-based philosophy. I also recognized my profound love and fascination with vastness where I sensed thoughts had no bounds and almost anything seemed possible.

At the age of 28, I couldn't determine a proven understanding to thoroughly explain vastness. I realized many varied disciplines and physical elements had to come together to explain vastness. For example, I understood astrophysicists could explain the creation of crystalline structures, which occurred in all natural settings, while geologists could explain how rocks had been laid down to form the base structural elements which underlay areas of wilderness. Additionally, aerologists could explain how winds that sculpted wilderness were generated. However, for me to understand how all of these different elements came together to explain what we witnessed as vastness felt elusive. I may not have been able to describe such thoughts in words, back when I was younger, but such questioning manifested through a profound sense of awe.

I had grown up in the suburbs of London, where I never felt

particularly satisfied. When I became a teenager, I joined a youth group at my local church. I rarely attended church services, but I enjoyed the group gatherings. One spring, the group leaders proposed a week-long hiking trip, during our summer holidays, in the Lake District. I signed up after my parents agreed, they probably felt grateful to not have my grumpy teenage attitude around for the week. I loved hiking among these small English mountains. No matter if the weather was sunny, cloudy, snowy or pouring with rain, I found a peace and a deep sense of satisfaction in the mountains' embrace.

I continued to join the annual outings to the Lake District until I turned 18 years of age. I'd discovered that despite my lanky 6' 3" frame, I had a surprisingly high level of endurance and developed a strong set of leg muscles. I prided myself on being first to the top of each peak, first to be back to the hostel, and first to have recovered from the day's exertions ready to go out for an evening at the local pub.

In college, I spent my summers in the Alps or Norway climbing and hiking. During those trips, I first encountered the sense of the endless vista. To sit on a snowy peak and look out over a sea of surrounding mountains and valleys entranced me. Their weaving, unpredictable patterns extended to a point where they appeared as no more than a thin blurred line of purple gray which melted into the lower strata of the sky. The horizon, at best, became visually ill-defined and to me, it also lost meaning in the circumstance. It wasn't a line—it was more like a conceived construct. It was where the discernible became indiscernible.

Such experiences became the motivation to climb taller peaks from which more magnificent vistas could be observed. To be present to Mother Nature and all that she had created prompted a humbling shift in how I saw myself. I began to understand how I represented a tiny speck in comparison to the forces that endowed the earth with such soaring mountains. At the same time, I couldn't fathom the mystical circumstances that had conjured this body, mind, and spirit, which had all come together as 'me' and how their union overcame hardships to gain the summits of a few of these lofty peaks. In scaling peaks, I recognized a degree of danger, which heightened my sense of human vulnerability and frailty. I came to understand if I had an accident while I climbed these peaks, then there would be no easy way out. To face fears regarding my vulnerabilities, I was forced to learn self-reliance, courage, understand the underpinning of self-confidence, and understand my own limitations.

I was intrigued by the immensity of the world around me and the complexity of the human form. Such thoughts may have sent many youngsters rushing to the library, the source of information 40 years ago. Unfortunately, I detested reading at the time and so for me, the only means to explore such ideas was to experience them. I didn't realize I was making that choice at the time, and I now find comfort knowing that deep down I was driven to seek answers by whatever means I could find.

At later times and in different circumstances, I recognized feelings of joy and wonder whenever I took time to relax while I looked out over open ocean. How could such feelings be evoked in me by waves crashing over rocks, the gentle rhythm of waves breaking on the beach, or the swell moving through the open water? The waves were repetitious, forming a pattern and rhythm, which had no beginning and no end. I saw the ocean extending to the far horizon and through my imagination I felt certain it continued far beyond. I considered the concept of a molecule of water and how many millions were contained within a single gallon. I realized the word immense was insignificant compared to the number of molecules of water in the ocean. How could such an immense number of water molecules—H_2O—be so uniform, or what chaos would have reigned if they hadn't been so consistent?

Such fascinating thoughts prompted many more questions about my own sense of being and how I fit in with this amazing scheme. Even though I was only 28 years old, I had already learned the truth about youth's misguided sense of being invincible. A climbing accident when I was 21 almost crippled me. In my need to make sense of my thoughts, feelings, and experiences, especially during my two-year recovery from that accident, I ventured into uncomfortable thoughts about a higher power that had influence in our lives. I initially rejected these ideas; I had turned away from the church and conventional religion as a teenager. However, the more I allowed myself to be exposed to vast expanses, whether they be mountains, oceans or forests, I found myself returning to thoughts of an overarching power and sense of order that existed beyond my, or human, knowing.

I couldn't deny my thoughts and, gradually, I adopted a naturalist type of spirituality that dovetailed with concepts of spatial considerations, such as emptiness and vastness, as well as repeating patterns. This loosely evolved concept satisfied my developing view of the world and life, as well as my own place in it.

Two years before my climbing accident, I had been scaling one of my favorite buttresses in North Wales. I had ascended about 150 feet with my climbing partner. As I was about to move onto a ledge, I noticed a couple of pebbles where I wanted to place my foot. While I looked for another foothold, I happened to glance down between my feet. There, 150 feet below me, stood three other climbers, as they prepared to start a different route. My thoughts about where to place my foot stopped instantly. I was filled with amazing thoughts when I realized if I had dislodged one of these pebbles, it could have seriously injured or possibly killed one of the three climbers below me. It was a highly unlikely possibility, but it wasn't impossible. In my mind, I balanced the chances of this possibility against the sense of awe I had about the incredible complexity of the human form which could be destroyed by a small pebble. In my 20 years of life, I had never before really considered the complexity of the human form and how vulnerable it could be. Standing on that ledge, with those thoughts flooding through my mind, is a memory that has stayed with me through the years.

For a number of years, this partly spiritual, partly pattern-based, and partly nature-based philosophy percolated within me. As some answers may have come to me, they generated more in-depth queries. It was a period of seeking that I wasn't really consciously aware of most of the time. I recall times when I sat quiet, but amazed, seeing all that surrounded me as patterns and wondering why. In Arabia at the age of 29 or 30, the idea of immersing myself in the Empty Quarter, a wilderness of scorching sand and dried salt, was undeniably powerful. I had to experience it, to be at one with it. Could I be a speck within its patterns?

EPILOGUE

الله شاء إن   الله شاء إن   الله شاء إن   الله شاء إن   الله شاء إن   الله شاء إن   الله شاء إن

Part II
Transition from being 28 years of age to being 70 years old

I see change as an undeniable phenomenon, interwoven into life itself. If I didn't experience change constantly, I wouldn't have life. I've heard people say they haven't changed in years, which I find to be rather superficial. When I look at myself, as an example, every second millions of cells die in my body and millions of new ones are formed. I can only hope the new ones are healthy. Just in the act of having a living body, I inherently am subject to change. I'm exposed to situations in life, such as illness or simply driving to the store, that can cause incredible or disastrous changes. I can try to affect how unexpected changes impact me by living and eating well, driving defensively, and taking other precautions, but I know I have no guarantees. I used to find such thoughts rather depressing; however, I've come to realize that to openly face this reality is the most incredibly freeing and liberating blessing. This realization circles back around to my choice to live life more fully, every day, because I don't know what tomorrow will bring, or if it will even dawn for me. Today, while I'm still upright and breathing, I open myself to experience all I can. I do so, in every moment, because each moment is all that I have. My past cannot be relived and my future cannot be experienced yet; the only time I have to live is right now. Even my next in-breath isn't guaranteed.

After I started to integrate such ideas into my life, I began to see how much I had hidden from the richness that life had to offer. I found the true rewards of life aren't derived from material objects or thoughts in the mind; they are found in the openness and acceptance in my heart. Life has its highs and its lows, and to varying degrees I have limited control over them. But, in all circumstances, I have control over one aspect of any situation. I can decide my attitude to that circumstance, whether it feels good or bad. Both joyful and sad events will chart the course of my life. My attitude will direct how I react or respond to those events, affecting my mood and how I see my state of being.

I've heard a few people suggest their attitude and reaction to an event, especially a bad event, is like a knee-jerk reaction. I believe it takes work to learn how to interrupt such an immediate and impulsive response, and instead invoke an attitude or reaction based on equanimity and compassion. Sometimes, I have found compassion for myself to be the toughest response to engender and sustain.

Would I have had this outlook on life if I hadn't taken the journey? It's possible. However, I believe the intensity of experiences in the journey opened me to look more seriously at the meaning of life. I'm not sure other life circumstances would have shown me such a path of understanding. I feel I could easily have been lulled into complacency, if I had chosen a more conventional lifestyle. I'm pretty certain I wouldn't now live in California and wouldn't have had a story to tell.

At the age of 28, I thought myself to be infallible. I quickly learned how shallow and untrue that notion was. On a number of occasions during the trip, I felt fearful and vulnerable. Sometimes, my mistakes were immediately obvious, and others only showed their consequences later. It started a long internal journey that has taught me humility. That isn't to say that my egotistical and arrogant sides don't show themselves—they do, all too often. Now, I'm more aware of them and I have the opportunity to soften their sharper edges.

To say that this journey has had a profound effect on me is true, but it stands as just one of many experiences and journeys that have made me who I am today. I believe everybody has experiences that shape them profoundly. It may be that other people's experiences didn't have a distinct duration which they can identify.

In Part I of the Epilogue, I discussed the back story behind my decision to venture out into the Empty Quarter. I had previously realized a connection with a spiritual side of me when I exposed myself to circumstances of vastness and emptiness.

After my five days in such vast wilderness, I came to understand I had experienced a sense of transcendence. Through it, I recognized and acknowledged the power beyond our human knowing that held domain over all that surrounded me. I found rational thought and logic had no place in this discussion. To accept transcendence—existence or experience of a force beyond what we can witness—is to have faith. This isn't confined to what I comprehend in a religious sense. To try to fathom what underlies faith or determine how it influences my life are simply excuses for me to avoid accepting it. For me, faith is the understanding that we humans are both miracles and insignificant specks within the cosmos, and that these two points of view cannot have happened by chance. I see a rhyme and a reason for our existence, which is grounded in the unknowable. Each of us can find our own way to faith, however we define it. I believe faith transcends all individuals' beliefs—I see it as an essential element of human life. Other elements are to love—especially oneself, to be compassionate, and to understand that we cannot separate ourselves from the community of all living beings—not just humans. We each have a soul, a Buddha Nature, a spirit, however we express it, that is uniquely authentic to each of us. This, I believe, is what leaves our body at the moment of death. I have been with a man when he died and, in that instant, a change occurred, something was gone from the room.

I find it intriguing that all through my life, I've been drawn by openness, vastness, and emptiness. Now, I recognize it as my seeking connection with what is beyond human knowing or glimpsing a state of transcendence. I do wonder how this has borne fruit in a much-loved activity of mine. For about 20 years, I have volunteered as an interfaith spiritual care volunteer in a hospital setting. I am a member of an interfaith chaplaincy program, a totally comfortable role for me. Two years ago, I transitioned from seeing patients in the hospital and ICU to visiting those in an infusion/oncology clinic. These patients have chronic or life-threatening diseases and require frequent infusion treatments. It isn't for me to try to convert these people who are suffering to a certain faith, but to honor and support them in their own personal spiritual journeys. I see their suffering as a universal trait of life, and their understanding of what it means to seek comfort from the spiritual as individually unique. To me, it doesn't matter if the patient is Christian, Muslim, Buddhist, Wiccan, atheist or agnostic; they are all suffering human beings and they all express, and some need to explore, their own spiritual understanding of their condition. When I've talked with the terminally ill or those with chronic diseases, I've learned I'm able to walk alongside them with compassion, allowing them to voice their thoughts and feelings. In their suffering, they are facing an openness, an emptiness, and uncertainty. Am I wrong to think nothing exists that is as empty, uncertain, or vast as the specter of death? Hopefully, my willingness to walk into that void with these patients brings them peace, comfort, and maybe at times a touch of joy. It isn't for me to fix their suffering; it is not for me to say I understand their suffering, because I cannot. Let me be pedantic here. It isn't a matter of *"I will not"* or *"I don't want to"*—it truly is *"I cannot"* understand their suffering. It is for me to simply witness, acknowledge, and where appropriate, suggest a way to reframe their pain. When I visit with patients, I conclude our meeting by offering to say a prayer. It isn't a standard prayer nor from any published book. The basic shell of the prayer has come from within me—I listen to what the patients say and try to modify the base to incorporate something that is specific to the story they have shared. I don't need to know the patient's faith because I offer a simple prayer which I hope is couched in universal language that speaks to suffering and offers it to a higher power. I have been surprised by how this simple prayer moves patients, even those who talk about not having any real faith. I hope my life's experiences allow me to walk a little further along their paths and to continue to offer these patients support and comfort.

My work with these infusion patients is the realization of lessons/understandings I have gained over time. I learned to live life fully when I feared the two Syrian soldiers might shoot Penny, Ron, and I. From Buddhist teachings, I understood that compassion is one of the basic tenets of a joyful life. Comparing my life to many who I have met as I have explored the world demonstrated that I am extremely fortunate to have been given opportunities that others could only dream of having. And more importantly, despite many of these people being in poverty and having to endure hardships, they have a joyfulness that I rarely see here, in the land of plenty. Similarly, infusion patients undergo suffering that I cannot imagine. I am struck by their level of resiliency, their depth of strength, their thankfulness for learning what is truly important or unimportant in their lives, and their appreciation of the love of family and friends. Those who let go of the unimportant elements in their lives express gratitude for their learning, they walk more lightly along life's path despite being weighed down by disease. Many gain the openness to recognize that death is real, allowing them to see death is actually walking alongside all of us, every day. Death is not an enemy, it is a companion along life's path. For me to accompany these patients along their journeys encourages me to live my life fully, live it with compassion, and to give thanks for my own situation. I will never understand patients' circumstances or their courage. Perhaps I glimpsed parallel situations when I struggled to climb mountains, when I felt vulnerable in vicious sandstorms in the Empty Quarter, when I felt overwhelmed while sailing in 6-foot seas, and when I endured the soul-sucking 800 mile drive alongside the pipeline. These memories don't allow me to walk in my patients' shoes, but they prepare me to walk by their sides.

For me, the most amazing part of this chaplaincy work is that while hopefully helping these patients in even the smallest way I, myself, am blessed in performing the work. The patients with whom I come in contact have become my most valued teachers. They teach me about mortality, love, courage, and priorities. Many people have wondered how I can do this work and not be depressed by it. On the contrary, it is an uplifting and beautiful part of my life. I will be sad the day when I must stop.

Lastly, here is the basic version of the prayer I share with patients.

> *Oh Divine*
> *I ask that you will be with 'name' in their times of trial and pain.*
> *Answer their prayers when they feel lost or are in need.*
> *Be there as a beacon of light, shining light upon the path,*
> *That they may be given the will and courage to face each day.*
> *And may they be given the strength to 'activity.'*
> *May 'name,' along with their family and friends, go out into the world,*
> *To spread your love and compassion to all those who are in need.*

I substitute the patient's name in the second and seventh lines, replacing the *'name.'* In the sixth line, I substitute a detail that the patient has discussed in our visit for the *'activity,'* e.g. "join her friends for a game of cards and to share childhood memories" or "take his dog, Roxie, for a walk along the ridge." These, often, are not special occasions. They are simple, everyday events that have become profoundly precious points of connection to what has real meaning in the lives of these people. I am honored and humbled to have these patients share their journeys with me.

APPENDIX

الله شاء إن   الله شاء إن   الله شاء إن   الله شاء إن   الله شاء إن

In the headings to each of the chapters, a line of Arabic script follows the chapter's title. The line contains five repetitions of the same word "الله شاء إن"—*Inshallah*, which means "God Willing." This word was frequently heard in camp where ex-pats adopted the word, as well as in all Arabic communities. The word still echoes in my head under certain circumstances.

The photographs that have been included in the book, as well as additional ones, are available in color on my website at: www.bdhwrites.com.

ACKNOWLEDGEMENTS

الله شاء إن   الله شاء إن   الله شاء إن   الله شاء إن   الله شاء إن   الله شاء إن   الله شاء إن

Many people have helped me throughout the writing of this book and I want to acknowledge their contributions.

First, I want to thank my wife Judi and my daughter Emily who have lovingly allowed me the time and resources to work on this memoir, have been willing to listen to both my angst and joy, have encouraged me throughout, and given me many great pieces of advice and suggestions. I should also add my thanks to Gracie, our pug. She has sat calmly in my lap during hours of writing and editing.

Over the course of my writing, I've taken classes, attended writing workshops and have learned so much about the craft of writing. I want to particularly thank the following: Linda Joy Myers and Brooke Warner at Write-Your-Memoir-in-6-Months.com, Aline Soules at OLLI-Concord, and Jill Morris at OLLI-Concord.

I would imagine writing a book like this would be quite a difficult and lonely endeavor without the support of fellow writers who critiqued the work regularly. For this challenging task, I need to thank the following: Bunny Duhl, Barbara Hill, Patrick Kelly, Katherine Thomas, Harriet Chamberlain, and Thomas Bauer. I must give a special thank you to Heidi Eliason who has walked along a parallel path to me and given me excellent feedback as she negotiated the writing and publication of her own travel based memoir *Confessions of a Middle-Aged Runaway*—recently published.

One group of people who contributed many hours of reading and thought to this effort are those who took on the task of beta reading one of the draft versions. Their dedication and amazing feedback pointed out areas needing my attention, suggestions of ways to clarify the story, and simple grammatical and spelling errors that needed to be corrected. For this task, I need to thank: Eric Owers, Bob Tattle, Debra Lobel, John Garvin, Heidi Eliason, Rowell Matt, Rod Haug, Ivars Krievans and Tim Taylor. Their encouragement gave me the confidence, which I needed to publish this book. A special thanks to all of you.

I have heard Brooke Warner repeat a piece of sagely advice multiple times in the last couple of years—"If you are going to self-publish, then make your book look as professional as you can." To this end, I have engaged with a couple of excellent experts in their fields. My editor, Lyn Roberts, has given me so much advice, guidance and cajoling as I've tried to bring this writing process to completion. She has forced me to rethink areas that I thought to be fine, but she knew I could do better. And she was correct, every time. Second, Marianne McBride worked with me to make the final version clean through her hours of copy editing. I needed her expert eyes to feel confident that the manuscript was ready to be published. My wife, Judi, gave me great advice and guidance as I went through the intimidating process of final proof-reading. Lastly, Andrew Benzie has walked me through the processes necessary to self-publish this book in both paperback and e-book format. His skills have made this nerve-wracking last step much less painful.

And finally, I want to thank the readers who have made it to the end. I hope you enjoyed the journey and see your own lives somewhat differently from when you started.

ABOUT THE AUTHOR

الله شاء ان الله شاء ان الله شاء ان الله شاء ان الله شاء ان الله شاء ان الله شاء ان

Barry Hampshire didn't know he was an adventurer when he started his career in England in 1971. He became a computer system architect and over 45 years he worked in London, Saudi Arabia, Houston, and San Francisco. Barry learned to develop computer systems and he also learned to calmly respond to unanticipated scenarios. This trait served him well during the journey described in these pages.

Before retirement, Barry started writing stories about his earlier adventures which have become the basis of this memoir covering his drive from London to Saudi Arabia and what has resulted.

CPSIA information can be obtained
at www.ICGtesting.com
Printed in the USA
LVHW030738111119
636962LV00011B/4782